Kings and Kingdoms
of early
Anglo-Saxon England

Barbara Yorke

To the several generations of King Alfred's College History students who have explored kings and kingdoms in early Anglo-Saxon England with me

941.01

© Barbara Yorke 1990
First published 1990
Reprinted 1992

Typeset by Inforum Typesetting, Portsmouth
Printed by
Biddles Ltd, Guildford, Surrey, Gt Britain
for the publishers
B A Seaby Ltd
7 Davies Street
London W1Y 1LL

Distributed by
B A Seaby Ltd
7 Davies Street
London W1Y 1LL

ISBN   1 85264 027 8

British Library Cataloguing in Publication Data
Yorke, Barbara 1951–

Kings and Kingdoms of early Anglo-Saxon England.
1. England. Kings, to 1154
I. Title
942.010922

Contents

FOREWORD

There are many excellent general surveys of Anglo-Saxon history, but their drawback for anyone interested in the history of one particular kingdom is that there is not usually an opportunity to treat the history of any one kingdom as a whole. This study surveys the history of the six best-recorded Anglo-Saxon kingdoms within the period AD 600–900: Kent, the East Saxons, the East Angles, Northumbria, Mercia and Wessex. The chapters, like many of the available written sources, approach the histories of the individual kingdoms through that of their royal families. Dynastic history is a major concern of the book, but the intention is to go beyond narrative accounts of the various royal houses to try to explain issues such as strategies of rulership, the reasons for success or failure and the dynamics of change to the office of king. More generalized conclusions suggest themselves from the studies of individual kingdoms and these are brought together in the final chapter which examines four main facets in the development of kingship in the period under review: kingship and overlordship; royal resources; royal and noble families; and king and church. The first chapter is also a general one and deals with the difficult issue of Anglo-Saxon kingship before 600 and introduces the main classes of written record.

Another aim of the work is to alert the general reader to the exciting research into early Anglo-Saxon England which has been carried out in recent years by historians and archaeologists, but which may only be available in specialist publications. Any writer is, of course, dependent on the primary and secondary works which are available and differences in the material which has survived or the type of research which has been done have helped dictate the shape of the chapters for the individual kingdoms. Readers who wish to follow up individual references will find full details through the notes and the bibliography. Notes have been primarily used for referencing secondary works, but there are some instances in which additional commentary has been provided through them. The reader is alerted to many major problems of interpretation through the text, but shortage of space and the nature of the book have prevented detailed discussion of the more complex issues.

Although I have been able to indicate the written works to which I have been indebted, it is more difficult to demonstrate the immense benefit I have gained from discussions with other Anglo-Saxonists. It would be impossible to name all those from whom at one time or another I have received advice and encouragement, but I hope that if they read this they will know that I am grateful. My thanks go, in particular, to Professor Frank Barlow with whom I began my study of Anglo-Saxon kingdoms for my doctoral thesis and to Dr David Kirby who very kindly read the book in manuscript and generously made many suggestions for its improvement. I am also most grateful to those who provided me with photographs and captions and to a succession of editors at Seaby's for their patience and assistance. Finally, on the home front, I must thank my husband Robert for without his continuing support I doubt if this book would ever have been completed.

WINCHESTER 30 SEPTEMBER 1989

LIST OF TABLES AND ILLUSTRATIONS

Conventions used in the tables

d = died; k = killed; m = married; † = died in infancy; A broken line in the tables indicates a hypothetical link.

For further information on the chronologies and family relationships of the Anglo-Saxon royal houses see the *Handbook of British Chronology* (Dumville 1986b) with which these tables are broadly in agreement.

Figures 1–7 appear on plates between pp. 90–91 and figures 8–14 on plates between pp. 106–107.

Chapter One

INTRODUCTION: THE ORIGINS OF THE ANGLO–SAXON KINGDOMS

There is a sense in which the history of the early Anglo-Saxon kingdoms can be said to have begun with the arrival of Augustine and a band of nearly forty monks at the court of King Æthelbert of Kent in 597. Augustine and his followers had been despatched by Pope Gregory the Great 'to preach the word of God to the English race' and, as far as we know, their mission was the first sustained attempt to bring Christianity to the Anglo-Saxons.[1] Not surprisingly the arrival of Augustine and his followers was an event of the utmost signifi- cance to Bede, whose *Ecclesiastical History of the English People* (completed in 731) is our main narrative source for the seventh and early eighth centuries, and he began his detailed discussion of the history of the Anglo-Saxon king- doms at this point. Bede as a monk naturally believed that the conversion of his people began a new phase in their history, but it would also be true to say that it was only after the arrival of the Augustine mission that Bede was able to write a detailed history of his people. For Augustine and his fellow monks not only brought a new religion to the Anglo-Saxons; they also brought the arts of reading and writing.

Although the arrival of the Gregorian mission clearly marked a very import- ant stage in the religious history of the Anglo-Saxons and in the production of written records, it is not an ideal point at which to begin an investigation into the history of the Anglo-Saxon kingdoms. For it is evident that the majority of Anglo-Saxon kingdoms were already in existence by 597 and that the complex political pattern of interrelationships and amalgamations which Bede reveals in his *Ecclesiastical History* had its origins in the pre-Christian period. This is frustrating for the historian for it means that many vital stages in the early growth of Anglo-Saxon kingdoms took place offstage, as it were, before the provision of adequate written records had begun. Fortunately the history of the country between AD 400 and 600 is not purely dependent upon written records and the evidence of place-names and archaeology has transformed our appreciation of the period. As new archaeological sites are constantly coming to light, and as much work which has already taken place has not yet been fully written up, the full potential that the archaeological evidence has for the understanding of the sub-Roman period is far from being realized.

Written sources: British

The settlement of the Anglo-Saxons in Britain and the origins of the Anglo-

Saxon kingdoms are two closely related, but not identical problems. Our nearest contemporary written source for the period of the Anglo-Saxon settlements is the homiletic work 'The Ruin of Britain' (*De Excidio Britanniae*) in which a British cleric called Gildas reviews the events of the fifth century from the vantage point of one of the surviving British kingdoms in the western half of Britain at a date (probably) around the middle of the sixth century.[2] Gildas' subject is not so much the advent of the Anglo-Saxons, but the sins of the British which, to his way of thinking, were ultimately responsible for provoking the vengeance of God in the form of Germanic and other barbarian piratical attacks. Gildas briefly sketches a picture of Saxons being utilized by the British as federate soldiers in eastern England following the recall of the Roman legions, of the federate settlements growing in size and confidence until they were strong enough to overthrow their paymasters, and of the Saxons then wreaking havoc on the hapless British until the famous victory of *Mons Badonicus* (Mount Badon) some forty-four years before the time that Gildas was writing.[3] The account is brief and lacks dates, and is clearly inaccurate on certain points such as assigning the building of the Hadrian and Antonine Walls to the fourth century. Gildas was relying on oral tradition rather than written records and gives an impressionistic version of events that had taken place before his birth; however, his is the only narrative we possess for the period of the Anglo-Saxon settlements and so it has provided the framework for a discussion of the events of the sub-Roman period from the time of Bede onwards.

Although Gildas is best known for his information on the *adventus* of the Anglo-Saxons, his testimony is equally important for the nature of British society in the sixth century when he was writing from personal knowledge. The castigation of this society was the real focus of Gildas' polemic and among his principal targets were British kings ruling in south-western England and Wales.[4] These areas had been part of the Roman province of Britain, but by the sixth century little that was characteristic of the late Roman world apparently survived except adherence to Christianity (which Gildas evidently saw as rather half-hearted). Control had passed to kings whom Gildas characterized as 'tyrants' and whose basis of power was their armed followings. It was a society in which violence was endemic. Gildas' brief sketch of British society in the west in the sixth century is broadly in accordance with what can be discerned from later charters, saints' *Lives* and annals from Wales.[5] There would also appear to have been many points of similarity between the exercise of royal power in Wales and in the Celtic areas of northern Britain,[6] and the ruler and his warband are portrayed in rather a different, heroic, light in the poem *Gododdin* which recounts a disastrous raid made from the kingdom of the Gododdin (in south-east Scotland) against the Deiran centre of Catterick.[7]

The tradition of events in the fifth century which Gildas reports seems to have been, in summary, that in part of eastern Britain those on whom power had devolved following the withdrawal of the Roman legions attempted to provide for their defence by hiring Germanic forces who eventually seized power from them, whereas in the western half of Britain comparable circumstances saw the rise of native warlords who filled the power vacuum and established kingdoms within former Roman *civitates*.

Written sources: Anglo-Saxon

When Bede wrote his *Ecclesiastical History* in 731 he used earlier narrative sources to provide some history of Britain before the advent of the Gregorian mission and took the basis of his account of the Anglo-Saxon settlement from Gildas' work.[8] Gildas did not provide any identification of the Saxon leaders who commanded the federates 'in the eastern part of the island', but Bede interpolated a passage in which he identified the leaders as two brothers, Hengist and Horsa, who were claimed to be the founders of the royal house of Kent.[9] The information presumably came from Abbot Albinus of Canterbury who was Bede's chief Kentish informant.[10] More detailed versions of the activities of Hengist and Horsa appear in the *Anglo-Saxon Chronicle* and in the 'Kentish Chronicles' included in the *Historia Brittonum*, a British compilation written in 829-30 and attributed to Nennius.[11] The *Anglo-Saxon Chronicle* also contains accounts of the arrival of Cerdic and Cynric, Stuf and Wihtgar and Ælle and his sons, the founders respectively of the kingdoms of the West Saxons, the Isle of Wight and the South Saxons.[12] These founding fathers arrived off Britain with a few ships and, after battling against British leaders for some years, established their kingdoms. Briefer notices for Northumbria and the Jutes of mainland Hampshire seem to conform to a similar pattern of events. By the eighth and ninth centuries it had apparently become conventional to depict the founders of royal houses arriving fresh from the Continent to set up their kingdoms. There seems to have been a standard 'origin tradition' which was utilized to explain the establishment of the various Anglo-Saxon royal houses; even Gildas' account may have been influenced by such a convention.[13] It would be unwise to assume that these foundation stories are historically valid.

Bede introduced his information about Hengist and Horsa with the phrase 'they are said . . .' (*perhibentur*), a formula he used elsewhere in his history when he was drawing on unverifiable oral tradition. Bede's comment suggests that we should use the information on the Kentish *adventus* with caution and certainly when one looks at the fuller narratives of the foundation of Kent and at the activities of Cerdic and Cynric one can see further reasons for questioning their historical validity. One must remember that these sources are not contemporary with the events they describe, but written some three to four hundred years later. They contain a number of features which can be found in foundation legends throughout the Indo-European world.[14] Particularly suspicious are the pairs of founding kinsmen with alliterating names, who recall the twin deities of the pagan Germanic world, and other characters whom the founders defeat or meet whose names seem to be derived from place-names. Thus the *Chronicle* describes a victory in 508 by Cerdic and Cynric over a

British king called Natanleod after whom, it is said, the district *Natanleaga* was named. In fact the name of this rather marshy area of Hampshire derives from the OE word *naet* 'wet' and it would appear that the name of a completely fictitious king has been taken from the place rather than the other way around.[15] There are many other examples of this type, and the Kentish foundation legends also contain other traditional story-telling motifs such as 'the night of the long knives' in which the Saxons lured many British nobles to their death by means of a ruse also found in the legends of the Greeks, Old Saxons and Vikings.

The chronologies of these foundation accounts are also suspect. Gildas provided no actual date for the Anglo-Saxon *adventus*, but Bede interpreted his words to mean that the first invitation to the federates was given between 449 and 455.[16] The arrival of Cerdic and Cynric is said to have occurred in 494 or 495, but it can be demonstrated that the chronology of the earliest West Saxon kings was artificially revised and traces of the rather clumsy revision remain in the repetitive entries within the *Anglo-Saxon Chronicle*.[17] David Dumville has argued that other versions of the West Saxon regnal list imply that the reign of Cerdic was originally dated to 538-54 which (following the time sequence of the *Chronicle*) would place the arrival of Cerdic and Cynric in 532.[18] The detailed critiques which have been made of the foundation accounts in recent years make it difficult to use them with any confidence to reconstruct the early histories of their kingdoms in the way which earlier generations of historians felt able to do. Even if there was a genuine core to the stories of Cerdic and Hengist it is impossible to separate it out from the later reworkings which the stories have evidently received. The accounts as they survive show how later Anglo-Saxons wanted to see the foundation of their kingdoms, rather than what actually occurred.

Cerdic was the founder king of the West Saxon dynasty from whom all subsequent West Saxon kings claimed descent. We know for a number of other kingdoms who the founders of their royal houses were believed to be and what their positions in regnal lists and genealogies were. As in the case of Cerdic (if we accept the revised date for his reign), these other examples suggest a sixth-century date for the formation of kingdoms. Bede, for instance, reveals that the kings of the East Angles were known as Wuffingas after Wuffa, the grandfather of King Rædwald.[19] As Rædwald died in c. 625, his grandfather presumably ruled around the middle of the sixth century. The key figure for the East Saxons was Sledd, from whom all subsequent East Saxon kings traced descent, and whose son was ruling in 604. Sledd must have come to power in the second half of the sixth century.[20] Although these dates could represent the limits of oral tradition when genealogical information was first written down, as they stand they suggest that the Anglo-Saxon kingdoms were creations of the sixth century rather than the fifth century and do not go back to the earliest origins of the Anglo-Saxons in Britain.[21]

Archaeological evidence

Archaeological evidence has a great potential for reconstructing the nature of the Anglo-Saxon settlements and the circumstances in which kingdoms developed. However, archaeologists have naturally been influenced in their interpretation of the material from settlement sites and cemeteries by the surviving written sources, although currently there is a greater appreciation of the written material's evident inadequacies.[22] It has been realized for some time that the date of around the middle of the fifth century for the Saxon *adventus*, which Bede derived from his reading of Gildas, was too specific. Germanic settlement in Britain may have begun before the end of the fourth century and seems to have continued throughout the fifth century and probably into the sixth century.[23] Nevertheless Gildas' explanation of why the Anglo-Saxons were allowed to settle in Britain has remained very influential. Confirmation of the use of Anglo-Saxons as federate troops has been seen as coming from burials of Anglo-Saxons wearing military equipment of a type issued to late Roman forces which have been found both in late Roman contexts, such as the Roman cemeteries of Winchester and Colchester, and in purely 'Anglo-Saxon' rural cemeteries like Mucking (Essex).[24] The distribution of the earliest Anglo-Saxon sites and place-names in close proximity to Roman settlements and roads has been interpreted as showing that initial Anglo-Saxon settlements were being controlled by the Romano-British.[25] However, it is not necessary to see all the early settlers as federate troops and this interpretation has been used rather too readily by some archaeologists.[26] A variety of relationships could have existed between Romano-British and incoming Anglo-Saxons.

The broader archaeological picture suggests that no one model will explain all the Anglo-Saxon settlements in Britain and that there was considerable regional variation. Settlement density varied within southern and eastern England. Norfolk has more large Anglo-Saxon cemeteries than the neighbouring East Anglian county of Suffolk; eastern Yorkshire (the nucleus of the Anglo-Saxon kingdom of Deira) far more than the rest of Northumbria.[27] The settlers were not all of the same type. Some were indeed warriors who were buried equipped with their weapons, but we should not assume that all of these were invited guests who were to guard Romano-British communities. Many, like the later Viking settlers, may have begun as piratical raiders who later seized land and made permanent settlements. Other settlers seem to have been much humbler people who had few if any weapons and suffered from malnutrition. These have been characterized by one archaeologist as Germanic 'boat people', refugees from crowded settlements on the North Sea which deteriorating climatic conditions would have made untenable.[28]

The settlers were of varied racial origins. In one of his additions to Gildas' narrative Bede says that the settlers came from:

> Three very powerful Germanic tribes, the Saxons, Angles and Jutes. The people of Kent and the inhabitants of the Isle of Wight are of Jutish origin and also those opposite the Isle of Wight . . . From the Saxon country . . . came the East Saxons, the South Saxons, and the West Saxons. Besides this,

from the country of the Angles . . . came the East Angles, the Middle
Angles, the Mercians, and all the Northumbrian race.[29]

Bede's account is in part a rationalization from the political situation of his
own day, but he does seem to have been broadly correct in identifying the
main North Sea provinces from which the bulk of the Germanic settlers in
Britain came and their main areas of settlement within Britain, though the
artefact evidence for Jutish settlement is less substantial than that for the
Angles and Saxons.[30] However, archaeology reveals that the detailed picture is
more complex. There seems to have been considerable racial admixture in all
areas reflected in variations in dress and burial custom. 'Mixed' cemeteries, in
which both cremation and inhumation were practised, occur throughout
southern and eastern England.[31] Other Germanic peoples also settled in Britain, as Bede acknowledged in a later passage in the *Ecclesiastical History*.[32]
Scandinavian settlers have been located in East Anglia and elsewhere along the
eastern seaboard,[33] and there seems to have been some Frankish settlement
south of the Thames.[34] However, there is always a difficulty in deciding
whether archaeological material from a specific area of Europe is an indicator
of movement of peoples from that area to Britain or merely of trade or gift-
exchange of various commodities.[35] Although there does seem to have been
some Frankish settlement in Britain, the bulk of the Frankish material which
has been recovered is more likely to reflect the close links which existed
between Francia and south-eastern England, and Kent in particular, in the
sixth century.[36]

But what was happening to the Romano-British population while the Germanic settlement of Britain was taking place? Archaeology has been particularly useful in showing that many Roman communities throughout Britain
experienced substantial changes during the fourth century before Anglo-
Saxon settlement began.[37] The changes appear to have included a shift from
an urban to a rural-based economy. In Wroxeter (Salop) and Exeter stone
town houses were replaced in the late fourth and early fifth centuries by
simpler, flimsier buildings made entirely of timber, while some areas of the
towns were abandoned altogether or were farmed.[38] Comparable drastic
changes seem to have occurred in towns like Canterbury and Winchester in the
eastern half of the country.[39] The eventual result was the virtual abandonment
within Britain during the fifth century of towns as centres of population. Some
rural villas initially gained advantage from the changing economic circumstances, but there are also signs of villas being adapted in the fourth and fifth
centuries to become more self-sufficient.[40] At Frocester (Gloucs) and
Rivenhall (Essex) the villa buildings were allowed to decay or were turned into
barns while new timber buildings, more typical of the early Middle Ages, were
erected.[41] Although attacks by Anglo-Saxons (and in the west of Britain by
Irish) exacerbated a difficult situation, they did not cause it, as Gildas' account
seems to imply. The complex problems which caused the decline of the
Roman empire affected the inhabitants of Britain well before Anglo-Saxon
settlement began on any scale,[42] and, by the time the Anglo-Saxons arrived,

the Romano-British inhabitants had already begun to adapt themselves to a way of life that can be described as 'early medieval'.

By the end of the fifth century different settlement patterns are discernible between eastern Britain (which had been settled by Anglo-Saxons) and western Britain (which had not). One sign of changing circumstances in the west of Britain was the re-emergence of hill-top settlements which, it has been argued by Leslie Alcock in particular, may have functioned as chieftain centres and be linked with the emergent British kingdoms we can dimly discern in the written sources.[43] The reoccupation of the impressive Iron Age hill-fort of South Cadbury (Som) is a good example of the type.[44] The whole of the innermost rampart of nearly 1100 m in length was refortified in the subRoman period and a substantial timber hall built on the highest point in the interior. Yet there were very few finds of artefacts from the South Cadbury excavations, and this helps to explain why the British generally have proved very hard to detect in the subRoman period.[45] After the Romano-British lost access to Roman industrial products, they become all but invisible in the archaeological record as they were no longer using on any scale artefacts which were diagnostically Romano-British or, at least, not of a type that survives in the soil. The Britons of the west country received the occasional consignment of pottery from Mediterranean kilns brought by foreign traders;[46] the Britons in the east presumably made use of Anglo-Saxon craftsmen. We should not assume that every owner of an artefact of 'Germanic' type in eastern England was of Germanic descent.

In fact, the majority of the people who lived in the Anglo-Saxon kingdoms must have been of Romano-British descent.[47] The large pagan Anglo-Saxon cemeteries like Spong Hill (Norfolk) which contained over three thousand burials, might at first sight seem to suggest that Anglo-Saxon settlement was on such a substantial scale that the native British population would have been completely overwhelmed by the newcomers – which is rather what Gildas seems to imply. However, when it is remembered that these cemeteries were in use in many cases for upwards of two hundred years it is apparent that the communties they served cannot have been that numerous; Spong Hill may have serviced a population of approximately four to five hundred people, though these would appear to have been dispersed over a wide area of countryside, rather than concentrated within one settlement.[48] Outside eastern England and Kent it is rare to find a cemetery of more than one hundred burials and, even allowing for the fact that the most westerly shires were not conquered until after the time the Anglo-Saxons were converted and had abandoned their distinctive burial customs, it is unlikely that the newcomers outnumbered the Romano-British, in spite of evidence for a substantial drop in the size of the Romano-British population in the fifth and sixth centuries.[49] Place-name evidence also provides indications of British survival even in the areas of densest Anglo-Saxon settlement.[50]

The Anglo-Saxons did not settle in an abandoned landscape on which they imposed new types of settlement and farming, as was once believed. Recent landscape studies have suggested a high degree of continuity between rural settlement in the Roman and Anglo-Saxon periods and this links with indications of early Saxon settlement taking place under the aegis of the Romano-British.[51] Landscape studies are a complex matter which draw upon a variety of topographical, archaeological and written sources. There are major problems in trying to relate Anglo-Saxon charter boundaries to those of Roman estates for which there are no written records, and by the end of the Anglo-Saxon period there had been major changes to the organization of the landscape which can obscure earlier arrangements.[52] Interpretation is also hindered by uncertainty about late Roman administrative arrangements. Nevertheless, studies carried out throughout the country, in 'British' as well as 'Anglo-Saxon' areas, have found examples of continuity of territorial boundaries where, for instance, Roman villa estate boundaries seem to have been identical with those of medieval estates, as delineated in early charters, though settlement sites within the defined territory might shift.[53]

What we see in these examples is probably continuity of the estate or territory as an unit of administration rather than one of exploitation. Although the upper level of Roman administration based on towns seems to have disappeared during the fifth century, a subsidiary system based on subdivisions of the countryside may have continued.[54] The basis of the internal organization of both the Anglo-Saxon kingdoms and those of their Celtic neighbours was a large rural territory which contained a number of subsidiary settlements dependent upon a central residence which the Anglo-Saxons called a *villa* in Latin and a *tun* in Old English.[55] These vills were centres of royal administration and visited by the kings and their entourages on regular circuits of their kingdoms when food rents which had to be rendered at the royal vill would be consumed.[56] In Anglo-Saxon England of the seventh and eighth centuries groups of royal vills and their dependent territories formed *regiones*, discrete territories within kingdoms for administrative purposes.[57] If this recent research is correct it suggests that the basic infrastructure of the early Anglo-Saxon kingdoms was inherited from late Roman or subRoman Britain.

In recent years a number of royal vills of the early Anglo-Saxon period have been identified from fieldwork and aerial photographs and some have been excavated. One of the best known is Yeavering in the kingdom of Northumbria, which is identified in the *Ecclesiastical History* as a *villa regalis* (royal vill) and seems to have been used by Northumbrian kings in the late sixth and seventh centuries, after an earlier history as a British cult and administrative centre.[58] Yeavering is a remarkable site and in addition to a series of large timber halls and a protective fort, had a unique wedge-shaped building which resembles a segment of a Roman amphitheatre (see Fig. 8). One notable feature of Yeavering is the small yield of diagnostic Anglo-Saxon finds or buildings; only a couple of sunken-featured buildings and a handful of pottery and other small finds betray their presence. All the other structures appear to have British or Roman antecedents. Nothing quite like Yeavering has been excavated further south, but comparable halls have been excavated at Cowdery's Down, near

Basingstoke (Hants) which were in use during the sixth and seventh centuries.[59] Although the Basingstoke area was part of the West Saxon kingdom at the end of the seventh century it is not clear what the political organization of the area was at the end of the sixth century. The size and sophistication of its large timber halls suggest that it too could have been a royal vill. Like Yeavering, the halls of Cowdery's Down have no exact parallels in the Germanic world, though they cannot be exactly matched in Romano-British tradition either (see Fig. 9). The great halls of the early Anglo-Saxon kingdoms seem to represent a fusion of Germanic and Romano-British building traditions.[60] They symbolize one of the most important contributions which archaeology has made to our understanding of the early Anglo-Saxon kingdoms, namely the demonstration of the importance within them of Romano-British as well as Germanic roots.

We cannot expect archaeology to show us the exact point at which Anglo-Saxon leaders became kings, but as the sixth century progresses we can trace the evolution of a class of male burial which has a number of distinctive characteristics and is substantially richer than the average warrior burial. By the end of the sixth century particularly significant individuals were being buried under mounds, either on their own or as part of a cemetery of similar barrows, and with a rich array and variety of gravegoods including foreign imports and objects made from gold, silver and semi-precious stones.[61] Such burials are commonly referred to as 'princely burials' and, as has been argued for the appearance of rich burials in the prehistoric period, the focusing of attention on the burials of the élite of the community may be an important indicator of 'state formation',[62] or, in Anglo-Saxon terms, the growth and development of kingship during the latter half of the sixth century. The princely burials could be seen as showing the insecurity of the parvenu who needs to proclaim his new status with ostentatious display.[63] The best known and the grandest of the princely burials is the ship-burial from mound 1 at Sutton Hoo which has often been claimed as the burial of King Rædwald of the East Angles (d. c. 625),[64] but two other early seventh-century burials at Taplow (Bucks) and Broomfield (Essex), which unfortunately were not excavated under modern conditions, approach it in richness and range of gravegoods.[65] The archaeological evidence thus provides some support for the indications we have from the more reliable of the written sources that the sixth century was the period when most Anglo-Saxon kingdoms came into existence.

The political structure of Anglo-Saxon England c. 600
We do not have sufficient sources for the fifth and sixth centuries to be able to reconstruct a political map of the time, but it is possible to infer from sources of the seventh century something of the political developments which had taken place by 600. It is clear from the *Ecclesiastical History* that there were a large number of small kingdoms in England during the seventh century, but the most informative source on the early political structure of England south of the Humber is a document known as the 'Tribal Hidage' which is reproduced below.[66]

Myrcna landes	30,000 (hides)	Hwinca	7,000
Wocensætna	7,000	Cilternsætna	4,000
Westerna	7,000	Hendrica	3,500
Pecsætna	1,200	Unecung(a)ga	1,200
Elmedsætna	600	Arosætna	600
Lindesfarona	7,000	Færpinga	300
mid Hæthfeldlande			
Suth Gyrwa	600	Bilmiga	600
North Gyrwa	600	Widerigga	600
East Wixna	300	East Willa	600
West Wixna	600	West Willa	600
Spalda	600	East Engle	30,000
Wigesta	900	East Sexena	7,000
Herefinna	1,200	Cantwarena	15,000
Sweordora	300	Suth Sexena	7,000
Gifla	300	West Sexena	100,000
Hicca	300		
Wihtgara	600		
Noxgaga	5,000		
Ohtgaga	2,000		
(Total)	66,100	(Total)	242,700
		(correctly	244,100)

Like many of the key documents for the early Anglo-Saxon period the text of the Tribal Hidage only survives in later manuscripts, the earliest of which dates to the eleventh century. The list's focus of interest seems to have been the Midlands and so it is generally assumed to have been a Mercian compilation.[67] It is most likely to have been drawn up in the second half of the seventh century, that is after the conversion of the Mercians, but before many of the people listed in it became incorporated into one of the larger kingdoms. The Tribal Hidage's most likely purpose was assessment for the collection of tribute and the reign of Wulfhere of Mercia (658-75) who is known to have been overlord of the other southern kingdoms is perhaps the most probable time for it to have been drawn up.[68] Thirty-five peoples are listed with assessments in hides, a unit of land used throughout the Anglo-Saxon period for a variety of assessment purposes, but which cannot be given a precise value in modern terms, though a hide may have originally been defined as the area of land sufficient to maintain one family and is sometimes given the notional equivalence of 120 acres.[69] The territories dependent upon royal vills which were discussed in the previous section could be as much as 100 hides in size. Although the assessments presumably do reflect to a large extent the relative size of the provinces, the list was not necessarily drawn up on a strictly pro rata basis: fertility of the soil, population density and a kingdom's exact relationship with the overlord province might all have affected the size of the hidage assessment.[70] The exceptionally large figure of 100,000 hides for the West

Saxons may be a later emendation to the source of our surviving manuscripts which reflects Wessex's later growth rather than its size when the list was originally composed.[71]

The peoples listed in the Tribal Hidage seem to represent political units of differing size within seventh-century Anglo-Saxon England. Some are large and well-attested kingdoms which continued into the eighth century, including the West Saxons (?100,000 hides), the East Angles and Mercians (30,000 hides) and the Cantwarena (people of Kent) (15,000 hides). Next in size are a number of peoples assessed at 7,000 hides: the Wocensætna (Wreocensæte), the Westerna (Magonsæte), the Lindesfarona (Lindsey), the Hwinca (Hwicce), the East Saxons and the South Saxons. All but the Wreocensæte are known to have had their own royal houses.[72] Little is known of the four peoples assessed at between 5,000 and 2,000 hides: the Cilternsætna (Chilternsæte)(4,000), the Hendrica (3,500), the Noxgaga (5,000) and Ohtgaga (2,000). The Cilternsætna (Chilternsæte) are usually presumed to be a people centred on the Chilterns, but the location of the other peoples is not known and the names Noxgaga and Ohtgaga may have become garbled in transmission. Finally there are twenty small peoples assessed at between 300 and 1,200 hides,[73] some of whom are known to have been ruled by kings in the seventh century. We have Bede's authority for kings of the Elmedsætna (Elmet) and the Wihtgara (Isle of Wight), both of which were assessed at 600 hides, and another 600-hide people, the South Gyrwe (who were probably based around Ely), are said by Bede to have had their own ruler, though he is called *princeps* rather than *rex*.[74]

Map 1 attempts to show the positions of those peoples of the Tribal Hidage who can be located with some confidence.[75] Although a large number of the peoples named in the Tribal Hidage are known from other written sources or from placenames, there are some names, such as Noxgaga, Ohtgaga and Unecungaga, which cannot be identified. Even for the names we can identify it is difficult to place them within exact boundaries on a map. In some instances this is because the people concerned, and this applies especially to the numerous small peoples of the east Midlands, lost their independence at an early date and cannot be linked with later adminstrative units. The map also includes one or two other provinces, such as Surrey and that of the Jutes of Hampshire, whose existence as self-governing areas seems well attested by other sources; they may be concealed beneath some of the unidentifiable names of the Tribal Hidage.

It is possible that although varying in size all thirty-five peoples of the Tribal Hidage were of the same status in that they were provinces which were ruled by their own royal houses and so assessed independently for payment of tribute.[76] Confirmation of this interpretation may come from Bede's account of the battle of the river *Winwæd* of 655 where it is said that Penda of Mercia, overlord of all the southern kingdoms, was able to call upon thirty contingents, each led by *duces regii* ('royal commanders'), to fight with him against the Northumbrians.[77] However, we should not assume that all the provinces in the

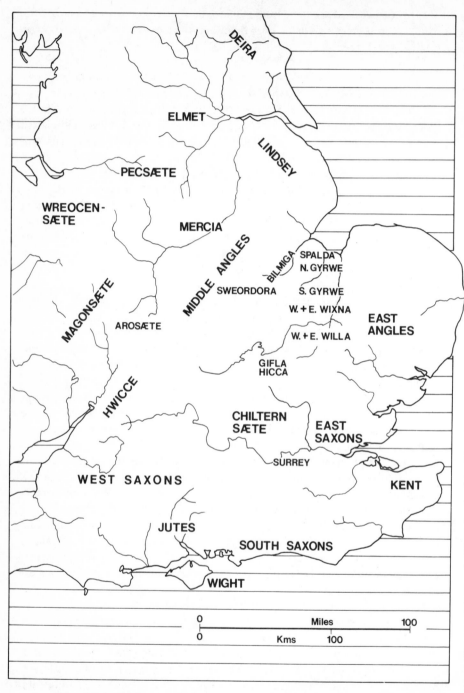

Map 1: Anglo-Saxon provinces at the time of the composition of the
Tribal Hidage (? late seventh century)

Tribal Hidage had rulers of Germanic birth. The kingdom of Elmet had a British ruler early in the seventh century[78] and it has been suggested that the Chilternsæte may have remained in native hands for most of the sixth century.[79]

Although the most westerly kingdoms listed, the Westerna/Magonsæte and Hwinca/Hwicce, may have been created in the course of the seventh century, it is likely that the majority of the provinces listed in the Tribal Hidage were in existence by the end of the sixth century. There is a concentration of small provinces in the east Midlands and it is not clear whether this distribution reflects a peculiarity of the political organization of the area or merely reflects Mercian interests.[80] It does, however, seem likely that in the sixth century there would have been more small independent provinces within eastern and southern England comparable to the group of 300-1,200 hides in the Tribal Hidage, for units of this type, described as *provinciae* or *regiones*, can be detected within many of the larger kingdoms of the seventh and eighth centuries.[81] Sometimes something distinctive in the administrative organization of the *regio* or in its political history will betray its previously independent existence. One of the best documented examples is the *regio* (or lathe in Kentish terminology) of west Kent. Throughout Kent's independent history the province of west Kent had its own ruler from the Kentish royal house, though at some points in the seventh century it was detached from Kentish control and ruled by East Saxons. The people of west Kent had their own bishopric at Rochester and in the sixth century their material culture seems to have had more in common with the Saxon provinces to their west and north than with the Jutes of east Kent.[82] However, none of our sources indicate just when and how the Oiscingas of east Kent conquered west Kent; it is one of the many unrecorded events of the sixth century. Several small provinces can also be detected in Hertfordshire, Middlesex, Berkshire and Surrey, but by the seventh century when our records begin these are dominated by other kingdoms and have a complex history of fluctuating overlordships.[83]

The existence of these numerous small provinces suggests that southern and eastern Britain may have have lost any political cohesion in the fifth and sixth centuries and fragmented into many small autonomous units, though late Roman administrative organization of the countryside may have helped dictate their boundaries. By the end of the sixth century the leaders of these communities were styling themselves kings, though it should not be assumed that all of them were Germanic in origin. There were also by the end of the sixth century some larger kingdoms and the majority of these were based on the south or east coasts. They include the provinces of the Jutes of Hampshire and Wight, the South Saxons, Kent, the East Saxons, East Angles, Lindsey and (north of the Humber) Deira and Bernicia (see map 2). Several of these kingdoms may have had as their initial focus a territory based on a former Roman *civitas* and this has been argued as particularly likely for the provinces of Kent, Lindsey, Deira and Bernicia, all of whose names derive from Romano-British tribal or district names.[84] The southern and east coasts were,

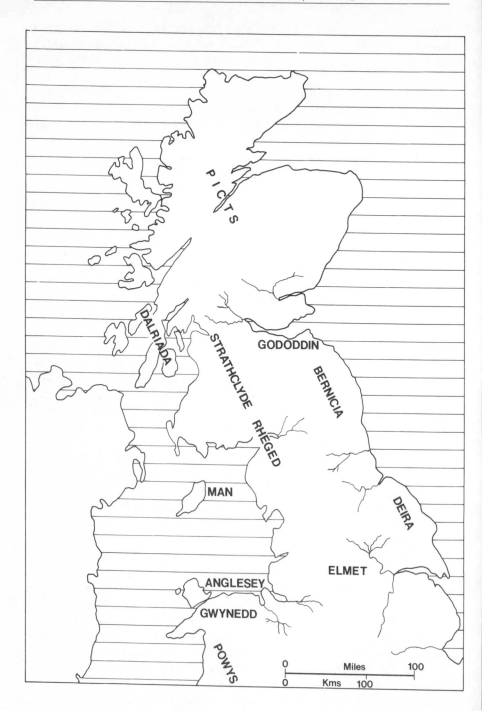

Map 2: Bernicia and Deira and their Celtic neighbours

of course, the areas settled first and in greatest numbers by the Germanic settlers and so presumably were the earliest to pass from Romano-British to Anglo-Saxon control. Once established they had the advantage of easy communication with other Germanic territories in Europe via the North Sea or the Channel. The east and south coast provinces may never have fragmented to the extent of some areas inland and by the end of the sixth century they were already beginning to expand by annexing smaller neighbours. Such aggressiveness must have encouraged areas which did not already possess military protection in the form of kings and their armies to acquire their own warleaders. By the time of the Tribal Hidage there were also two large 'inland' kingdoms, those of the Mercians and West Saxons, whose spectacular growth we can trace in part in our sources for the seventh century, but it is not clear how far this expansion had proceeded by the end of the sixth century.

The nature of early Anglo-Saxon kingship

Kingship seems to have been widespread in England by the end of the sixth century, but there is a limited amount which can be learnt about the nature of the office before the seventh century. Not only are the birth pangs of kingship among the Anglo-Saxons lost to us, but it is also difficult to say exactly what the position of king meant to an early Anglo-Saxon. Tacitus and other Roman writers show that some at least of the Germanic peoples had kings in the pre-migration period and two different strands of early Germanic kingship have been recognized: the traditional kingship of rulers who exercised various political and religious functions and military leadership.[85] Some of the Anglo-Saxon kingdoms claimed that their founders were scions of Continental royal houses. Hengist, the supposed founder of the royal house of Kent, may have been identical with the Jutish prince of that name who features in a Scandinavian context in the Anglo-Saxon poems *Beowulf* and the *Fight at Finnsburg*.[86] The Mercian kings included in their genealogies Wærmund and his son Offa, kings of Continental Angeln, who also appear in early Anglo-Saxon poems.[87] Clearly there was a desire by the eighth century to connect Anglo-Saxon rulers with some of the Germanic heroes of the fourth and early fifth centuries, the time at which much of Anglo-Saxon heroic poetry was set, but the inclusion of these heroic progenitors in the pedigrees is more likely to have been literary embellishment than solid historical fact.[88] However, the possibility cannot be ruled out altogether that some of those who became kings in Britain came from families which had been similarly successful on the Continent. The ship-burials at Sutton Hoo and Snape have been interpreted as implying a link between the East Anglian royal house and the Vendel dynasty of Sweden.[89]

Even if Anglo-Saxon kings were not descended from European royal houses they may have been influenced by inherited traditions of Germanic kingship. All the royal houses for whom genealogies exist claimed to be descended from one of the pagan gods. In the majority of cases the god was Woden,[90] but the East Saxons traced descent from Seaxnet, a god also worshipped by the Old Saxons of Germany,[91] and the kings of Kent who claimed to be Woden-born included in their genealogy Oisc who may also have been a god.[92] Whatever their origins Anglo-Saxon kings seem to have wanted to buttress their power by linking themselves with older traditions of sacral kingship which raised the king above his followers and – and this may be what was most significant – made their family the only one from which subsequent rulers could be chosen.[93]

But it would appear that Anglo-Saxon kings really owed their positions to their abilities as warleaders, as did the other Germanic leaders who created kingdoms for themselves out of former Roman provinces in Europe.[94] The accounts of the first Anglo-Saxon kings concentrate on their successes in battle and list their victories over British kings. The sixth-century entries in the *Anglo-Saxon Chronicle* are frequently problematic, but they do give a vivid impression of the aggressiveness of the early Anglo-Saxon kingdoms. Some of the fighting was concerned with expansion of territory and competition over land, but collection of tribute and booty were no doubt also important motives.[95] By the end of the sixth century the most powerful kings were able to claim an overlordship over the rest, sometimes referred to by historians as the bretwaldaship from the word 'bretwalda', meaning 'ruler of Britain', applied in the *Anglo-Saxon Chronicle* to the ninth-century overlord Egbert of the West Saxons.[96] The *Ecclesiastical History* lists the first seven great overlords beginning with Ælle of the South Saxons whose activities in the *Anglo-Saxon Chronicle* are placed between 477 and 491.[97] It seems doubtful whether Ælle really ruled at quite such an early date, especially as the second in the list was Ceawlin of Wessex whose *floruit* seems to have been the 580s and early 590s. Ceawlin was followed by Æthelbert of Kent who was ruling when the Gregorian mission came to England. The origins of this system of overlordship are obscure, but judging from what we can learn of overlords of the seventh century its basis was military strength. Although there have been various ingenious theories to account for the origins of the bretwaldaship,[98] it is not such a surprising institution in a society of rival kingdoms. Tacitus observed that amongst the warring Germanic tribes of the first century AD a particularly powerful king could win the submission of neighbouring tribes on the reputation of the size and effectiveness of his army alone.[99] It is quite possible that the most powerful sixth-century rulers exercised a similarly superficial overlordship over surrounding provinces, though, unlike the most powerful seventh-century rulers, they may not have commanded all the provinces south of the Humber.

Woden was an appropriate progenitor for rulers who were essentially warleaders because he was the god of battle.[100] Archaeology also indicates that war was an all-important concern for the elites of the early kingdoms. In male pagan burials weapons were the primary status symbol. The king buried, or commemorated, in Mound 1 at Sutton Hoo was not only provided with a veritable arsenal of everyday weapons, but took with him to the grave a magnificent set of war-gear, consisting of helmet, shield and an elaborate, jewelled harness and belt to support his sword.[101] The outfit must have been for ceremonial rather than practical wear and suggests the personification of the king as a great warrior. This picture is reinforced by the object generally interpreted as a sceptre which is in effect a giant whetstone; it seems the ideal symbol for a ruler whose basis of power was his military strength (see Fig. 3).[102] Helmets too may have been a symbol of royalty and they were used in coronations instead of a crown until c. 900.[103] Only two helmets have been recovered from burials, at Sutton Hoo and Benty Grange (see Figs 1 and 2).[104]

In a society where the success of a ruler and the people dependent upon him derived from effectiveness in war, the relationship of the king with his military followers was of vital importance. Tacitus saw the relationship of king and warband (*comitatus*) as central to the success and failure of the Germanic provinces he describes.[105] The interaction between the king and his warriors is also a major concern of Old English heroic poetry. Poems like *Beowulf* stress the reciprocal nature of the relationship of king and *comitatus*. The followers fought loyally for their lord, but the loyalty had been purchased beforehand by the upkeep the king provided for his warriors and by the giving of gifts; conspicuous acts of loyalty in battle would be rewarded by further gifts – appropriate generosity was what made a 'good king'.[106] When not in battle, the king's hall was the place where the necessary bonding of lord and follower occurred.[107] The *comitatus* ate and slept in the hall at the king's expense. It was at feasts in the great hall that pledges of loyalty were made and gifts in the form of weapons and other items of a warrior's equipment were handed over; anything made or decorated with gold was especially desired.

The excavated halls of Yeavering and Cowdery's Down form a bridge between the world of *Beowulf* and the reality of Anglo-Saxon life. These sites were probably royal vills to which the people of the surrounding district brought food rents to support the king and his followers. The reconstructions of halls from Cowdery's Down and Yeavering, based upon the surviving posthole evidence, show that they could have approached in grandeur the great feasting-hall of Heorot in which the Danish king entertained Beowulf and his followers.[108] We can fit the halls out for a feast with some of the items that were buried with the Sutton Hoo king: a vast cauldron with its iron chain which would have hung from the rafters over a central fire, drinking vessels of wood and horn, and plates and bowls of Byzantine silver.[109] Glass drinking vessels are a common item in other rich burials. It was a world of conspicuous display and personal adornment in which the wealth and power of the Sutton Hoo king would have been immediately apparent from his splendid appearance in regalia of silver, gold and garnets. In *Beowulf* the Danish coastguard knew instantly that Beowulf was a man of rank from his outward appearance and Beowulf's gift to the coastguard of a gold-hilted sword ensured that the receiver would be more honoured in the king's hall than he had been before.[110] *Beowulf* celebrated the bond betwen lord and follower, but also makes clear the economics behind the relationship; a good king was also a wealthy one.

By 600 royal lordship embraced not only the immediate followers of the king's warband, but the other members of his kingdom as well. So much seems clear from the earliest surviving lawcode, that of Æthelbert of Kent which was drawn up not long after his conversion.[111] The king is shown as exercising responsibility for the maintenance of law and order in his kingdom and his legislation covered all ranks of society – nobles, freemen (ceorls), unfree peasants and slaves. One of the major roles of the king was to set, and enforce, the payments which an injured party could claim from a transgressor by way of compensation, according to his or her status in society. Without such incentives to bring a claim for arbitration an accidental injury could easily turn into a full-scale bloodfeud.[112] Those who were not protected by Anglo-Saxon lordship or kinship ties, would be the particular responsibility of the king, and this included any resident foreigners, such as traders or missionaries;[113] breaches of the king's protection (*mund*) were particularly seriously punished. The king had a financial incentive for the maintenance of law and order for part of the fines for some of the most serious crimes came to him. Clearly there was a potential in the traditional law-enforcement duties of a king for the future development of royal powers.

Germanic traditions of kingship and lordship provided the basis of the authority of the earliest Anglo-Saxon kings, but there were additional influences which shaped the development of the early kingdoms. One of the most influential role-models from the contemporary Germanic world was Francia. There is evidence, recently gathered together by Ian Wood, to suggest that Francia exercised considerable influence in southern England in the sixth century and may even have taken tribute from some of the southern kingdoms.[114] Frankish influence can be seen most clearly in Kent which was connected with the Merovingian royal house of the Franks by marriage. Frankish goods are widely found throughout eastern Kent and the form of dress and tastes in food and drink of the Kentish nobility seem to have been modelled on those of their Frankish contemporaries.[115] Not only was there a demand for goods of Frankish craftsmanship and probably other items like wine, but Francia was the main route through which more exotic items like garnets and Byzantine silks and silver reached England.[116] These items were the expected accoutrements of kingship or the gifts the nobility desired from their royal lord and it was up to the kings to establish mechanisms for their acquisition. Although there is a concentration of Frankish goods in Kent, they are found throughout southern and eastern England in the sixth century, and no doubt less tangible influences from Francia were diffused with them, as certainly seems to have happened in later centuries. Although Francia was the most influential of the Continental Germanic kingdoms, ideas and influences may have come from other provinces as well, particularly those which also bordered the North Sea. The similarities between the Sutton Hoo ship-burial and those of the Vendel period in Sweden could be not so much the result of migration, but a pan-Germanic concept of the imagery of kingship.[117]

One of the greatest weaknesses of the *Ecclesiastical History* for the modern historian is that it gives little sense of the indebtedness of Anglo-Saxon England to its Romano-British background. In part this may be the result of a lack of adequate written sources, but Bede was also hostile towards the British because they had apparently not made any attempt to convert the Anglo-Saxons to Christianity.[118] Bede's history has been so influential that it is only recently that it has come to be appreciated that the organization of Anglo-Saxon kingdoms is likely to have owed much to Roman and sub-Roman administrative arrangements. As we have seen, a number of studies have suggested that territories dependent on royal vills, which formed the basis of Anglo-Saxon royal administration, had their antecedents in Roman organization of the countryside. The majority of inhabitants of Anglo-Saxon England were of Romano-British origin and many Anglo-Saxon kingdoms incorporated British principalities. The West Saxon royal house regularly made use of British name-elements which may be an indication of intermarriage with a British princely house. There were many basic similarities between the practices of Anglo-Saxon and British kings which must in part be a response to similar circumstances, but may also point to a complex interrelationship between rulers of the two nations. It may be significant that one of our few symbols of Anglo-Saxon royal power, the Sutton Hoo whetstone or sceptre, with its eight enigmatic carved heads and the delicate, naturalistic stag which surmounted it, seems to have been of Celtic manufacture.[119]

Whether because of their links with the Romano-British or not, the Anglo-Saxons were not unaware of the Roman past and their kings used its trappings to reinforce their own power.[120] Bede records of Edwin of Northumbria that:

So great was his majesty in his realm that not only were banners (*vexilla*) carried before him in battle, but even in time of peace, as he rode about among his cities, estates and kingdoms with his thegns, he always used to be preceded by a standard-bearer (*signifer*). Further, when he walked anywhere along the roads, there used to be carried before him the type of standard which the Romans call a *tufa* and the English call a *thuf*.[121]

It is thought that the standard at Sutton Hoo may have been a *tufa*, and the sceptre may have had its ultimate origins in Roman staffs of authority. A number of items of the impressive royal regalia have Roman prototypes, including the helmet and the shoulder clasps.[122] The segment of a Roman amphitheatre at Yeavering and the Roman amphitheatre which seems to have remained a feature of early Anglo-Saxon Canterbury were probably used for their own assemblies by Anglo-Saxon kings and suggest a similar desire to connect with the Roman past.[123] The Roman empire was the ultimate model for an upwardly-mobile Anglo-Saxon ruler and represented wealth and power beyond the dreams of the most ambitious Germanic prince. With the adoption of Christianity Anglo-Saxon kings acquired new links with the Roman world and inherited further skills from it, but even before the seventh century Anglo-Saxon kings were not unaware that they had taken over parts of a former Roman province and were the heirs of Roman emperors.

Sources for the study of kings and kingdoms from the seventh to ninth centuries
It is unfortunately only possible to discuss the history of a few of the Anglo-

Saxon kingdoms in any detail. Although written records began to be kept in the seventh century, the amount of material actually dating from this century is small. Many kingdoms simply did not exist for long enough as independent provinces to produce a body of written material. Even for kingdoms which continued well into the eighth century there is considerable variation in the survival rate of written sources. The kingdom of the South Saxons, for instance, was in existence as an independent unit until the reign of Offa of Mercia (757-96). It seems to have been one of the earliest dominant kingdoms and possesses a considerable amount of cemetery evidence for the pagan period. Yet it is impossible to write at any length about the history of the province in the seventh and eighth centuries. We know the names of some South Saxon kings and something of the history of the kingdom where it impinged on those of other provinces, but we do not have any genealogies or regnal lists which would help us to understand the relationship of different kings to one another and the internal history of the kingdom is obscure.[124]

Most of the documents which can be used to study individual kingdoms were introduced by the church, primarily for its own purposes, and they reflect the range of documentation which could be found in European churches during the same period. Kings were the most important benefactors of the religious houses within their kingdoms and naturally figure prominently in the archives of religious communities both through the records of their benefactions and in 'historical' records, such as saints' *Lives* and annals, produced by individual religious houses. Religious houses might also act as repositories for the archives of their royal families and produce classes of records such as king-lists and genealogies for them.[125] The historian is therefore dependent upon the survival of the archives of religious communities and as only a few religious houses enjoyed continuity from the early to the later Anglo-Saxon period and beyond, this is a major reason for the differential survival of material from individual kingdoms. For instance, the East Anglian royal house continued until 869 when King Edmund was killed by the Danes, but the subsequent Danish settlement seems to have led to the obliteration of most of the surviving religious communities with the result that no pre-Viking charters have survived from this important Anglo-Saxon kingdom.[126] Another eastern province, Lindsey, fared even worse and, apart from occasional references in works produced in other kingdoms, has left no historical records.[127]

It is in southern England and the west Midlands, the areas which were not settled by Vikings, that the greatest continuity of religious houses is to be found. Even so, few documents have survived in their archives as original manuscripts; most have been copied at various points in their history, and some are only preserved in the works of later medieval historians like William of Malmesbury. One of the most complex tasks of the historian is to decide whether a document has been altered, either deliberately or accidentally, in the course of transmission. The problems are particularly acute with charters, as it is evident that many of these have been 'improved' over the course of time. In the later Anglo-Saxon period, for instance, many religious houses sought to reclaim lands that had been lost in the ninth and early tenth centuries, and when earlier charters were found to be inadequate or were no longer in existence they might be rewritten with embellishments which would help to prove their owners' claims.

Although the question of a charter's authenticity is frequently problematic, charters are one of the most important sources of evidence for the study of kingship.[128] They record the name of the ruler making the grant and his title, the position of the land which was being granted and the conditions on which it was given, and they end with a list of prominent people who were witnesses to the transaction which can be of great value in establishing the power structure within a kingdom. There is some controversy about when charters were first introduced into England. Logic might suggest that they would have been introduced by Augustine, but the earliest surviving charter whose authenticity is not in doubt, for it is an 'original', is dated 679 from the reign of Hlothere of Kent, and consequently it has been proposed that the written charter may have been introduced in the time of Archbishop Theodore (668-90).[129] The truth may be, as Patrick Wormald has argued in a recent survey, that 'we are in no position to discover any single precise source, that there was probably more than one, and that, as it emerges into the historian's view, the Anglo-Saxon charter was neither Italian nor Frankish nor Celtic but simply *sui generis*'.[130] In introducing charters, the church was not only bringing in a new form of written evidence, but also a new concept of land tenure which was to bring some radical changes to the Anglo-Saxon kingdoms.[131]

Regnal lists and genealogies are two classes of record which may have pre-Christian antecedents. Bede records that a decision was taken by 'those who compute the dates of kings' not to record the names of two pagan, and spectacularly unsuccessful, kings of Northumbria who died in 634, but instead to consign the year of their reign to their successor Oswald.[132] However, although there may have been a native traditon of recording the reigns of kings and their pedigrees, the list and genealogies which have survived have done so in the archives of religious communities and show evident signs of clerical literary embellishment.[133] The most striking example of the latter is the West Saxon genealogy which traces Woden's descent from Adam. As the example of the Northumbrian kings cited above demonstrates, even such apparently simple documents as regnal lists and genealogies could be manipulated in a way which is likely to mislead the historian. The largest manuscript collection of genealogies and regnal lists is the so-called Anglian collection which its editor, David Dumville, believes was first assembled in Northumbria in the later eighth century.[134] The reasons for putting the Anglian collection together remain obscure; Dr Dumville suspects a political purpose connected with the claims of Anglian overlordship (Northumbrian or Mercian) over other areas of England. There is a certain artificiality about the pedigrees of the list for although the last people named in them died at varying points over a century and a half the genealogies are of a standard length.

Even the most secular of Old English poems also owe their survival to inclusion in ecclesiastical archives. Old English poetry is difficult to date and the most substantial pieces are only known from manuscripts written towards the end of the Anglo-Saxon period. There has been considerable debate about the date of the poem *Beowulf.* Until recently the poem had been considered to be a product of the seventh or eighth centuries,[135] but literary scholars seem to be increasingly favouring a date in the later Saxon period when the manuscript containing the poem was written.[136] To many historians and archaeologists it seems a work that belongs more naturally to the pre-Alfredian period and the milieu of Bede's *Ecclesiastical History* and the early *Lives* of Anglo-Saxon saints.[137] The value of *Beowulf* and other heroic poems to the historian is that they are virtually the only guide to the mentality of the secular aristocracy. *Beowulf,* which for all its dragons and sea-monsters has a strong Christian content, not only shows the secular values of lordship, but also how the vocabulary and morality of the institution was adapted by the church to convert the Anglo-Saxon aristocracy though not without some distortion of its basic message.[138]

Undoubtedly the most important of the surviving sources for a study of the early Anglo-Saxon kingdoms is Bede's *Ecclesiastical History of the English People.*[139] The work was completed in 731 or soon after, close to the end of Bede's life which had been devoted to the study and elucidation of sacred texts. In his last years Bede seems to have been increasingly preoccupied with the problems of contemporary Northumbria which included political decline abroad and unrest at home, and inadequate provision for the church and a falling away of Christian standards. In Bede's mind the different problems were closely interrelated for his study of the Bible had shown him that a people's worldly position was intimately linked with its standing with God. The *Ecclesiastical History* shows the Anglo-Saxons how their own history could be interpreted in Old Testament terms and Bede probably hoped that many would find the latter's message easier to absorb if they could relate it to people and places of which they had heard. As Bede says in his own Preface:

> Should history tell of good men and their good estate, the thoughtful listener is spurred on to imitate the good; should it record the evil ends of wicked men, no less effectually the devout and earnest listener or reader is kindled to eschew what is harmful and perverse.

Anglo-Saxon kings provided many of the examples of good and bad behaviour and the Old Testament provided Bede with models for his portrayals.[140]

Bede believed that the course of events would reveal God's will towards man and so he set out to reconstruct as accurately as he could the history of the Anglo-Saxons since their arrival in Britain and adoption of Christianity. Correspondents in monasteries and other religious foundations throughout the country provided him, at his request, with relevant material.[141] Some of the material came in the form of written documents and Bede has preserved material such as the extracts from early English synods and the *Life of St*

Æthelburh of Barking which would otherwise have been lost. However, most of his material came from oral tradition and some of it was certainly influenced by the conventions of both Germanic and Christian story-telling, so that we have set-piece scenes of heroic action, on the one hand, and miracle-working, on the other. One of Bede's greatest problems – and therefore one of his greatest boons to the modern historian – was to impose a consistent chronology. There was no universal means of dating events in Anglo-Saxon England, and correlation of events was a major problem with regnal years, for instance, beginning at a different point in every kingdom, depending on when each monarch came to the throne. Whenever possible Bede translated the dates he was given into *anno Domini* form and so pioneered this method of dating in England.[142]

Bede's achievements as a historian are impressive. Although he does use a story to point a moral and may emphasize certain aspects of royal behaviour and play down others, he provides enough information for readers to draw their own conclusions. He includes material for most areas of Anglo-Saxon England, though inevitably he has more on some kingdoms than others, and not surprisingly Northumbria has the best coverage. Bede cannot avoid some partisanship and is sometimes inclined to belittle Mercian successes to the advantage of Northumbria, and he has no time at all for Celtic areas which obstinately refused to abandon practices not approved of by the rest of the western church. One aspect that is perhaps more surprising is that the bulk of his work is concerned with the seventh century, and that the nearer we move to events of which Bede had personal knowledge, the less he has to say, particularly on political matters. No doubt this was a wise precaution; the work was dedicated to King Ceolwulf of Northumbria who had apparently already read the book in draft and even eminent theologians like Bede had to be careful what they said to kings.[143] It does not seem too fanciful to suggest that Bede hoped the king would be able to derive some practical assistance for the difficult days ahead of him from studying the history of his own people with its gallery of 'good' and 'bad' kings. But the details of political history were always subordinated to Bede's overriding ecclesiastical aims and as Bede remarked 'both the beginning and the course of his [Ceolwulf's] reign have been filled with so many and such serious commotions and setbacks that it is as yet impossible to know what to say about them'; God's intention towards man was not yet apparent to Bede from the events of his own day.[144]

Although Bede had no immediate successor, his work probably did act as a spur to the production of annals in Northumbria and Wessex. Between them the Northern annals and the *Anglo-Saxon Chronicle* provide a framework of events for the later eighth and the ninth centuries, though the lack of annals from Mercia, the dominant kingdom for much of this period, is a considerable disadvantage. Nor must we overlook the continuing importance of other disciplines which also study the Anglo-Saxon past. Archaeological evidence continues to be of the greatest importance and can show us the products of royal orders and decisions. Numismatic studies become increasingly useful for understanding political as well as economic developments.[145] Sources for individual kingdoms will be introduced in the relevant chapters for it is now time to review the history and regnal practices of the kingdoms for which sufficient written evidence survives. From these we can hope to learn more of Anglo-Saxon kingship and the factors which enabled some kingdoms to thrive while others disappeared from view.

Sources

No major narrative source written in Kent has survived, but Kent ranks as one of the best recorded of the early Anglo-Saxon kingdoms and can be studied through a variety of written sources. Bede was well-informed on Kentish affairs, one of his chief informants being, as he explains in his Preface, Abbot Albinus of the monastery of St Peter and St Paul, Canterbury (subsequently St Augustine's). Bede was also able to make use of the correspondence of the Gregorian mission which the priest Nothhelm copied for him from the papal archives.[1] In addition to the regnal and genealogical information included in the *Ecclesiastical History*, there is a genealogy of Æthelbert II of Kent in the Anglian collection[2] and a regnal list (which also ends with Æthelbert II) copied in the twelfth century.[3] The surviving charters come from the archives of the ecclesiatical foundations of Christ Church and St Augustine's Canterbury, Rochester, Minster-in-Thanet, Lyminge and Reculver. The charters are of great value not only for their information on relations between church and state, but also for the light they shed on royal administration and on individual members of the royal house. Unfortunately accurate dating is a problem with many of the charters and some of their chronological information is hard to reconcile with that provided by Bede and other narrative sources.[4] Lawcodes survive from the reigns of Æthelbert I, Hlothere and Eadric, and Wihtred.[5]

These sources present a rather bland picture of the Kentish kings, but insight into tensions within the royal house is provided by a series of related texts which are known as the 'Legend of St Mildrith'.[6] The various versions of the Legend bring together a number of traditions concerning members of the royal house of Kent and their Mercian and East Anglian relatives who were regarded as saints. At the heart of the Legend is an account of the murder of the Kentish princes Æthelbert and Æthelred by their cousin King Egbert which led to the foundation of the monastery at Minster-in-Thanet where Mildrith was abbess in the early eighth century. David Rollason, who has studied the texts in detail, argues that the archetype of the Legend dated to the second quarter of the eighth century, and that, in spite of its various hagiographical and traditional story-telling elements, it incorporated reliable historical traditions. It is also possible to receive some interesting insights into the lives of members of the royal house who were correspondents of the missionary St Boniface.

The origins of the kingdom of Kent

Kent has the most detailed surviving origin legends of any Anglo-Saxon kingdom. In addition to the brief references to Hengist and Horsa in the *Ecclesiastical History*, there are the fuller narratives in the *Historia Brittonum* and the *Anglo-Saxon Chronicle* which seem to be variant versions of the same traditions about Hengist, Horsa and the British king Vortigern.[7] Recent detailed studies by Patrick Sims-Williams and Nicholas Brooks have confirmed that these accounts are largely mythic and that any reliable oral tradition which they may have embodied has been lost in the conventions of the origin-legend format.[8] Rather less is known about Oisc from whom Bede says the Kentish royal house took the name of Oiscingas which implies that Oisc was originally seen as the more significant founder of the dynasty (though Oisc's name suggests that he may have been more god than man).[9] According to Bede Oisc was the *cognomen* of Hengist's son Œric and his son was Octa, but a variant on these traditions represented by the *Historia Brittonum* and the genealogy of Æthelbert II in the Anglian collection has Octa as Hengist's son and Oisc (though in a variant form) as Hengist's grandson. Such variations serve to underline the point that the stories about the origins of Kent belong to the literary world of saga rather than genuine historical tradition. To reach a clearer understanding of what may actually have occurred in the fifth and sixth centuries we have to use archaeology, landscape studies and place-names, plus what can be inferred from the earliest reliable written sources.

Bede recorded that the people of Kent were of Jutish origin and the claim is reflected in the choice of Hengist, who appears in Old English poetry as a warleader of the Jutes, as the founder of the dynasty.[10] The case for a Jutish origin receives support from fifth-century finds from eastern Kent, though the pottery and other artefacts cannot tell us in what capacity the Jutes first came to the province.[11] Objects made on the Jutland peninsula were still reaching Kent in the sixth century, but the dominant influence reflected in the archaeological record for the sixth century was Frankish. Frankish fashions in dress, weaponry and drink are reflected in the burials, though these are never exclusively Frankish suggesting 'influence' rather than settlement.[12] The Frankish connection receives support from the earliest reliable information we have about the Kentish royal house, which is discussed below, and in claims by the Merovingian royal house of the Franks to overlordship of some part of Britain in the sixth century.[13] Whatever the exact nature of the connection, it would appear to have been of material advantage to the Kentishmen; Kentish burials are not only distinguished from those of other Anglo-Saxon provinces by a greater range of imported goods, but are also significantly richer whether this wealth is measured in terms of precious metals or range of objects buried.[14]

The archaeological record cannot show when the balance of power passed from Romano-British to Germanic hands though it does show that the material culture of the province was predominantly Germanic by the sixth century. Although the province's major Roman town at Canterbury seems to have been abandoned during the fifth century (to be reoccupied at the end of the sixth century)[15] and there is a striking contrast between the small finds of the Roman and early Anglo-Saxon periods, there seems to have been greater continuity in rural settlement. Alan Everitt's study of the historical geography of Kent shows how the infrastructure of the Germanic kingdom may have grown out of the Romano-British organization of the province. Germanic settlement was concentrated in the same areas that had the greatest centres of population in the Roman period, especially the fertile area of the east of the county between the downland and the sea. The major estates and the 'regions' or lathes into which they were grouped for administrative purposes may also reflect the earlier Roman organization of the province to some degree and the estate centres of the Anglo-Saxon period, based at river- or spring-heads, were in many cases the sites of villas or other significant Roman settlements.[16] The Germanic settlers also adopted the Romano-British name of the province (*Cantium*) and this provides further encouragement for the idea of a subRoman province passing from British to Germanic hands with its basic structure preserved intact – which is what the legends of Hengist and Vortigern could be seen as embodying.[17]

The distinctive Kentish culture discussed above is confined to eastern Kent, and archaeological finds from western Kent are rather poorer and different in character, being more typical of 'Saxon' finds from Surrey, Essex and the Thames valley.[18] Kent is unique amongst the Anglo-Saxon kingdoms in having had two bishoprics (Canterbury for east Kent and Rochester for west Kent) from the early days of its conversion. The division into east and west Kent also seems to have been a political one with the two provinces each having its own king for much of the period in which the independent kingdom of Kent existed.[19] The combination of this evidence suggests that the Kentish kingdom originally comprised only east Kent, but that at some point probably in the sixth century west Kent was annexed and incorporated into the kingdom, though remaining a distinctive province in certain respects. The Saxon provinces to the north were the most obvious areas into which the men of Kent could expand with good communications provided by Watling Street as well as by sea.[20] Expansion to the south-west was hindered by difficult communications because of the Weald. The only other option for expansion was by sea and it seems likely that the sixth-century rulers of Kent also had an interest in the only other two areas which Bede said were settled by Jutes, the Isle of Wight and the area of Hampshire opposite it. The connection between Kent and Wight seems particularly likely as the mythological ancestors of the Kentish royal house included Wecta and Wihtgils whose names seem to be derived from the Latin name for the Isle of Wight (*Vecta/Vectis* anglicized as Wiht-), as was that of Wihtgar the eponymous founder of the royal house of Wight.[21] Material from Isle of Wight cemeteries suggests Kentish connections and one very rich female burial from Chessell Down was so overwhelmingly Kentish in character as to provoke the hypothesis that she was a Kentish princess married into royal house of Wight.[22]

The history of the kingdom of Kent
The historical horizon of the Kentish kings can be said to begin with Eormenric, the father of King Æthelbert. The name of Eormenric is only recorded in the Kentish genealogies, but the contemporary Frankish historian
Gregory of Tours alludes to the marriage of Æthelbert and Bertha, the daughter of King Charibert of Paris and Ingoberg, as having occurred while
Æthelbert's father was ruling in Kent.[23] Unfortunately Gregory does not
provide the date of the marriage, though he implies that Bertha was not born
until after 561 and his words could be taken to mean that Eormenric was still
ruling in 589.[24] Eormenric's name reinforces the archaeological evidence for
Frankish connections being of great importance in Kent by the middle of the
sixth century; its first element 'Eormen' is rare in Anglo-Saxon nomenclature,
but relatively common among the Frankish royal house and aristocracy.

Gregory of Tours provides contemporary evidence for the reign of
Æthelbert and although his information on the chronology of Kentish reigns
lacks precision, it does suggest that Bede's statement that Æthelbert died in
616 after a reign of 56 years must be mistaken as this would place Æthelbert's
accession in 560 – before the birth of the wife he is supposed to have married
while he was still a prince! 56 is in any case improbably long for a reign in the
early Saxon period, and it is perhaps more likely that Æthelbert died *aged* 56.[25]
Bede tells us that Æthelbert was able to exercise overlordship over the other
southern kingdoms[26] and we have seen some evidence for an extension of
Kentish power to neighbouring provinces. Exactly how and when Æthelbert
achieved his pre-eminence we do not know, but the previous great overlord
Ceawlin of Wessex fell from power in 592, according to West Saxon tradition.

The reality of Kentish power in the kingdom of the East Saxons is apparent.
Æthelbert's sister Ricula was married to Sledd of the East Saxons and as Sledd
seems to have been the first of his line to rule, it is possible that Kent played a
key role in bringing the family to power.[27] By 604 Sledd's son Sabert was
ruling the East Saxons and was nominally in charge of the London area, but it
was Æthelbert who took the responsibility, and the credit, for founding the
first cathedral of St Paul's. Links with the East Angles may also have been
particularly significant. The East Angles are the only other Anglo-Saxon
people whom Æthelbert is recorded as having tried to convert and though
King Rædwald refused to abandon his pagan gods completely, Paulinus, one of
the Italian missionaries, does seem to have been introduced into his court.[28]

Although Æthelbert married a Frankish princess, albeit a not particularly
prestigious one, the circumstances of Æthelbert's conversion suggest that he
was at some pains to distance himself from too close an association with
Frankish power. His Frankish bride Bertha, like the majority of the Franks,
was Christian and came accompanied not by a mere chaplain, but by a bishop
called Liudhard.[29] Although Bede does not specifically say so, the intention
was surely that Æthelbert would agree to consider conversion at Frankish
hands as a condition of the marriage. Analogy with similar unions between
Christian princesses and pagan kings from elsewhere within Europe and

within Anglo-Saxon England support such an interpretation and suggest that for Æthelbert to have received conversion via the Frankish court would have been an explicit recognition that he was politically subordinate to Francia.[30] By receiving conversion through Rome – and one of Pope Gregory's letters hints that Æthelbert had indicated a willingness to receive a papal delegation[31] – Æthelbert effectively asserted his independence from Frankish control.

None of Æthelbert's successors exercised the same level of authority outside Kent which Æthelbert had enjoyed, but Kentish power should not be underestimated in the reigns of Eadbald (616-40), Eorcenbert (640-64), Egbert I (664-73), Hlothere (673/4-85) and Eadric (685-87). References to events during their reigns are few, so it is probably significant that a number of them show Kentish influence outside Kent itself or suggest Kent enjoyed particular prestige among the early kingdoms. The Frankish connection was strengthened when Æthelbert's son Eadbald also took a Frankish bride – once his archbishop had persuaded him that he could not marry his stepmother.[32] Kentish tradition knew her as Ymme and believed her to be a Frankish princess, though the historian Karl Werner has recently suggested that she was the daughter of Erchinoald, mayor of the palace of Neustria (western Francia).[33] Within England there seems to have been a certain demand for Kentish princesses from the other royal kingdoms, though we are exceptionally well-informed about the marriages of Kentish royal women through the hagiographic traditions surrounding St Mildrith.[34] Bede pays particular attention to the marriage arranged during the reign of Eadbald between his sister, Æthelburh, and Edwin of Deira which brought Christianity to Northumbria, and apparently assured a special relationship between the two provinces for Bede claims that when Edwin was overlord of the southern English he did not exercise authority over Kent.[35]

Kentish interests in the areas immediately north and west of the province seem to have continued. The bond with the East Saxon royal house weakened, but the laws of Hlothere and Eadric reveal continuing Kentish interests in London where there was a Kentish royal residence (*cyngæs sele*), a reeve to represent Kentish royal interests (*cyninges wicgerefan*) and where men of Kent might be expected to make considerable property transactions.[36] King Egbert was in a position to found the monastery of Chertsey in Surrey and may have controlled all the eastern part of the province.[37] There may even have been some Kentish influence amongst the South Saxons, though the only clear reference concerns rather unusual circumstances in which Eadric raised the South Saxons against his uncle, Hlothere, and was thereby able to deprive him of the throne.[38]

However, the position of Kent could not remain entirely unaffected by the new forces coming to power in the seventh century. Traces of Northumbrian intervention are slight, though Oswald threatened the infant heirs of Edwin of Deira whom Æthelburh had taken back to Kent,[39] and Oswiu appears to have tried to intervene in the appointment of a new archbishop of Canterbury in

664.[40] In 676 Æthelred of Mercia invaded Kent and caused so much destruction in the Rochester diocese that the see had to be abandoned for a while.[41]
The reasons for his attack are not given by Bede; enforcement of overlordship
or an attempt to discourage Kentish influence in Surrey and London are
possibilities.[42] A more serious invasion seems to have brought Eadric's reign to
an end. A raid on Kent by Cædwalla of Wessex and his brother Mul is recorded
in 686, and shortly afterwards Mul as king of Kent confirmed previous royal
grants to the monastery of Minster-in-Thanet.[43] Possibly Cædwalla and Mul
joined forces with the East Saxons as a charter (admittedly rather problematic)
in which Cædwalla granted away land in Kent refers to the invasion of King
Sigehere who apparently witnessed the document.[44] Mul's reign came to an
abrupt end when he and twelve others were burnt to death in 687 : Cædwalla
ravaged the kingdom again and the West Saxons ultimately had to pay appropriate compensation for the murder to his successor, Ine.[45] The exact fate of
Eadric while these events occurred is not certain, but according to a Frankish
source he died on 31 August 687.[46]

The abdication of Cædwalla in 688 was followed by further upheaval in
Kent. East Saxon interests were inherited by Swæfheard, son of Sæbbi who
ruled in the western half of Kent probably until 694.[47] The other half of the
kingdom was ruled by Oswine who was a member of the Kentish royal house,
but apparently not considered eligible for the throne by Bede's informants or
by those who kept the regnal lists as he does not appear in the latter.[48] It is
possible that both men owed their positions to help from Æthelred of Mercia
who confirmed charters of both rulers and whose enmity towards the main-
stream Kentish royal house had been demonstrated in 676.[49] However, in 690
or 691 Wihtred, the brother of Eadric, and, according to Bede, 'the rightful
king', toppled Oswine,[50] though, as has already been mentioned, Swæfheard
may have lingered until 694. There is no reason to think that Wihtred's
position was weaker than that of his predecessors who ruled before 686. One of
his grants was issued at Berkhamsted, suggesting that Wihtred may have
exercised power north of the Thames and had his revenge on the East
Saxons.[51]

Bede's last Kentish notice records the death of Wihtred in 725 and that he
left three sons, Æthelbert, Eadbert and Alric, as his heirs.[52] From this point
the chronology of the Kentish kings becomes much less certain and, as
Thomas of Elmham, a medieval chronicler who grappled with the problems of
Kentish dating observed, there are severe problems in reconciling charter and
chronicle evidence.[53] Alric is not heard of again, and according to the *Anglo-
Saxon Chronicle* Eadbert died in 748 and Æthelbert in 762. The charter
evidence implies that Æthelbert was the senior and in command from the
death of his father and that both Æthelbert and Eadbert were alive and ruling
in 762 (though it should be noted that there are no charters for Æthelbert or
Eadbert between 748 and 761).[54] Clearly both sets of evidence cannot be
correct. The *Chronicle* evidence for Eadbert's death in 748 receives some
support from evidence for an Eardwulf, son of King Eadbert, ruling in the

Rochester diocese in the latter part of the period (though unfortunately none of his charters or letters is securely dated).[55] However, to accept Eadbert's death in 748 one also has to accept that a second Eadbert came to the throne in 761 and that subsequently the regnal years of his charters were altered to make it appear as if he was the same person as the earlier Eadbert. One can hypothesize about which solution is likely to be correct, but overall it seems safer to live with some uncertainty over the exact nature and chronology of the reigns of Æthelbert, Eadbert and Eardwulf.

Æthelbert and Eadbert were ruling at the time of the great Mercian overlord Æthelbald and, although he does not seem to have interfered with their sovereign rights in Kent, Kentish outside interests were certainly affected when London became a Mercian city. Kentish religious houses who wished for favourable tolls now had to seek them from Æthelbald, and a grant from King Æthelbald to Abbess Eadburh of Minster-in-Thanet which is witnessed by King Eadbert helps to underline a shift in the relationship of Kentish and Mercian kings.[56] Another sign of changing times was the appointment of Mercians as archbishops of Canterbury. Tatwine (731-4) came from the monastery of Breedon (Leics); Nothhelm (735-9) was a priest in London; and there is a possibility that Cuthbert (740-61) had been bishop of Hereford before his appointment to Canterbury.[57]

Æthelbert died in 762 and Eadbert is found sharing power in the same year with King Sigered who conceivably, from the form of his name, was a member of the East Saxon royal house; a charter in which Sigered and Eadbert both appear is Eadbert's last appearance.[58] Subsequently Sigered ruled with a king Eanmund,[59] but the reigns of both men seem to have ended in 764 when Offa of Mercia took control in Canterbury with a determination to enforce Mercian overlordship in a way that Kent had not experienced before. Offa apparently claimed the right to control the Kentish royal lands and that Kentish kings could only grant land with his consent. Offa demonstrated his control in 764 by regranting in his own right land which Rochester had previously received from Sigered with the consent of Eanmund.[60] Native kings were at first allowed to rule under Offa's authorization, and Heahbert and Egbert II are found sharing power in 765.[61] Heahbert soon disappeared and it is possible (but not certain because of the dubious nature of the charter texts) that Offa ruled Kent in his own right between 772 and 774. However, Egbert seems eventually to have led a successful counterattack and it would appear that the men of Kent were the victors over the Mercians at the battle of Otford in 776.[62] In 778 and 779 Egbert was able to grant charters without reference to Offa,[63] and it is possible that this period of relative Kentish independence extended to 784 when a King Ealhmund made a single appearance in a charter.[64] However, from 785 Offa is found in sole control of the province and grants which Egbert had made in his own right were rescinded.[65]

The main representative of the royal house from this time seems to have been Eadbert Præn who like other displaced Anglo-Saxon princes took refuge at the court of Charlemagne in the latter part of Offa's reign.[66] On Offa's death in 796 Eadbert returned to Kent and was able to take control of the kingdom for two years until defeated and captured by Offa's successor Cenwulf.[67] Cenwulf's claims were strengthened by the fact that Eadbert had been in holy orders which he had illegally renounced in order to become king.[68] As a sop to Kentish independence Cenwulf created his own brother Cuthred subking of Kent, but when Cuthred died in 807 Cenwulf treated the Kentish kingdom as part of his own patrimony, as Offa had done before him.[69] There was possibly a last surge of independence c. 823-25 when we know, chiefly from the numismatic evidence, that Baldred was in power in Kent, but Baldred could equally be a Mercian prince and a relative of King Beornwulf who took power from Cenwulf's successor Ceolwulf in 823.[70] Baldred was expelled by Egbert of Wessex in 825 and from this time the former kingdom was under West Saxon control. Kent together with Sussex, Surrey and, probably, Essex formed a subkingdom of Wessex until 858 when it was fully integrated with the main kingdom.

The Kentish royal house

Although the surviving versions of the Kentish regnal list show only single reigns, it is clear from Bede and the charter evidence that it was normal for two kings to rule together in Kent even if one of these was generally dominant. A sequence of joint reigns can be traced from the reigns of Hlothere and his nephew Eadric, who issued a joint lawcode, and joint rule even persisted during periods of foreign conquest (Table 1).[71] The evidence for joint king-ship before the accession of Hlothere and Eadric is not so substantial, but there are hints of it. Forged charters of Canterbury and Rochester preserve a tradi-tion that Eadbald ruled with his father Æthelbert.[72] During Eadbald's own reign letters from the papal archives transcribed in the *Ecclesiastical History* seem to distinguish Eadbald 'Audubald' from a Kentish ruler 'Aduluald' (Æthelwald) who must have been his contemporary.[73] The 'Legend of St Mildrith' preserves a tradition that Eormenred was a junior Kentish king probably during the reign of Eadbald (presumably in succession to Æthelwald).[74]

In some cases there is evidence that the kings possessed separate courts based in east and west Kent which is what one might expect from the evidence for the separate dioceses. When after the death of Æthelbert the missionaries were faced with a reaction against Christianity, King Eadbald seems to have been brought back to the true faith by Archbishop Lawrence while his co-ruler Æthelwald was saved from apostasy by Bishop Justus of Rochester.[75] The charters of Æthelbert II and Eadbert show their different spheres of activity in east and west Kent and there is a clear indication of their separate courts in a charter of 738 which was witnessed by each brother with his own entourage.[76] The king based in east Kent and Canterbury tended to be the dominant partner, but relations between the two rulers varied with individual circum-stances. Wihtred, for instance, seems to have delegated some royal powers to his eldest son Æthelbert II, but Æthelbert did not use the title of king until

Kings of East Kent	Kings of West Kent
Æthelbert I d. 616	?Eadbald
Eadbald 616–640	Æthelwald
Eorcenbert 640–664	?Eormenred
Egbert I 664–673	
Hlothere 673/4–685	Eadric
Eadric 685–687	
Mul 687	?Sigehere of East Saxons
Oswine 688–690	Swæfheard of East Saxons (688–694)
Wihtred 690/1–725	Æthelbert
Æthelbert II 725–762	Eadbert 725–?762 Eardwulf c. 747–?762
Eanmund c. 762–c. 764	Sigered c. 762–c. 764
Heabert c. 764–c. 765	

Mercian control of the province began in 765, but was interrupted by the following reigns of Kentish kings:

> Egbert II c. 764–c. 785
> Ealhmund c. 784
> Eadbert Præn 796–798

Mercian subkings of Kent

Cuthred 798–807
Baldred c. 823–825

West Saxon subkings of Kent

Æthelwulf 825–839
Æthelstan 839–c. 851
Æthelbert c. 851–860

Table 1: Regnal list of the kings of Kent

after his father's death. When Æthelbert became the dominant king he shared power with his brother Eadbert who enjoyed more freedom of action than Æthelbert apparently had under their father.[77] Possibly the brothers did not always agree on their relative powers as in one charter we find Bishop Ealdwulf of Rochester apologizing because he had not known he needed Æthelbert's confirmation for a grant made by Eadbert.[78] Oswine and the East Saxon Swæfheard provide the best evidence for an equal division of authority as each witnessed the other's charters. It would appear from the charter donations that Swæfheard was based in west Kent, which of course was closest to the East Saxon kingdom and may originally have been a 'Saxon' province, and Oswine in the eastern part of the kingdom.[79] A similar clearcut division into two provinces seems to have occurred in 762 when Sigered (who from his name could also have been an East Saxon) described himself as 'king of a half part of the province of the *Cantuarii*'.[80] Rather surprisingly, as Sigered's untidy title illustrates, there does not seem to have been any term in common use for the two halves of the kingdom. Although for administrative purposes the kingdom of Kent was usually divided between two courts which might go their own way at times of foreign conquest, the kingdom generally seems to have been regarded as an entity with one king who was dominant.

The division into the two provinces presumably goes back to the sixth century when west Kent is most likely to have been taken over by the rulers of east Kent. By the ninth century the administrative division into two provinces had become so fossilized that they were kept as separate ealdormanries of east and west Kent after Kent was incorporated into Wessex.[81] It was not unusual for Anglo-Saxon kingdoms to turn a newly acquired province into a sub-kingdom, but it was unusual for such a subkingdom to persist for longer than one or two generations. Presumably the internal subdivision of the kingdom was a matter of some significance to the rulers of Kent which even the most powerful kings wished to preserve. One reason for its persistence may have been the opportunities it presented for manipulation of the succession. For one of the distinctive features of kingship in Kent is its pattern of restricted succession in which only those who were themselves sons of kings succeeded to the throne.[82] The subkingship provided an opportunity to establish and maintain such a system of succession if, as certainly occurred in a number of cases, the junior king followed his senior partner to the dominant position.[83]

However, this system of succession could not eliminate rivalry within the royal house. Eadric seems to have served as junior king to his uncle Hlothere which would presumably have meant that he would have succeeded to his uncle's position in due course. Eadric, however, preferred to anticipate events and with the aid of the South Saxons brought about his uncle's untimely death;[84] perhaps Hlothere had sons of his own whom Eadric feared may have ultimately been preferred to himself. One of the clearest accounts of the tensions within the royal house is contained within the Kentish hagiographical collection known as 'The Legend of St Mildrith' and concerns the circumstances which led up to the deaths of Mildrith's uncles Æthelred and

Æthelbert.[85] According to the Legend, Eadbald had two sons, Eorcenbert and Eormenred, and was succeeded by the former. Some of the older versions record that Eormenred was the elder of the two and give him the title of *regulus* which may imply that he held the junior kingship under his father. Eormenred seems to have predeceased his brother, and left two sons, Æthelbert and Æthelred, under Eorcenbert's protection. When Eorcenbert died his own son Egbert succeeded him and in order to safeguard his position Egbert had Æthelbert and Æthelred murdered. The two princes are presented as young children, but in fact they are more likely to have been adults and a genuine threat to Egbert's position (see Table 3).

The account of the murder of Æthelred and Æthelbert reveals very clearly the problems inherent in the type of restricted succession which was practised in Kent. A king might be succeeded by two or more sons, but usually only the offspring of one of these sons would inherit the throne. Rivalry between first cousins was consequently likely to be intense and Egbert's actions reveal one course of action which could resolve the situation. The expectation in Kent, as in Francia, seems to have been that only those who were the sons of kings succeeded to the throne; more distant relatives seem to have been excluded and had to resort to force of arms if they wished to accede. This is what Oswine had to do, and he seems to have turned to the East Saxons and Mercians to assist him. His exact relationship to the main line is not known, though a case has been made for him being a descendant of Eormenred whose wife, according to the Mildrith Legend, was called Oslafa.[86] However, Bede, no doubt reflecting the views of the descendants of Egbert who soon regained power, says that Oswine was *dubius* and not the rightful king.[87] Rules of succession seem to have been sharply defined in Kent, as they were in Merovingian Francia, and they generally seem to have been vigorously enforced.

These observations only apply up to the time of Æthelbert II and Eadbert for we do not know how any of the subsequent kings were related to the main line or to each other. The names of Eanmund, Ealhmund, Egbert II and Eadbert Praen follow the naming traditions of the dominant branch, but that is as far as one can go. Sigered and Baldred may not have been Kentishmen at all, but members of East Saxon and Mercian dynasties respectively. Heahbert's origins are obscure. On the face of it the Kentish kings did not experience any of the eruptions of distant cousins and rival royal lineages which upset the succession plans of other Anglo-Saxon dynasties, but our knowledge of what occurred in the kingdom's final days is incomplete.

We do not know much about what happened to male members of the royal house who, like Oswine, were apparently considered ineligible for the throne. One might have expected them to take their place amongst the ranks of the higher nobility and assist in royal government, but none of the nobles who witnessed royal charters can be definitely identified as members of the royal house, though King Heahbert may be the individual of that name who was among the nobles who witnessed a charter of Sigered.[88] Some of the surplus princes might have gone into the church, like Eadbert Præn, which theoretically prevented them from having any claim on the throne.[89] Some of the kinsmen of Abbess Eangyth and her daughter Heahburh (who were related to the royal house though it is not known exactly how) seem to have been forced into exile because of the hostility of the main line.[90]

On the whole we are rather better informed about the roles allowed to women of the royal house. Female relatives were in the first instance of value for the links which they could form with other royal houses through marriage.[91] Kentish princesses married three of the most powerful rulers of the seventh century, namely Edwin and Oswiu of Northumbria and Wulfhere of Mercia. The marriage of Edwin and Æthelburh, sister of Eadbald, was not only important for the spread of Christianity, but also sealed an alliance between the two kingdoms which was advantageous to Kent when Northumbria became militarily pre-eminent.[92] When Edwin was killed, Æthelburh returned to Kent with her daughter Eanflæd, who must have been an important bargaining counter for her cousin Hlothere when Oswiu of Northumbria wished to marry her to help strengthen his command of the two Northumbrian

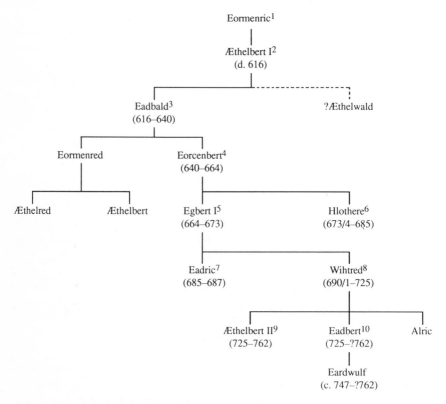

Table 2: Genealogy of the Oiscingas kings and princes of Kent

The kings are numbered in the order in which they ruled as dominant kings of Kent; the intrusive foreign rulers of Kent and Oswine who cannot be placed in the genealogy are omitted here, but see table 1.

provinces.[93] Eanflæd seems to have been a particularly forceful queen of Northumbria, and though her power derived in part from the fact that she was a Deiran princess, her Kentish links may also have been significant; for instance, she mobilized her cousin Hlothere to help her promote the career of Wilfrid who like her favoured the customs of Deira rather than Bernicia over such issues as the celebration of Easter.[94]

Kentish royal women also played an important role in the church in Kent. In the council of Bapchild King Wihtred granted privileged rights to eight royal minsters; five of these – Minster-in-Thanet, Folkestone, Lyminge, Sheppey and Hoo – were double monasteries of a type first found in Francia, that is mixed communities of nuns and monks or secular clergy under the control of an abbess.[95] All but Hoo were founded, according to the Mildrith Legend, by or for queens or princesses of Kent and their foundresses were subsequently honoured as saints.[96] Minster-in-Thanet is the best recorded of these royal double monasteries as its early charters were preserved at St Augustine's, Canterbury which acquired the monastery and its estates in the

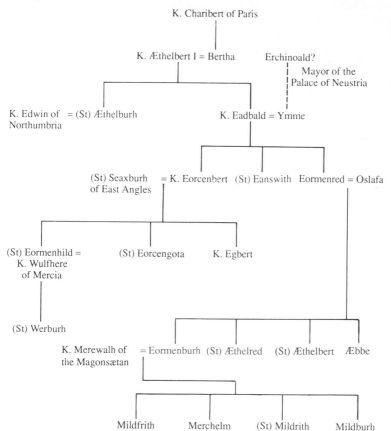

Table 3: Female members of the Kentish royal house and their connections by marriage

reign of Cnut.[97] The foundation of Minster is a major concern of the Mildrith Legend for, after the murder of the princes Æthelred and Æthelbert, Egbert was obliged to atone for his crime by founding the monastery on the Isle of Thanet. Its first abbess was a sister of the murdered princes; she appears in the Mildrith Legend as Domne (i.e. Domina) Eafe and in the Minster charters as Abbess Æbbe.[98]

Control of Minster seems to have passed among female members of the Kentish royal house and gives us some insight into the workings of a royal proprietary monastery. Æbbe was succeeded by her niece Mildrith, the subject of the Mildrith Legend, and she in turn was succeeded by Eadburh, who was probably also a member of the Kentish royal house though her exact relationship is uncertain.[99] Eadburh actively promoted the cult of Mildrith and was later regarded as a saint herself. The next abbess to appear in the charters is Sigeburh who was conceivably related to King Sigered whose reign overlapped with her term as abbess.[100] All the abbesses were active in obtaining grants and privileges from Kentish kings or from Mercian overlords when appropriate. Eadburh seems to have been highly regarded by fellow religious and was treated with great respect by the Anglo-Saxon missionary Boniface who commissioned her to copy the epistles of St Peter in gold.[101]

It is likely that the other double monasteries would provide a similar history if their charters had survived. Boniface's correspondants also included Abbess Eangyth and her daughter Heahburh who eventually succeeded her as abbess. They were related to King Æthelbert II and presumably controlled one of the other proprietary monasteries of the royal house.[102] Like Eadburh they were literate, pious and wrote respectable Latin. These proprietary houses allowed the royal house to endow the church, but retain use of it for their relatives, though as Eangyth's letter to Boniface reveals the endowments were not always sufficient and kings, queens and their officials might make oppressive demands (presumably financial) on such houses.[103] The proprietary houses may also have been linked with the administration of the kingdom for a number of them seem to have been based in the central places of major estates for whose spiritual needs they would have been responsible.[104]

Pope Gregory had advised Augustine to make certain compromises with Anglo-Saxon custom in order to ensure the success of their mission.[105] This principle also seems to have been adopted by Archbishop Theodore, who, for instance, was prepared to allow the existence of double monasteries as an established local custom although he could find little canonical support for them.[106] The result seems to have been (as far as we can tell) harmonious relations between Kentish kings and their archbishops. The kings conscientiously endowed and protected the churches as their legislation indicates, though they retained certain rights over church lands, and the archbishops refrained from objecting to such institutions as proprietary monasteries in which in any case, if two of the double monasteries are a reliable guide, standards of religious observance were high. Whether matters would have continued in such a harmonious strain if the Kentish kings had not been ousted in the last quarter of the eighth century we shall never know. But when the Mercian kings and their kinswomen attempted to take over the proprietary rights of the Kentish royal house in Minster-in-Thanet, Lyminge and Reculver they were actively opposed by successive archbishops of Canterbury who successfully asserted episcopal rights over such monasteries in opposition to the interests of the new rulers.[107]

Royal resources and government

Unlike most other major Anglo-Saxon kingdoms, it is not Kent's military prowess which emerges most clearly from the available sources as the reason for its success. This is not to say that military successes did not play an important role; there are scattered references to Kentish battles and the Kentish army was apparently strong enough to defeat a Mercian army of Offa in 776. Rather it is that the sources available for the study of the Kentish kingdom enable us to concentrate on other factors which help explain the power of its kings.

One thing which distinguishes Kent from other Anglo-Saxon kingdoms is the strength of its Frankish connections. As we have seen, Frankish finds and fashions are a notable feature of the archaeology of the province in the sixth century. The arrival of Frankish goods can be linked with the personal ties between Kent and the Neustrian (west Frankish) court seen most clearly through the marriages of Æthelbert and Eadbald. We should not underestimate the importance of these family links. When Æthelburh, the sister of Eadbald, fled from Northumbria after the death of her husband Edwin, she sent her children to the court of King Dagobert in Francia for safety, as she feared they might otherwise fall victim to dynastic intrigue. Bede calls Dagobert her *amicus*, but he was also, if rather distantly, her kinsman.[108] Frankish names like Eorcenbert, Eormenred and Hlothere (Leutharius) continued to be favoured by the royal house. At least one Kentish princess, Eorcengota, the daughter of Eorcenbert, entered a Frankish double monastery (Faremoûtier-en-Brie).[109]

We cannot know the exact circumstances in which the link between the Kentish and Frankish royal houses was established though, as Ian Wood has shown, it fits into a pattern of Frankish expansion and overlordship of areas bordering the North Sea in the sixth century.[110] As a province on the periphery of the Frankish kingdom the Kentish kings received various advantages, both tangible and intangible, which may have helped them emerge as one of the dominant kingdoms of southern England in the late sixth and seventh centuries. The tangible advantages of the connection were the imported goods already referred to which are in such abundance that they must represent commerce rather than just gift-exchange between royal courts.[111] Exactly when Kentish kings came to control trade in Kent is debated. Royal interest in the supervision of trade and protection of merchants is evident in the Kentish lawcodes of the later seventh century.[112] One way in which traders could prove an important source of royal revenue was through the levying of tolls and royal officials whose duty it was to collect such tolls (*theolonearii*) appear in a number of Kentish charters.[113] Grants of remissions of tolls at Kentish ports to religious houses imply that such tolls were normally burdensome. The exemptions from toll also show the involvement of the royal proprietary houses in foreign trade and many of them, including Minster-in-Thanet, Lyminge and Reculver, were ideally sited for that purpose on coasts or navigable channels in eastern Kent. The combination of sources suggests that commercial interests were of great importance to the Kentish royal house during the seventh and early eighth centuries.

What is not so certain is how far this royal domination of trade can be projected back into the sixth century. The cemeteries associated with two early ports at Sarre and Dover contain an unusual number of burials well-equipped with weapons which has led to the suggestion that they were the graves of men charged with the supervision of traffic at the ports, the predecessors of the royal reeves who carried out the same role in the late seventh and eighth centuries.[114] Sarre, Dover and another early port (OE *wic*) at Fordwich were either the centres of royal estates in the seventh and eighth centuries or closely associated with royal vills and there is a likelihood that royal control originated before our written sources begin; it has been proposed that one of the achievements of Æthelbert was to create a monopoly of trade that had previously been carried out by the aristocracy.[115] In the seventh century trade was a significant aspect of Kentish royal power, even if it is not clear what Kent was exporting in exchange for the luxury items which it imported.[116] Revenue from trade was one significant aspect, but the virtual monopoly which Kent enjoyed on various commodities, including amethyst, crystal and wheel-thrown pottery (and the liquids it may have contained), gave it an important bargaining point in its relationships with other Anglo-Saxon kingdoms.[117] The Kentish kings could offer gifts which other kingdoms would find hard to match. Kent's expansion of its interests to London (described by Bede as an emporium for many nations) by the end of the sixth century was a logical expansion of existing commercial interests.[118] The laws of Hlothere and Eadric refer to a Kentish reeve in the *wic* of London and a king's hall in which transactions could be witnessed.[119]

Corroboration that trade with Francia was important in the seventh and eighth centuries is provided by the numismatic evidence. Kent seems to have taken the lead in the production of coin in England and, as its first issues and subsequent adaptations are in line with what happened in Francia, it is likely that exchange with Francia was a main function of the coinage. The first Kentish coins were probably struck in the late sixth century and imitated Merovingian gold tremisses.[120] These are the coins to which the holy messengers, who came to claim the soul of Princess Eorcengota of Kent from the monastery of Faremoûtier, alluded when they said 'that they had been sent to take back with them the golden coin which had been brought thither from Kent'.[121] The Kentish gold coins are rare until the second quarter of the seventh century when some seem to have been struck in London as well as in

Kent itself and one of the London issues apparently carries the name of King Eadbald. It was not normal in this period for the monarch's name to appear on coins and consequently it has been questioned whether kings enjoyed a monopoly on the production of coin before the introduction of the named penny coinages of the late eighth century.[122]

In both Francia and Kent the gold coinage was increasingly debased by the addition of silver, until in the late 660s it was replaced in Neustria by a totally silver coinage, with the Kentish coinage following suit soon after. The Kentish and London mints took the lead in the production of the new coinage, usually known in England as sceattas, and Kent is the main findspot of the primary series (see Fig. 14.1).[123] However, from the early eighth century the production of sceattas became much more widespread within England. This may be an indication that direct trade with Francia was now more widespread, and it coincides with the period of Kentish political decline. Further reform because of debasement became necessary in both England and Francia in the 760s, and the first 'pennies' in imitation of the Frankish deniers of Pepin the Short are probably those of the Kentish kings Egbert and Heahbert (see Fig. 14.2), though the Canterbury mint seems to have been taken over subsequently by Offa and coins were minted in his name alone.[124]

Coins and imported goods are tangible evidence of the influence of western Francia on Kent and its kings, but we should look for intangible signs as well. Not just objects, but also ideas and concepts were likely to have been diffused from Francia to Kent and the kings of Kent may have acquired through their Frankish contacts not only material wealth, but also practical knowledge of Frankish government which they were able to use in order to enhance their own royal authority. The introduction of written law into Kent provides an example of the type of borrowing which may have taken place. Bede says that Æthelbert produced the first written lawcode for Kent *iuxta exempla Romanorum*, but in practice the king seems to have been more influenced by Frankish than Roman forms.[125] The provision of a written lawcode was a sign, like the adoption of Christianity, that Kent had joined the more advanced Germanic kingdoms of Europe and the writing down of Æthelbert's lawcode may have had a symbolic as well as a practical value. Although there are major differences between the Kentish and Frankish lawcodes, there are also some interesting parallels which are particularly striking when the Kentish laws are compared with those from Wessex. For instance, the Kentish wergilds follow the same proportions as those of the Franks and differ from those found in the West Saxon codes. The West Saxon code has two levels among the nobility whereas the Kentish and Frankish codes only recognize the equivalent of the West Saxon lower noble class, which both refer to as *leudes/leode*.[126] Although this material has been seen as evidence for large-scale Frankish settlement in Kent,[127] it is more likely to be an indication of how pervasive Merovingian influences were among the upper echelons of Kentish society, and of how such influences could have affected the definition of relations between the kings of Kent and their nobles.

Frankish influence can be found in other areas of Kentish life as well. Its double monasteries seem to have been modelled on those of northern Francia and like many of the Merovingian houses remained intimately connected with the royal house. The apparent rules governing royal succession in Kent may be modelled on the practices of the Merovingian royal house. But disentangling Frankish from other influences is not always an easy matter, for the kings of Kent and Francia were heirs to common Germanic and imperial traditions. The right the Kentish kings claimed to collect tolls at Kentish ports could have been an imitation of Frankish practice, but might also have been a legacy from Roman control of the province or a derivation from Germanic traditions of the ruler as protector and supervisor of strangers such as traders.[128]

A Germanic king could only control his kingdom and win his battles with the aid of the nobility, but the Kentish nobles are elusive and are generally only glimpsed witnessing charters, attending councils or approving lawcodes. Unfortunately the charters with witness lists surviving are not sufficiently numerous to allow a detailed analysis of the leading nobles and only one charter from a Kentish nobleman survives from the period when Kent was an independent kingdom. Nevertheless one can see, from the earliest surviving charters from Hlothere's reign (673/4-85) onwards, a tendency for a small number of nobles to regularly witness after the king and ecclesiastical dignitaries, and such nobles often continue to appear during times of political change. For instance, Ecca, Osfrith and Gumbert, who appear regularly in leading positions in Hlothere's charters, also dominate the charters of Oswine and Swæfheard.[129] Ecca seems to have been particularly significant as he frequently attests first and is the only one of the three to witness all the five charters of Oswine and Swæfheard. Similar instances of dominant nobles can be found in eighth-century charters in which they occasionally are given titles though there does not seem to be much consistency in the terms used. An individual called Baldheard (there are various spellings) appears regularly in key positions in charters of both Æthelbert II and Eadbert, once with the title *dux* and once described as *comes*.[130] Ecgbald who leads the attesting nobles in a grant of Sigered is described as *comes atque praefectus*[131] and Abbess Eangyth complained that the *praefectus* was one of those from whose exactions she suffered.[132] Possibly these dominant nobles filled roles similar to those of the mayors of the palace in contemporary Francia.

Certainly we need not doubt that the kings of Kent possessed a well-organized administration and Eadbert in one of his charters refers to a whole string of royal officials – *patricii, duces, comites, actionarii, dignitates publici* and *theolonearii* – though unfortunately it is not clear whether they all possessed clearly defined fields of activity, though the last named were probably specifically concerned with the collection of tolls in which the Kentish kings were so interested.[133] Such officials would have been responsible for the smooth running of the administration which seems to have been based around a series of royal estate centres which were grouped into lathes for the purpose of collecting royal dues and imposing royal justice.[134]

We learn more of some noble families from the period after Kent became a Mercian dependency. Offa's control of Kent was achieved in part by ruling with the co-operation of the Kentish nobility. Among those who benefited from the Mercian take-over were Ealdbert and his sister Selethryth whose father is known to have been a Kentish landowner.[135] Selethryth became abbess of Lyminge, and possibly of Minster-in-Thanet as well, and her brother, who is described as *minister* of Offa, may have exercised some sort of supervisory or protective role over the foundations. A relative of theirs called Oswulf subsequently became an ealdorman and inherited their interests. Jænbert, archbishop of Canterbury (765-92), during the reign of Offa, seems to have been a member of an important Kentish family. His kinsman Eadhun had been Egbert II's reeve in Kent and Jænbert himself was on close terms with Egbert.[136] Jænbert did not work as harmoniously with the new order as Ealdbert and Selethryth had done and after his death the Mercians reverted to a practice initiated under Æthelbald of appointing archbishops who came from outside Kent from various Mercian dependencies. Æthelheard (792-805) had been abbot of Louth in Lindsey, and Wulfred (805-32) seems to have been a member of a distinguished Middle Saxon noble family.[137]

Conclusion

We can appreciate how Kent's geographical position favoured its development as one of the most successful Anglo-Saxon kingdoms in the latter part of the sixth century. The North Sea area seems to have been particularly significant in Europe at this time as a result of Merovingian expansion and as the part of Britain closest to northern Francia Kent was a natural area to be included within the Merovingian sphere of influence. Of course, there were possible disadvantages in too close an association with Merovingian power and Æthelbert I of Kent seems to have been aware of potential dangers when he made arrangements for his conversion to Christianity. But for the kings of Kent any disadvantages seem to have been outweighed by the advantages of the association. The kingdom benefited from commerce with Francia, and the kings learnt from their Merovingian role-models how to effectively dominate and organize their kingdoms. The early Kentish kings, of course, were not unaware of their Anglo-Saxon neighbours, but the areas in which they seem to have been most active – London and the East Saxon province, the East Anglian kingdom and the Jutish provinces based on the Solent – were ones which also had a coastline and so had potential connections with the continent of Europe.

Kent's geographical position was not so advantageous when the kingdoms of Mercia and Wessex became more dominant in the late seventh and eighth centuries. For unlike Wessex and Mercia Kent was not ideally placed for expansion within Britain, and when Mercia became dominant in the London area and Wessex over Hampshire and Sussex the Kentish kings lost the possibility of extending their own kingdom into these areas. At the same time they lost their near monopoly of cross-Channel trade-routes and this is reflected in the spread of the sceatta coinage and the growth of new *wics* such as Hamwic (Hants). But neither the Mercians nor the West Saxons initially found Kent as easy to conquer as some of the other southern kingdoms and only a determined assault by Offa of Mercia over a number of years reduced the province to a Mercian dependency. The evidence of lawcodes, estates, proprietary religious houses, coinage and the pattern of royal succession all bear witness to a well-organized kingdom in which there was effective royal control. Kentish kings led the way in Anglo-Saxon England in many areas, not least in the acceptance of Christianity, and their Anglo-Saxon neighbours had much to learn from them just as the kings of Kent had learnt from their counterparts in Francia.

Chapter Three

THE EAST SAXONS

Sources
It would be impossible to write at length on the history of the East Saxon kingdom without the help of Bede's *Ecclesiastical History*. Bede's main sources on East Saxon affairs were Abbot Albinus of Canterbury and the brothers of Lastingham (N.Yorks) whose founder Cedd had been bishop of the East Saxons.[1] Bede also was able to make use of a written work now lost to us containing miracles associated with Abbess Æthelburh of Barking, and he may have had a regnal list which provided him with the sequence of reigns.[2] Other material seems to have reached Bede by chance; his information on the apostasy of part of the East Saxon kingdom in the great plague of 663-4 depended upon speaking with a priest who had accompanied the bishop of Mercia on a mission to reconvert the province.[3] Bede's narrative provides us with the framework of East Saxon history until the early years of the eighth century, but his information is inevitably very selective. Through Bede we have to approach East Saxon history via the history of its conversion and relations with more powerful kingdoms.

The most important additional sources are genealogies and charters. There is no East Saxon entry in the Anglian collection of genealogies and regnal lists, but the pedigrees of three East Saxon kings, Offa, Swithred and Sigered, are given in a ninth-century West Saxon manuscript and were also known to the post-Conquest historians William of Malmesbury and 'Florence of Worcester'.[4] Charters granted by East Saxon kings survive for the East Saxon episcopal church of St Paul's, London,[5] and the nunneries or double monasteries of Minster-in-Thanet (Kent), Barking and Nazeing (Essex).[6] The charters granting land to Nazeing have only recently come to light, and the site of the nunnery may have been located in recent excavations at Nazeingbury.[7] East Saxon kings also appear in charters of their ecclesiastics and their Mercian and West Saxon overlords. The pedigrees and the charters supplement the information in the *Ecclesiastical History* and, with the aid of occasional references in the *Anglo-Saxon Chronicle* and other annals, allow us to continue the narrative beyond the days of Bede though the picture is far from complete.

Archaeology can provide additional information about the East Saxon kingdom. Sites like that of the Roman villa at Rivenhall and Roman town at Great Chesterford seem to show the peaceful interaction of Romano-British and Germanic peoples and throw light on the circumstances through which the late

Roman *civitas* of the Trinovantes became an Anglo-Saxon kingdom.[8] Recent studies of the Essex landscape and the relationship between Roman and Saxon sites suggest that the structure of the Roman countryside largely survived and that any changes in rural settlement were a gradual response to changing economic and political circumstances.[9] Saxon settlers would have been in the minority and their cemeteries are centred on the coast and eastern waterways.[10] One of the first archaeological signs of kingship may be the exceptionally rich burial at Broomfield whose gravegoods have close parallels with those of Sutton Hoo and Taplow (Bucks) and so may also be early seventh century in date.[11] Unfortunately the burial was poorly excavated in the nineteenth century and has never been the subject of a major study. Excavations of the religious houses at Nazeing, Barking[12] and (possibly) Waltham Abbey[13] may indirectly show the results of patronage by the royal house, and the causeway linking Mersea Island to the mainland could be a royal public building work.[14]

The origins of the East Saxon kingdom
Sites like Mucking show that the territory of the East Saxon kingdom was among the first areas of Britain to receive Anglo-Saxon settlers in the early years of the fifth century.[15] However, the history of the East Saxon royal house cannot be traced back nearly this far. The common ancestor from whom descent was traced in the genealogies was Sledd whose son Sabert was ruling when the East Saxon see was founded in 604. A post-Conquest source places Sledd's accession in 587 and, although experience suggests little confidence can be placed in such dates, his main sphere of influence must have been in the latter part of the sixth century.[16] Sledd was married to Ricula, the sister of Æthelbert of Kent, and when the *Ecclesiastical History* opens Æthelbert is found exercising an unusually high degree of authority over the East Saxons.[17] Interestingly the two versions of the name of Sledd's putative father, Erken-wine and Æscwine, are both more typical of the nomenclature of the Kentish royal house than that of the East Saxon which tends to favour names beginning with 'S'. Although the evidence is slight it is possible that the rise to power of the Sledd dynasty in the second half of the sixth century was connected with Kentish expansion into Saxon areas bordering the Thames;[18] any earlier regnal arrangements for the province are lost to us.

The question of the bounds of the East Saxon kingdom is complex and would be clearer if we knew more of what must have occurred in the sixth century. The original bounds of the diocese of London, that is the East Saxon see, seem to have included not only Essex, but also Middlesex, south-eastern Hertfordshire and Surrey.[19] Charter evidence confirms that the diocesan areas outside Essex were controlled by East Saxon kings in the seventh and early eighth centuries, though Surrey was only intermittently under their rule and had a very complex history of changing overlordship until it was formally transferred to the Winchester diocese early in the eighth century.[20] The East Saxon kings never seem to have been as secure in Middlesex and Hertfordshire as they were in Essex itself. When East Saxon kings granted land in

Hertfordshire or Middlesex they frequently made reference to their foreign overlords whereas in Essex they granted land freely. In the course of the eighth century the Hertfordshire and Middlesex lands, together with London, were detached altogether and became part of Mercia, whereas Essex continued to be ruled by the East Saxon dynasty until it was taken over by the West Saxons in the ninth century.[21]

The Hertfordshire and Middlesex lands were known as 'the province of the Middle Saxons' from the early eighth century at least.[22] It is not entirely clear whether the Middle Saxon province was formerly an integral part of the East Saxon kingdom which was detached by the Mercians in the eighth century or if it was once an independent province which came under East Saxon over-lordship in the late sixth century.[23] However, the fact that it always seems to have been treated rather differently from the main East Saxon province provides some support for the latter hypothesis. The name of Surrey is one of the main reasons, in addition to the diocesan evidence, for thinking that it was once attached to the Middle Saxon province. Bede gives the name as *Sudergeona* 'the southern district', and its corresponding northern district would presumably have been Middlesex.[24] The element 'ge' is early and the administrative arrangements which the name seems to imply presumably are also early in date because for much of the seventh century Surrey had a different history from the lands north of the Thames. In the reign of Wulfhere Surrey had its own subking called Frithuwold.[25] On the whole Frithuwold seems more likely to have been a Mercian and related to Frithuric *princeps* who was active in eastern Mercia in the late seventh century than a member of an indigenous Surrey dynasty, but his existence could suggest a tradition of independent rule in Surrey.[26] The situation in the lower Thames was clearly very complex. A number of distinct administrative districts (*regiones*) can be recognized within Middle Saxon territory and Surrey itself seems to have been composed of two distinct areas with separate *regiones* within them.[27] Other small *regiones* which do not ever seem to have been under East Saxon overlord-ship adjoin to the north and west.[28] The lower Thames in the sixth century may not have contained a dominant province at all, but may have been divided between a number of diverse *regiones* which were subsequently subject to different overlords and combined in a variety of ways to form provinces until Mercian domination was paramount in the eighth century.

The history of the East Saxon kingdom c. 600–825
A major problem in reconstructing East Saxon history is that the available sources tend to concentrate only on certain aspects of the province's past, notably the various attempts to convert the East Saxons to Christianity and to gain overlordship of the province. The two topics are not, of course, uncon-nected. At the beginning of the seventh century Kentish influence was domi-nant in the province. King Sabert was converted through the intervention of his uncle King Æthelbert of Kent in 604.[29] According to Bede it was Æthelbert not Sabert who built and endowed St Paul's in accordance with

Pope Gregory's plan to base the southern metropolitan see in London. The reaction against Sabert following Æthelbert's death in 616 was probably as much a reaction against Kentish domination as against Christianity, and Bede specifically says that Eadbald was not able to recover his father's overlordship of the East Saxons.[30] Sabert's three sons who succeeded him returned the kingdom to paganism and expelled the Gregorian missionaries from London, and so inadvertently ensured that Canterbury remained the metropolitan centre. According to Bede, their sacrilegious actions were avenged shortly afterwards when all three were defeated and killed in battle against the West Saxons – possibly they were battling for control of Surrey.[31]

Virtually nothing is known beyond his existence of the next ruler Sigebert 'Parvus', but his successor Sigebert 'Sanctus' was persuaded by the Northumbrian overlord Oswiu to adopt Christianity in c. 653, a period in which Oswiu was mobilizing opposition to Penda of Mercia.[32] As a result of Oswiu's initiative a group of missionaries was despatched from Northumbria led by Cedd who subsequently became bishop of the East Saxons. Several churches were established at this time including that at Bradwell-on-Sea (see Fig. 12), which still stands, and another at Tilbury; all were presumably dependent upon Lindisfarne. Once again there was a reaction which Bede represents purely as opposition to Christianity, but which may also have been linked to resistance to a foreign overlord. According to Bede Sigebert was killed by two kinsmen because 'he was too ready to pardon his enemies', an interesting observation of a clash between Christian and traditional values for in the code of the latter loyal supporters would feel undervalued if appropriate vengeance was not taken against the disloyal. It may well be that Sigebert's successor Swithhelm was one of the murderers, and Swithfrith who appears to have been king during the same period, could have been his brother.[33] Swithhelm was subsequently himself baptized as a Christian at the court of King Æthelwald of the East Angles and Cedd continued to act as bishop.[34] Unfortunately none of these events can be dated, but Bede implies that Swithhelm's death occurred at about the same time as the great plague of 664.[35]

Wulfhere moved quickly while the new kings, Sæbbi and Sigehere, were establishing themselves to make himself overlord of the province. A mission was sent under Bishop Jaruman of Mercia to reconvert part of the East Saxon people who had apostasized during the plague and Wulfhere subsequently provided a new bishop of London when he sold the see to Wine.[36] But there was keen competition to control the East Saxons and their satellite provinces in the latter part of the seventh century. While Wulfhere was overlord north of the Thames, Egbert of Kent was dominant in Surrey and remembered as the founder of Chertsey abbey, probably in 666.[37] However, in 672x674 when Frithuwold issued his charter to Chertsey he described himself as *subregulus* of Wulfhere.[38] After Wulfhere's death in 675 the Kentish kings may have been able to reassert themselves in London for the laws of Hlothere and Eadric (673-85) refer to Kentish commercial interests there.[39] Cædwalla of Wessex during his brief but spectacular period of overlordship in southern England

(685-88) was certainly in control of Surrey where he oversaw the foundation of a series of minster churches,[40] and the presence of West Saxon witnesses in East Saxon charters suggests overlordship of the main province as well.[41] After Cædwalla's departure for Rome, Æthelred was able to reassert Mercian over-lordship, as is acknowledged in various charters of the time,[42] but Surrey seems to have remained under West Saxon control. The fact that Surrey was still in the London diocese seems to have caused various disputes between Ine of Wessex, on the one hand, and the East Saxon and Mercian kings, on the other, until Surrey was formally transferred to the Winchester diocese after a synod at Brentford in c. 705.[43]

The above seems to present rather a bleak picture of East Saxon kingship at the end of the seventh century with the local rulers apparently allowing them-selves to be trampled upon by a series of foreign invaders, and some effort must be made to view things from an East Saxon perspective for the biases in the surviving evidence encourage us to dwell on the foreign overlords. The two kings Sæbbi and Sigehere who succeeded on the death of Swithhelm were not that closely related being first cousins once removed.[44] The two rulers seem to have followed different policies in separate areas of the kingdom for in 664 Sæbbi and his portion of East Saxon people seem to have remained Christian while Sigehere and his province apostasized.[45] Such internal con-flicts provided opportunities for foreign intervention and the rival candidates appear to have looked to different outside kingdoms for support. Sigehere may have thrown in his lot with Cædwalla. A charter of Cædwalla, which Sigehere appears to have witnessed, refers to Sigehere's conquest of Kent.[46] As any such conquest would have occurred at about the same time that Cædwalla's brother Mul became ruler of Kent it is possible that the two men worked together and briefly ruled Kent between them.[47]

Sæbbi, on the other hand, seems to have sided with the Mercian kings, and may have done so as early as 664. After Cædwalla's abdication in 688 Mercian support ensured the supremacy of Sæbbi's family. Sæbbi's son Swæfheard took the throne of West Kent in 688 or 689 after the Kentishmen had revolted and killed Mul. His co-ruler in East Kent was a member of the Kentish royal line called Oswine. Both men acknowledged the overlordship of Æthelred in charters and it is possible he provided them with military support.[48] Oswine had been replaced by Wihtred by 691, but Swæfheard continued to rule until 694.[49] There was a distinction between the nature of Æthelred's overlordship over the Middle Saxon province and over the East Saxon kingdom itself, both during the reign of Sæbbi and those of his two sons, Sigeheard and Swæfred who succeeded him in 693 or 694 and shared power for at least part of the time with Offa (son of Sigehere).[50] Æthelred possessed land in the Middle Saxon province and was able to appoint a *comes* to oversee Mercian interests in London and the sur-rounding area, but seems to have possessed no corresponding authority in the East Saxon homelands.[51] The East Saxon kings of the late seventh and early eighth centuries sometimes, but not invariably, acknowledged Mercian overlord-ship when granting land in Hertfordshire or Middlesex, but never for grants

they made in Essex.[52] This balance of power continued in the reigns of
Æthelred's nephew Cenred and son Ceolred.[53]

When Cenred abdicated and journeyed to Rome to become a monk in 709
he took with him Offa of the East Saxons. It is not clear whether the two men
were really impelled by the desire for the monastic life, as Bede implies, or
whether they were departing as political exiles.[54] Although Æthelred of Mercia had retired to become abbot of Bardney he still seems to have been
influential in Mercia[55] and by abdicating Cenred allowed the succession of
Æthelred's son Ceolred. Offa too was in a difficult position as junior ruler to
his two second cousins Sigeheard and Swæfred. Whatever may have lain
behind it, Offa's departure marks an important stage for the historian for he is
the last ruler referred to by Bede. Unfortunately the charters of the East Saxon
kings also come to an end in the first decade of the eighth century so that
reconstruction of East Saxon history becomes extremely difficult. We know
the names of various rulers over the next century, but can provide only a few
dates for them. We do not know when Sigeheard and Swæfred ceased to rule,
but their successors were Swæfbert whose death is recorded in 738,[56] and
Selered who died in 746 according to the *Anglo-Saxon Chronicle*. Selered
appears in one of the pedigrees as a descendant of a brother of Sabert, a
collateral line which is not known to have produced any earlier kings. It is not
clear how the reigns of Swæfbert and Selered interrelated and whether they
ruled jointly or consecutively. Swithred, whose genealogy in the East Saxon
collection shows that he was a grandson of the former king Sigeheard, may
have been Selered's successor.[57]

Any further light on East Saxon affairs must come through consideration of
the relations between their province and the great Mercian kings Æthelbald
and Offa. The Mercian rulers granted land freely in Middlesex and
Hertfordshire without reference to East Saxon rulers, and the Middle Saxon
province must have become fully Mercian during the reign of Æthelbald.[58]
The port of London would have been an important prize for the Mercian kings
and the remissions of tolls to certain religious houses on ships using the port
are one sign of the kings' interest in commerce.[59] London was an important
mint for both Æthelbald and Offa,[60] and Offa may have done much to develop
the city both as a trading base and as a royal centre.[61] However, we have no
evidence for the Mercians exercising any direct authority within Essex itself
and this negative evidence combined with the admittedly scanty evidence for a
continuing succession of East Saxon kings suggests that the East Saxon kingdom managed to survive as an independent kingdom during the eighth century, though probably under strong Mercian influence. Possible confirmation
of this view comes from an issue of sceatta coinage whose distribution is
concentrated in Essex and London. The reverse is a design of wolf-heads
found on issues which have been associated with Æthelbald of Mercia, but the
obverse with a standing sphinx is distinctive. The sceatta issue could be
interpreted as an East Saxon coinage issued by the East Saxon kings, but under
licence from Æthelbald.[62]

One cannot be certain that an East Saxon king continued to rule throughout the reign of Offa when several of the other Mercian satellite kingdoms lost their rulers, but the East Saxon royal house were still in existence after Offa's death. King Sigeric I, son of King Selered, seems to have witnessed a charter of King Egfrith, but departed for Rome soon afterwards.[63] His son Sigered appears with the title of king in two charters of King Cenwulf for 811, though thereafter his status vis-à-vis the Mercian ruler seems to have declined and he was reduced to the status of *dux*.[64] But in the end it seems to have been the West Saxons rather than the Mercians who brought the East Saxon kingdom to an end. In 825, after the defeat of their Mercian protectors, the *Chronicle* records that the East Saxons together with the South Saxons and the people of Kent and Surrey surrendered to Egbert of Wessex. These defeated peoples were formed into a subkingdom of Wessex which was ruled by Egbert's son Æthelwulf.[65] But that was not quite the end of the East Saxon dynasty, for a Sigeric styled king of the East Saxons appears as a *minister* of King Wiglaf of Mercia in a lease of land in Hertfordshire to be dated between 829 and 837, that is after Wiglaf had returned from his expulsion by Egbert.[66] When so much treachery is recorded in the relations between different Anglo-Saxon kingdoms it is refreshing to discover that the alliance between the royal houses of Mercia and the East Saxons apparently continued beyond the independent history of the East Saxon kingdom.

Sabert (ruling 604) d. c. 616

Sæward, Seaxred and ?Seaxbald d. c. 618–623

Sigebert 'Parvus'

Sigebert 'Sanctus' (ruling 653)

Swithhelm d. c. 664

Sigehere c. 664– c. 688 and Sæbbi c. 664–693/4

Sigeheard and Swæfred acc. 693/4

Swæfbert d. 738

Selered d. 746

Swithred

Sigeric I ab. 798

Sigered ?798–825

Sigeric II

Table 4: Regnal list of the kings of the East Saxons
(Only dominant kings have been listed)

The East Saxon royal house

Although lacking evidence on many facets of East Saxon history, it is possible thanks to the surviving pedigrees, charters and the regnal information in the *Ecclesiastical History* to make various observations about the royal family and the nature of its kingship.[67] Until the eighth century all the rulers were descendants of Sabert who was ruling in 604, though by the end of the seventh century two rival branches can be discerned which traced descent from different sons of Sabert. In the course of the eighth century members of a collateral branch descended from a brother of Sabert began to rule (Selered,

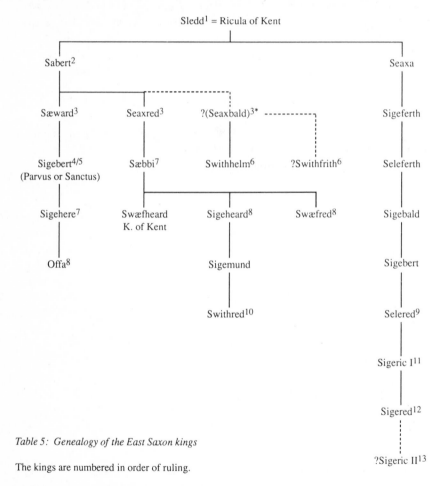

Table 5: Genealogy of the East Saxon kings

The kings are numbered in order of ruling.

*HE III, 22 states that Swithhelm was the son of Seaxbald and, as suggested by Chadwick 1905, 276, it is possible that Seaxbald was the otherwise unknown third son of Sabert.

Sigeric I, Sigered and probably Sigeric II) and eventually monopolized the throne; however, no members of this branch are known to have ruled in the seventh century. All rulers could therefore trace descent from Sledd in the male line and seem to have emphasized the fact by a striking conformity of nomenclature. For with the exception of Offa and a kinsman of Sæbbi called Œthelred, all the East Saxon rulers and their relations who appear in the pedigrees have names which begin with the letter 'S'.

A significant number of joint reigns are recorded, that is reigns where power was shared between two or more rulers. These include the well-attested instances of the three sons of Sabert who shared power on their father's death, of Sigehere and Sæbbi and of Sigeheard and Swæfred. Other possible joint rulers are Swithhelm and Swithfrith, and Swæfbert and Selered, but we do not know enough about how their reigns interconnected. The joint reign of Sigehere and Sæbbi is of particular interest as although the two men are described as co-heirs (*coheres*),[68] they were, according to the pedigrees, first cousins once removed. Whereas the sons of Sabert are depicted as taking joint action in expelling the missionaries and fighting with the West Saxons, Sigehere and Sæbbi seem to have followed different policies and sided with the West Saxons and the Mercians respectively. Their separate actions are not so surprising as they seem to have been ruling geographically distinct areas for Bede describes Sigehere 'with his part of the people' apostasizing, while Sæbbi and his people remained Christian.[69] An obvious territorial division within the area governed by the East Saxons in the seventh century would be between the East Saxon homelands and the province of the Middle Saxons. It is quite conceivable that during the disputes over succession following the death of a king members of different kin-groups might establish themselves within the two provinces and that is probably how the reigns of Sigehere and Sæbbi should be interpreted. Joint reigns were not always of the same type in the East Saxon province. Brothers, like the sons of Sabert and Sæbbi, might act in concert, but the subdivisions within the kingdom meant that there was also the possibility of rival candidates sharing power in which case co-operation was less likely to occur.

In addition to the dominant East Saxon kings there seem to have been further subsidiary rulers of rather more ambiguous status. Offa is the best attested of these. On the one hand, he was able to grant land in his own right and appears as *rex* in charters;[70] his pedigree is one of the three which has survived. On the other hand, he is also described in one grant as *subregulus* and Bede says that he was an expectant heir, rather than a full king, when he left for Rome.[71] Offa was the son of King Sigehere and so presumably inherited rights from his father. Œthelred, who simply describes himself as *parens* '?kinsman' of Sæbbi,[72] may have occupied an analogous position for although he did not use the title of king, he was able to make generous grants of land to the double monastery of Barking,[73] and it has been suggested that he was a subking of Surrey.[74] Both Offa and Œthelred appear as witnesses (without titles) in one of the recently discovered grants of Swæfred.[75] The witness-list also includes a Saba who appears immediately before Œthelred and who is likely to have been another member of the royal house, perhaps of similar status to Offa and Œthelred. Administrative subdivisions of the two main provinces of the East and Middle Saxons are known. The *pago* of Hemel (Hempstead) and the *regio* of Dengie (Essex) appear in charters,[76] and two Essex district names *Vange* and *Ginges* contain the element *ge* meaning 'district' which is also found in the name of Surrey which we know had its own ruler at one point in the seventh century.[77] West Kent when it was ruled by Swæfheard c. 688-94 seems to have been considered subsidiary to the main East Saxon kingdom for Swæfheard acknowledged the authority of his father Sæbbi.[78]

Although we cannot appreciate all its ramifications the East Saxons seem to have possessed an interesting system of multiple kingship which apparently allowed several members of the royal house to be ruling at the same time though not all rulers were necessarily of the same status. Kings who were not particularly close relatives might be ruling concurrently and the existence of separate provinces within the East Saxon kingdom probably facilitated this occurrence. However, a powerful dominant king would naturally try to promote his own kin-group to key positions and that is what Sæbbi, whose thirty year reign can be considered one of the most 'successful' of the East Saxon kings, apparently did. Sæbbi's son Swæfheard became king in West Kent and another relative Œthelred also ruled, possibly as ruler of Surrey. It is not certain whether Sæbbi's sons Sigeheard and Swæfred held positions as subsidiary rulers while their father was alive. The only evidence to suggest it is that their names appear with the title of king below that of their father in two East Saxon charters, but the names could represent later confirmations.[79] Certainly Sigeheard and Swæfred were able to take over their father's position on his death, though they were not able to exclude their second cousin Offa (son of Sigehere) from some share of power.

It is even more difficult to discuss members of the royal house who did not have the status of king. As in other Anglo-Saxon kingdoms, female members of the royal house seem to have played important roles within the church as abbesses of religious houses. Osyth, the founder of a religious house at Chich in Essex where her cult was venerated in the later Saxon period, was reputedly the wife of King Sigehere. Various post-Conquest lives of Osyth exist, but by the time they were written her cult had become hopelessly confused with that of a namesake, St Osyth of Aylesbury and can add little to our appreciation of East Saxon history in the seventh century.[80] Charters survive for two East Saxon nunneries or double monasteries; Nazeing founded by Swæfred for 'ffymme' (the form of her name has probably been corrupted during copying),[81] and Barking founded for Æthelburh by her brother Eorcenwald, according to Bede, though the foundation grant seems actually to have come from King Swithfrith.[82] There is no direct evidence that 'ffymme' and Æthelburh were members of the royal house, but we can see from looking at other kingdoms, for instance Kent and Northumbria both of which had close early connections with the East Saxon kingdom and its emergent church, that women to whom kings gave generous grants of land in order to found religious houses tended to be their own kinswomen.

The endowment of Nazeing is known from two recently discovered charters of Swæfred granting 30 and 10 hides respectively. The nunnery seems to have been founded on a large estate bounded by natural and archaeological features and which may have existed as a territorial unit in the Roman period. Particular interest attaches to it because of recent excavations at Nazeingbury which seem to have revealed the site of the nunnery itself and possibly even the tomb of its first abbess 'ffymme'.[83] The excavations revealed two successive wooden churches of substantial and sophisticated construction and most of the cemetery which was dominated by the burials of elderly, well-nourished women who do not seem to have given birth. Some of the bodies of men and children buried in the cemetery showed severe signs of ill-health suggesting that they had lived in the community as invalids. The nunnery seems to have ceased to function in the ninth century, though this should not necessarily be seen as the result of Viking attacks, for the disappearance of the East Saxon royal house is just as likely to have been the cause of its termination. Its lands probably then passed to Barking abbey and were used in the twelfth century by an abbess of Barking to endow a hospital at Ilford which ultimately accounts for the survival of its two charters to the present day.

Three charters for the double monastery at Barking survive and have been discussed in detail by Dr Cyril Hart.[84] One is the original charter of Œthelred, and another obligingly lists the early endowments of the monastery. In addition to the substantial grants from Swithfrith and Œthelred, Barking was also patronized by Wulfhere and Æthelred of Mercia and Cædwalla of Wessex. It was standard practice for foreign overlords to try to ingratiate themselves with their subject provinces by endowing religious houses, particularly those controlled by members of the provincial royal house; Swæfheard did the same thing when as king of West Kent he patronized Minster-in-Thanet.[85] All the seventh-century donations were of land which lay on the banks of the Thames or its tributaries. Like the double monasteries of Kent, Barking seems to have been well-sited for trade and in Domesday Book Barking was a port with its own fishing fleet.[86] The economic picture of Barking can be supplemented by the miracles associated with Æthelburh which Bede cited in the *Ecclesiastical History* from a book which is now lost.[87] Current excavations promise further insights into the community's life.[88]

The likelihood that Æthelburh was a member of the East Saxon royal house is particularly important because if it is accepted it must mean that her brother Eorcenwald, bishop of London, was also of royal East Saxon birth. There has been some reluctance to assign Eorcenwald and Æthelburh to the East Saxon royal family because their names do not conform to the 'S' nomenclature so clearly attested among males of the royal house and are instead typical of the Kentish royal house where the only other instances of names using the Frankish element 'Eorcen' are found.[89] However, the East Saxon royal family had links with that of Kent through the marriage of Sabert with King Æthelbert's sister, and the 'S' nomenclature may only have been used by those eligible for the main East Saxon kingship because, for instance, they were descendants in the direct male line. If Æthelburh and Eorcenwald were descended through the female line it could explain the different name-forms. Significantly one of the major patrons of Barking was Œthelred whose name also departs from the 'S' nomenclature and has the first element 'Œthel' which may be a variant form of 'Æthel', but who was nevertheless probably a kinsman of Sæbbi. There must be a possibility that Œthelred and Eorcenwald and his sister Æthelburh were related and were all members of an East Saxon royal kin-group, but one whose males were not eligible for the throne.

Eorcenwald was a person of some significance in the early Anglo-Saxon church and in the complicated political situation in the lower Thames in the second half of the seventh century.[90] He was the founder of Chertsey abbey in c. 666 and became the fourth bishop of London in c. 675. He secured substantial endowments for Chertsey, beginning with 300 hides acquired from King Egbert of Kent and Frithuwold of Surrey, which included 10 hides by the port of London 'where ships come to land',[91] and oversaw the endowments of his sister's foundation at Barking which included grants from both Mercian and West Saxon overlords. Eorcenwald worked with Cædwalla and Bishop Wilfrid of Northumbria (who was acting as bishop of the South Saxons) in establishing a proper ecclesiastical structure for Surrey and assisted in the reconciliation of Wilfrid with Archbishop Theodore.[92] Ine grandly referred to him as 'my bishop' (though probably only the Surrey part of Eorcenwald's diocese was controlled by Ine) and consulted him when drawing up his lawcode (one wonders whether the East Saxon kings already had a lawcode by this time).[93] Ine's sister Cuthburh was a nun at Barking in this period and Aldhelm (who was probably their kinsman) produced his treatise on virginity for the community.[94] Literary influence spread outwards from the London diocese as well. A distinctive group of charters is linked by associations with Eorcenwald and it seems that he may have played a major role in the development of the diplomatic of the English charter and influenced charter production in Mercia and Wessex as well as in his own diocese.[95] Eorcenwald seems to have shared the talents of his putative kinsmen of the family of Sæbbi for turning competition among the more militarily powerful kingdoms to his advantage.

Bede says that Eorcenwald was renowned for his holy life which was vouchsafed by miracles.[96] His relics were kept at St Paul's and his cult revived with some success in the twelfth century.[97] Within a few years of Eorcenwald's death St Paul's was able to claim a second East Saxon saint, King Sæbbi who was apparently so religious that 'many people thought and often said that a man of his disposition ought to have been a bishop rather than king' (though he was sufficiently practically minded to survive as king for thirty years).[98] Sæbbi was able to become a monk shortly before his death when his essential holiness was revealed by a miraculous lengthening of a sarcophagus to take his body. He too was buried at St Paul's.

Sæbbi died in London, and his death and cult are an important reminder that in the seventh century London was in the first instance an East Saxon city, even if it not infrequently attracted the attention of foreign overlords. Bede describes London as 'an emporium for many nations' and traces of its *wic* or trading base have come to light in excavations in the Strand, that is, outside the Roman walled town where St Paul's was situated.[99] London's early commercial importance is also demonstrated by a rare gold coinage of the early seventh century and an issue of primary series sceattas from the later seventh century.[100] It must have been an important asset of the seventh-century East Saxon kings who presumably played a key role in London's early development as a commercial centre even if we have little in the way of direct evidence for this. However, the charters of Barking and Chertsey do reflect something of the royal house's interest in the port and are an indicator that participation and control of foreign trade were likely to have been an important facet in the developing kingship of the East Saxons.

Conclusion

For the historian of Anglo-Saxon kingdoms the East Saxons are of considerable interest even if one is constantly regretting that more information has not survived. They are particularly of interest for their complex, if at times enigmatic, system of kingship and for the light the kingdom throws on the practice of overlordship among the Anglo-Saxons. The East Saxon kingdom never produced one of the great overlords of the Anglo-Saxons, though the East Saxons were for some time overlords of the Middle Saxons and even for a brief period rulers of part of the kingdom of Kent, thus neatly reversing the tables on a people who had dominated them at the beginning of the seventh century. They were frequently subject to foreign overlords, but not necessarily unduly repressed by them and there is evidence to suggest that East Saxon kings and ecclesiastics were quite capable of manipulating a complex political situation to their advantage. West Saxon and Mercian overlords cannot be shown exercising within the main East Saxon province the same rights of authorizing grants of land which they exercised among the Middle Saxons. What is perhaps more remarkable and significant than the fact that the East Saxon province often had foreign overlords is that it survived as an independent kingdom for so long. Even though the East Saxons lost control of London and the Middle Saxon province to Æthelbald and Offa, they retained their own royal family who at the beginning of the ninth century were one of the five Anglo-Saxon royal lines which we can be certain were still in existence.

Chapter Four

THE EAST ANGLES

Sources

The East Anglian kingdom was one of only four kingdoms still in existence
when the Great Heathen Army arrived in 865, but unlike Northumbria, Mercia and Wessex very few records have survived from its period as an independent kingdom. It is unlikely that the East Anglian kingdom did not possess the
usual range of early Anglo-Saxon documentation, and the poor survival rate
can be linked with the events of the ninth century when the Viking raids and
settlements resulted in the disappearance (or severe impoverishment) of the
major archive-holders, the two episcopal sees and the major religious houses.[1]
Without Bede's information we would scarcely be able to attempt the history
of the East Anglian kingdom. He received some information about the East
Angles from Albinus and Nothhelm, and the rest was discovered 'partly from
the writings or the traditions of men of the past, and partly from the account of
the esteemed Abbot Esi'.[2] Bede's sources included a *Life of St Fursa*[3] and
probably oral traditions about St Æthelthryth. Although Bede does provide
the sequence of East Anglian kings, he had very little specific chronological
information about them and does not indicate how long any of them ruled. As
no regnal list with reign lengths has survived, the chronology of the East
Anglian kings presents a major problem though the better evidence for the
dates of some of the early East Anglian bishops provides some help. The lack
of charters is a severe handicap for this and many other aspects of East Anglian
history.

The shortage of dates in the early sources has led some writers to turn to
post-Conquest historians to fill the gap. 'Florence of Worcester', William of
Malmesbury, Roger of Wendover and Matthew Paris do apparently provide
dates for events not dated elsewhere, but these writers are committed to an
annalistic format; they have to date events in order to fit them into their
histories and so if there were no relevant dates in their sources they presumably had to make intelligent guesses. As the post-Conquest historians frequently misdate events which can be authoritatively dated from pre-Conquest
sources, any unsupported dates must be treated with the greatest caution.
There is little sign that these writers did have access to East Anglian sources
that are otherwise unknown to us; for instance, they purport to give regnal lists
of the East Anglian kings, but do not name rulers known from the coin
evidence. 'Florence' apparently provides additional genealogical information,

but as Sir Frank Stenton was able to show, all he did was to produce his own interpretation of the genealogy of Ælfwald (which fortunately survives separately in the Anglian collection) and so mislead a number of subsequent historians.[4] Remarkably little historical information survived the fall of the East Anglian kings, and even the monastery of Ely which was revived in the tenth century seems to have known very little about the royal house which had provided its first patrons.[5]

The *Lives* of four saints provide us with some additional information about the East Anglian province and its rulers. The most valuable of these is Felix's *Life of Saint Guthlac* which was actually written in East Anglia at the request of King Ælfwald (d. 749) and so, among other things, throws light on standards of learning in the kingdom.[6] Its hero is a saint distantly related to the Mercian royal house, who died c. 715 after spending most of his adult life as a hermit in the fenland area which was disputed between Mercia and the East Angles. The two kingdoms were also rivals in their promotion of the saint's cult.[7] An account of the life of Foillan, half-brother of the East Anglian missionary Fursa and at one time abbot of the monastery of *Cnobheresburg*, was written at Nivelles in the middle of the seventh century and, as Dorothy Whitelock has shown, contributes to our knowledge of the establishment of Christianity in East Anglia.[8] The remaining two saints were kings of the East Angles who met violent deaths, but their *Lives* were written outside East Anglia and some considerable time after the events they describe. Æthelbert was a victim of Offa of Mercia and apparently murdered at a royal vill in Herefordshire in 794. He was eventually buried in Hereford cathedral and became one of its patron saints, though he also had a cult in East Anglia.[9] The circumstances of his death are interesting, but the three main versions of his *Life* were written in the twelfth and thirteenth centuries, although the oldest is probably based on a pre-Conquest account. The *Life* of the last native East Anglian king, Edmund, who was slain by the Vikings in 869 is also disappointing. It was written by Abbo of Fleury between 985 and 987 and Abbo says he based his information on an account Archbishop Dunstan had heard as a young man at the court of King Athelstan (acc. 925) from an old man who had been Edmund's armour-bearer.[10] However, the story seems to have lost something in the telling, and Abbo has written a rather bland account of the martyrdom which has little of substance to say about the East Anglian kingdom.

Some compensation for the shortage of written sources for the East Anglian kingdom is provided by the famous ship-burial in Mound 1 at Sutton Hoo, though it would also be true to say that, if the written sources for the seventh century were fuller, interpretation of aspects of the burial would be easier. The contents of the ship-burial have been admirably described and discussed by Dr Bruce-Mitford in three volumes,[11] but some basic matters still remain unresolved. No definite traces of a body have been recovered and although, as subsequent excavations on the site have shown, the acidic soil may have dissolved the bone, there is a possibility that the ship-burial was really a cenotaph or that the body was subsequently removed.[12] Nor can one be completely certain of the date of the burial and so of the identity of the individual it honoured. The gravegoods which potentially can be dated with the greatest precision are the thirty-seven Merovingian coins, though, of course, they cannot provide the actual date of burial, only a date after which the burial must have taken place. Merovingian coins do not carry dates and so can only be dated fairly broadly from the references to kings, bishops and minters contained upon them. However, a method has been derived to date them more narrowly by analysis of their gold content which declined as the seventh century progressed, though the decline did not take place at a steady pace as some kings such as Dagobert I (acc. 623) temporarily returned to higher standards.[13] Consequently different interpretations of the results of metal analysis are possible, and the conclusion of Dr Kent that the latest coin from the Sutton Hoo burial was minted c. 620-25 and that most of the coins were several years earlier has not gone unchallenged, though it seems generally agreed that the coin collection was put together at some point in the 620s.[14]

The favourite candidate for the burial is King Rædwald who is known to have been overlord of the southern English and whose recorded encounter with Christianity, but final commitment to paganism, is thought by some to be reflected in the choice of gravegoods.[15] What is not always appreciated is that the exact date of Rædwald's death is as difficult to establish as the date of the latest coin in the purse (see Fig. 4). The date of 624 is provided by the thirteenth-century chroniclers Roger of Wendover and Matthew Paris, but we do not know the source of their information. Some support for this as a likely date for Rædwald's death has been derived from Bede's information that Paulinus was created bishop of Northumbria in 625 prior to Edwin's conversion in 627; neither of these events, it is suggested, is likely to have occurred before Rædwald's death as Edwin was beholden to Rædwald.[16] The last entry Bede records for Rædwald is the battle of the river Idle of 616 which enabled Edwin to succeed to the Northumbrian throne.[17] Rædwald must have been dead by 627 when his son Eorpwald seems to have been ruling in East Anglia.[18] A date towards the end of the range 616-27 in which Rædwald must have died seems most likely as Rædwald cannot have become bretwalda until after the death of Æthelbert of Kent (probably in 616) and presumably held the position for a number of years to have earned his place in the *Ecclesiastical History*'s list.

The identification of the burial as Rædwald's cannot be regarded as definite. Although the Mound I burial at Sutton Hoo is the richest known Anglo-Saxon burial it is only one of several burial mounds in the Sutton Hoo cemetery some of which may have rivalled it in wealth. Mound 2 had been robbed, but enough traces of its original gravegoods survived to show that it too had been an exceptional burial in which a ship was included.[19] It seems reasonable to infer that Sutton Hoo was an élite cemetery of the East Anglian royal house and that information derived from the finds in Mound 1 can be used to increase our knowledge of the dynasty, but we must be more cautious in using them as evidence for bretwaldaship.

The origins of the East Anglian kingdom

Rædwald is the first of the East Anglian kings definitely known to have ruled though the origins of the dynasty can be traced back further. Bede gives Rædwald's father's name as Tytil and his grandfather's as Wuffa 'from whom the East Anglian kings are called Wuffingas'.[20] It would appear that Wuffa's position was analogous to that of Oisc in the Kentish genealogy as the ancestor from whom the right to rule was claimed though a note in the *Historia Brittonum* states that Wehha, father of Wuffa, was the first to rule.[21] These traditions suggest an origin for the royal house in the second or third quarters of the sixth century. Roger of Wendover gives dates of 571 and 578 for the accessions of Wuffa and Tytil respectively.

As in most kingdoms there is a not inconsiderable gap between the first appearance of the royal house and the earliest Anglo-Saxon settlement in the province. It has been argued that East Anglia was the first region to receive independent Anglo-Saxon settlers in the fifth century.[22] In the sixth century there is some evidence, particularly the use of distinctive sleeve- or cuff-clasps to fasten shirts or trousers, for additional settlement from Scandinavia.[23] Scandinavian influence can be seen in the Mound 1 ship-burial from Sutton Hoo. Not only is the rite of ship-burial restricted within this period to Scandinavia and East Anglia, but there are striking iconographic parallels between objects from Sutton Hoo and burials of the Vendel period in Sweden; in the words of Bruce-Mitford, Swedish influence permeates the Sutton Hoo assemblage.[24] It has even been suggested on the strength of these parallels that the Wuffingas were descendants of an eastern Swedish dynasty.[25] An alternative theory sees them as members of the royal house of the Geats, who feature in the poem *Beowulf*, and who, it is proposed, fled to England with their treasure after their conquest by the Swedes (Svear) in the sixth century.[26] Now that some of the objects previously thought to be heirlooms from Sweden are believed to have been manufactured in England, such arguments have lost some of their force.[27] Certainly there would seem to have been contacts between the East Anglian and Scandinavian courts and craftsmen may have moved between them,[28] though some of the iconographic parallels between Anglo-Saxon and Swedish pieces, such as the birds of prey (see Fig. 4), may reflect motifs common to the aristocratic and royal circles of a number of Germanic peoples, many of which stem ultimately from the late Roman world.[29] However, one of the characteristics of many of the Sutton Hoo pieces is that they cannot be paralleled exactly anywhere else.

Norfolk and Suffolk together seem to represent the original territory of the Iceni, but the province may not have had a united history throughout the subRoman period. The distinctive rites of ship-burial which have been associated with the Wuffingas dynasty are concentrated in south-eastern Suffolk and this may represent the family's original centre from which they came to dominate the whole East Anglian province.[30] The names of the North Folk and South Folk of Norfolk and Suffolk may reflect a basic subdivision within the kingdom which had its origins in the lost events of the subRoman period.[31]

The history of the East Anglian kingdom

East Anglia first appears in the *Ecclesiastical History* as a rising power under King Rædwald. Rædwald's was one of the kingdoms in which Æthelbert could claim some authority and whose conversion he attempted, but although Rædwald did erect an altar to the Christian god, he also persisted in honouring pagan deities.[32] Rædwald's display of independence from Æthelbert also seems to be reflected in a passage which has provided some difficulties in interpretation, but seems to say that when Æthelbert was overlord Rædwald retained the *ducatus* over his own people, that is the full military command of his own forces.[33] When Æthelbert died in 616 Rædwald succeeded to his position as the chief king in southern England, and just as Æthelbert had tried to underscore his authority in some provinces by the conversion of subject kings, so Rædwald may have been responsible for ensuring that the East Saxons and Kent (temporarily) returned to paganism. Rædwald gave shelter at his court to Edwin of Deira who was being pursued by King Æthelfrith of Northumbria, and, although initially attracted by the payments offered by Æthelfrith for a dead Edwin, Rædwald used his military power to defeat Æthelfrith in 616 at the battle of the river Idle on the borders of Deira and Mercia and so helped Edwin to the Northumbrian throne.[34] No doubt Edwin expressed his gratitude and obligation through appropriate payments.

Edwin followed Rædwald as overlord of the southern English and it was no doubt to reinforce the changed positions of the two kingdoms that he persuaded Rædwald's son and successor, Eorpwald, to accept Christianity probably in 627.[35] There was a pagan reaction and Eorpwald was slain in 627 or 628 by one Ricbert who may then have ruled the country for the next three years, though Bede is not clear on this point. In 630 or 631 Sigebert, brother of Eorpwald (half-brother according to 'Florence of Worcester' and William of Malmesbury) who had been in exile in Francia and was a Christian succeeded to the throne.

The accession of Sigebert brings in a period in which the East Anglian kings appear in two main roles in our sources: as patrons of the church and as victims of Mercian aggression. Bede is full of praise for the practical piety of Sigebert and his successor Anna. Sigebert eventually retired to become a monk at a monastery he had founded and entrusted control of the kingdom to his kinsman Ecgric who had previously been ruling part of the kingdom.[36] However, when the kingdom came under serious attack from the Mercians under Penda, Sigebert was brought from the monastery to join the army 'in the hope that the soldiers would be less afraid and less ready to flee if they had with them one who was once their most vigorous and distinguished leader'. The date of the battle in which both Sigebert and Ecgric were slain is not known, but may have occurred in the early 640s as Anna was ruling when Cenwalh of Wessex came to the kingdom in exile in 645.[37]

The source of conflict between Mercia and East Anglia was presumably control of the amorphous East Midland peoples known collectively as the Middle Angles whose south-eastern territories lay between the two kingdoms.

Anna seems to have been a serious challenge to the rising power of Penda of Mercia. The *Life of St Foillan* refers to a serious attack on East Anglia c. 650 which led to the destruction of the monastery of *Cnobheresburg* (possibly Burgh Castle, Norfolk) and temporary expulsion of King Anna, perhaps to the territory of the Magonsæte who seem to have had strong links with the East Angles at about this time.[38] A second attack from Mercia brought about Anna's death and this would appear to have been a significant point in Penda's career.[39] It is one of the few East Anglian events to have found its way into the *Anglo-Saxon Chronicle* where it is dated to 653/54. Bede does not provide a date for Anna's death, but he does show that it was about the time that Anna died that Penda created his son Peada king of the Middle Angles, an event he dates to 653.[40] Although the Mercians were still pagans, a bishop was provided for the Middle Angles perhaps suggesting that they had already been converted under East Anglian influence. Penda was also responsible for the death of a fourth East Anglian king as Anna's brother and successor, Æthelhere, died in 655 at the battle of the *Winwæd* where he was leading the East Anglian contingent in Penda's army.[41]

The reigns of the next three kings – Æthelwald (655-63), Aldwulf (663-713) and Ælfwald (713-49) – are rather more securely dated than those of their predecessors, but are in other ways more poorly recorded. Aldwulf was the last East Anglian king of whom Bede knew.[42] His reign of about fifty years seems suspiciously long, but his accession is fixed by the synod of Hatfield of 679 being dated to his seventeenth year and the date of his death is provided by Frankish annals.[43] The only other kings whose regnal years are cited in the Hatfield proceedings are those of the kings of Northumbria, Mercia and Kent, and so the inclusion of East Anglia gives some idea of its importance at this time. Swithhelm of the East Saxons was baptized in East Anglia during the reign of Æthelwald with the king as his sponsor which, judging from the circumstances surrounding comparable conversions, could imply that the East Angles had some sort of overlordship of the East Saxons at the time.[44] A continuing interest in the Middle Angles can be demonstrated. It was probably in the reign of Æthelwald or Aldwulf that the East Anglian princess Æthelthryth married Tondbert, *princeps* of the South Gyrwe, though her career is very hard to date accurately.[45] Through this marriage the East Angles seem to have won control of the area based on Ely where Æthelthryth founded a monastery in 673.[46] Further East Anglian influence in Middle Anglian areas is suggested from the way a Mercian exile like the future king Æthelbald could safely retreat to the Crowland fens during the reign of Ceolred of Mercia (709-16),[47] and from the interest taken by King Ælfwald in the life of the Middle Anglian saint Guthlac, in spite of Guthlac being a member of the Mercian royal house.[48]

In 749, according to the Northern annals of the *Historia Regum*, Ælfwald died and the kingdom was divided between Hun, Beonna and Alberht.[49] We know no more than this of the events in 749, but it would appear that Beonna emerged as the dominant king as he was the only one to mint coins in his own name (see Fig. 14.3). His coins are provisionally dated to the late 750s or early 760s, but, as a substantial number more have been discovered recently, these dates may be subject to change.[50] At the moment we cannot be certain when Beonna's reign ended. His successor may have been Æthelred, the father of St Æthelbert, as the *Lives* of the latter claim, though no coins in Æthelred's name are known.[51] According to the *Lives* Æthelbert succeeded his father as king of the East Angles in 779. It is not clear when Offa of Mercia took control of the province, but by the early 790s he was minting a penny coinage there.[52] Æthelbert also minted pennies and the usual interpretation has been that this represents a rebellion by Æthelbert against Offa the end result of which was Æthelbert's death at the hands of Offa in 794.[53]

Offa may have controlled East Anglia only for a relatively short period in the 790s. The coin evidence suggests that a native king, Eadwald, took control of the kingdom after Offa's death and that he was eventually ousted by Cenwulf.[54] East Anglian autonomy seems to have been restored under Athelstan, the most prolific minter among these late East Anglian kings. It has been suggested on the basis of the coin evidence that Athelstan made his first bid for the throne after Cenwulf's death, was subsequently ousted by Ceolwulf and then re-emerged after Ceolwulf's death.[55] Athelstan was probably the un-named East Anglian king who is recorded in the *Chronicle* as the slayer of the Mercian kings Beornwulf (d. 826) and Ludeca (d. 827), who was the last Mercian king to use the East Anglian mint.[56] Athelstan's successors in the East Anglian coinage were Æthelweard and Edmund. According to later Anglo-Saxon accounts Edmund came to the throne in 855; his death at the hands of the Great Heathen Army in 869 is recorded in the *Chronicle* and was greatly elaborated in later sources.[57] East Anglia then passed under the control of Danish kings until its conquest by Edward the Elder, though coins in the names of Æthelred and Oswald which bear a resemblance to known East Anglian issues, may be evidence that the Danes followed their practice attested elsewhere in England of leaving part of the kingdom under native control.[58]

Sources of royal power

The East Anglian kings appear in the written sources as doughty fighters who were able to offer an effective resistance to Mercian plans for eastern expansion and ultimately played a major part in ending Mercian dominance in southern England. Control of the fenland Middle Anglian peoples was a major source of conflict with Mercia and the respective influences of the two kingdoms fluctuated during the period. Although Penda attempted to unify the Middle Angles as one kingdom with their own subking and bishop, it does not appear that they really were as unified as some other kingdoms and, as indicated in the Tribal Hidage, they consisted of a number of small peoples, some of which are recorded elsewhere as having their own rulers.[59] It can hardly be expected that each of these peoples had identical histories and the East Anglian kings had stronger control of some of the south-eastern ones than others; the South Gyrwe, for instance, seem to have been absorbed into East Anglia by the end of the seventh century, whereas the Crowland area where Guthlac had his hermitage and which probably belonged to the North Gyrwe remained debatable territory between the Mercian and East Anglian kingdoms.[60] The fenlands may have hindered East Anglian expansion, but they also made it more difficult for the Mercians to take over East Anglia and, in spite of determined efforts by the late-eighth- and ninth-century Mercian kings, the Mercian conquest of East Anglia was ultimately unsuccessful.[61] Expansion south was blocked by the East Saxons; the river Stour was the boundary at the end of the Saxon period and may have been so earlier as well. Æthelwald may have had some power over the East Saxons, but that is the only indication of any major contact between the two peoples.

Military effectiveness was one side of East Anglian royal power, but there must have been other facets. There are interesting parallels with Kent. In both kingdoms a period where Scandinavian contacts were important was superseded by one in which Frankish links became more significant, though the shift in foreign contacts occurred much earlier in Kent. The gravegoods from Mound 1 at Sutton Hoo can be seen as transitional between the two periods. The ritual of burial in a ship can only be paralleled in Scandinavia, though there are striking differences as well as similarities with the burials of the Vendel period in Sweden.[62] Many of the motifs of the jewellery and armour have their closest parallels in Scandinavia, but the techniques of manufacture are more likely to have a Frankish origin, and many of the raw materials, the sword and the Byzantine silverware are likely to have reached East Anglia via Francia.[63] The purse contained thirty-seven Merovingian coins and one interpretation of them is as a diplomatic gift from the Neustrian court.[64] Rædwald's son (or possibly stepson) Sigebert had a Frankish name.

With the accession of Sigebert the links with Francia became more pronounced. Sigebert had been in exile in Francia and had become a Christian there; Bede specifically says that the church in Gaul (Francia) provided the inspiration for the institutions which Sigebert established in his own kingdom.[65] His bishop Felix came ultimately from Burgundy, but had probably been a member of one of the foundations of Columbanus in Francia.[66] The Irish monk Fursa who founded *Cnobheresburg* in East Anglia also founded a monastery in Neustria, and when his brother and other monks had to flee to Francia because of Mercian attacks, they were initially received by Erchinoald, mayor of the palace of Neustria, whose interest in Anglo-Saxon England is well-attested and whose daughter may have married Eadbald of Kent.[67] Like the Kentish princess Eorcengota, East Anglian princesses entered double monasteries in Neustria and Anna's stepdaughter Sæthryth and daughter Æthelburh both became abbesses at Faremoûtier-en-Brie, while Hereswith, widow of Anna's brother Æthelric, went to Chelles.[68]

The written sources do not permit the same type of link to be made between kings and trade which was apparent in Kent, but excavations in Ipswich have demonstrated that it was a significant trading emporium from the early seventh century.[69] Ipswich is only 12 miles from Sutton Hoo and the nearby royal vill of Rendlesham and has generally been interpreted as being under royal control. It was the centre of a large-scale wheel-turned pottery industry, the only one of this standard known in southern England during the Middle Saxon period, and its wares have been found throughout East Anglia and in areas of Middle Anglia.[70] Finds of foreign origin show that there was trade with Neustria, but that trade with the Rhineland, usually believed to be in the hands of Frisian middlemen, was more significant.[71] The difference in trading patterns may help to explain why East Anglia did not produce its own coinage as early as Kent did. The earliest East Anglian coins were secondary sceattas produced during the reigns of Aldwulf and Ælfwald.[72] By the middle of the eighth century the production of coin had clearly become very significant in East Anglia and Beonna made the first attempt to restore the silver content of the southern coinage probably on the lines of Eadbert's reforms in Northumbria.[73] His coins are the first in southern England to regularly carry the king's name. The change to a penny coinage of the Carolingian type was probably the work of Offa in the early 790s, but as we have already seen, native kings minted pennies in their own names whenever they were in a position to do so.

In view of their common North Sea interests, it is not surprising that there was an early close link between Kent and East Anglia which is first demonstrated by Æthelbert's attempts to convert Rædwald. When East Anglia was finally converted to Christianity the connection was strengthened. The first bishop of East Anglia, the Burgundian Felix, was sent from Kent and for a period East Anglia was the only foreign kingdom to recognize the authority of the archbishop of Canterbury.[74] Anna's daughter Seaxburh married Eorcenbert of Kent and their daughter Eorcengota was at Brie with her East Anglian aunts.[75] Imma, a thegn in the Northumbrian army who was captured at the battle of the river Trent in 679 and sold into slavery in London, was able to obtain money for his ransom from Seaxburh's son, Hlothere, on the grounds that he had once been the thegn of Seaxburh's sister Æthelthryth.[76] Kentish connections may also have helped to establish links between East Anglia and the Magonsæte on the western borders of Mercia.[77]

The East Anglian royal line also had close links with the Northumbrian royal house. The links were initially with the Deiran dynasty for whom Rædwald formed a major service by defeating and killing the Bernician Æthelfrith.[78] Æthelric of East Anglia married Edwin's niece Hereswith and her sister Hild came to East Anglia before Aidan helped to facilitate a reconciliation between the two Northumbrian dynasties.[79] The Deiran monk Ceolfrith came to study the monastic practices of Botulf at Iken (Suffolk) before his appointment at Wearmouth.[80] Bede surprisingly does not mention this connection, but he had his own East Anglian contact in Abbot Esi whose monastery is not known.[81] The East Anglians had links with the Bernician dynasty as well. Æthelthryth the daughter of Anna married Egfrith of Northumbria, though the marriage can hardly be described as very successful.[82] Once we get to the eighth century references of any kind to East Anglia are few and far between, but references to East Anglian affairs in the northern annals preserved in the *Historia Regum* suggest continued contact and the most telling evidence is Beonna's remodelling of the coinage apparently under the influence of that from Northumbria. Northumbria and East Anglia were natural allies; both wished to restrict the power of Mercia and both were people of the North Sea littoral with similar commercial interests.

The royal family and administration
We know the relationship of most of the kings from Rædwald to Ælfwald whose genealogy is given in the Anglian collection.[83] The succession seems to have been kept within a narrow family group during this time. Rædwald was succeeded by his son Eorpwald, but the ancestry of Eorpwald's slayer and possible successor, Ricbert, is not known. Sigebert was Eorpwald's brother according to Bede, though William of Malmesbury and 'Florence of Worcester' record a tradition that they were only related through their mother, i.e.

Rædwald d. by 627

Eorpwald d. 627/8

?Ricbert 627/8–630/1

Sigebert acc. 630/1

Ecgric

Anna d. 653/4

Æthelhere 653/4–655

Æthelwald 655–663

Aldwulf 663–713

Ælfwald 713–749

Beonna acc. 749

Æthelred

Æthelbert ?779–794

Eadwald

Athelstan

Æthelweard

Edmund 855–869

Table 6: Regnal list of the kings of the East Angles

that Rædwald was not Sigebert's father.[84] This leaves the way open for an interesting hypothesis whereby Sigebert could be seen as a representative of a rival line which would explain Rædwald's recorded hostility towards him and his period of exile in Francia. However, as we do not know the source of William's and 'Florence's' information it cannot be accepted as authoritative. Sigebert eventually resigned the throne to a relative called Ecgric who had already been ruling with him. It has been suggested that Ecgric should be equated with Æthelric, the father of Aldwulf, but their first name-elements are two distinct forms, both well-attested among the Anglo-Saxons.[85] The throne next passed to first cousins of Eorpwald and Sigebert, the sons of Rædwald's brother Eni, who provide an interesting example of fraternal succession. Three brothers, Anna, Æthelhere and Æthelwald ruled in turn and Æthelwald was succeeded by his nephew, Aldwulf, the son of a fourth brother, Æthelric. The next king, Ælfwald, was the son of Aldwulf and there our genealogical information ends. There are grounds for suspecting, from the form of his name, that Beonna was not from the same family group, though Alberht with whom he apparently shared the kingdom could have been. The oldest *Life* of St Æthelbert claimed that he and his father Æthelred were descended from Rædwald and the earlier East Anglian kings[86] and their name-elements help to support this, but without a proper pedigree we can make no certain observations about patterns of succession after the time of Ælfwald. The pattern as

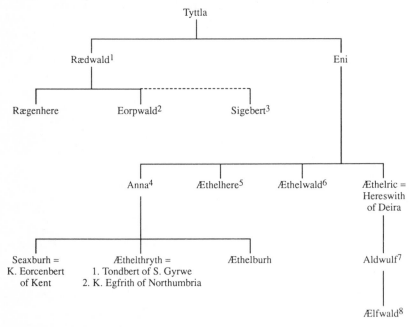

Table 7: Genealogy of the East Anglian royal house
The kings are numbered in order of ruling.

far as we can trace it recalls that in Kent whereby succession was generally contained within a restricted kin-group.

The lack of any records connected with royal administration in East Anglia makes any detailed appraisal of royal government impossible, though Peter Warner has detected within later arrangements traces of a pre-Danish organization of the province into letes and hundreds which recalls that of the Kentish lathes.[87] There are hints of a major subdivision within the kingdom comparable to the East/West division in Kent. East Anglia was originally provided with only one see based at *Dommoc* which is usually taken to be Dunwich, though a case has also been made for Felixstowe.[88] Sometime after the synod of Hertford of 672, Archbishop Theodore took advantage of the illness of the bishop of East Anglia and divided the see with a new episcopal centre at North Elmham.[89] The sees were separated by the river Waveney which divided – and still divides – the North and the South Folk. The names Norfolk and Suffolk are not found until the eleventh century, but obviously could be much older.[90] It is possible that in the provision of the two sees Theodore was following a political division of much older origin, as Augustine did in Kent when he formed the two dioceses of Rochester and Canterbury.

The best supporting evidence for a major political division comes from the reign of Sigebert. Bede records that when Sigebert decided to retire to a monastery, he entrusted the kingdom to his *cognatus* Ecgric who had previously ruled over part of the kingdom.[91] Clearly a bipartite division – though not necessarily an equal one – is implied. The only other possible indication of a similar joint reign is after the death of Anna. Bede separately describes both Æthelhere and Æthelwald as Anna's successor.[92] It is possible that not too much weight should be given to Bede's words, especially as Æthelhere only ruled for a year or so, but as they stand they imply that the two brothers originally ruled together and so provide some further support for joint kingship and a subkingdom among the East Angles. In the eighth century the *Historia Regum* records that Hun, Beonna and Alberht divided the kingdom between them. It is possible that such a tripartite division could be based on Norfolk, Suffolk and the lands around Ely, but we lack any real understanding of the political situation in 749. Although a threefold division is recorded, only Beonna produced coins in his name.

The Wuffingas were much more strongly associated with Suffolk than with Norfolk. The two major ship-burial cemeteries, Sutton Hoo and Snape, are in Suffolk,[93] and close to the royal vill of Rendlesham and *wic* at Ipswich. Two prestigious Middle Saxon sites at Burrow Hill and Brandon in Suffolk are currently under investigation.[94] The site of the first see was in Suffolk, if *Dommoc* is correctly identified as Dunwich or Felixstowe, and there seem to have been more important monasteries patronized by the royal house in Suffolk than in Norfolk. At the synod of *Clofeshoh* in 803 the bishop of *Dommoc* took with him two abbots (perhaps from Blythburgh and Iken) as well as priests whereas the bishop of Elmham was only supported by priests.[95] There may have been a double monastery at East Dereham in Norfolk,[96] but apart from that and Elmham the only major foundation which has been suggested for Norfolk is *Cnobheresburg*. For a long time it has been assumed that *Cnobheresburg* was Burgh Castle, but a recent assessment of the excavated evidence could find nothing conclusive to support the identification.[97] In any case the foundation appears to have been shortlived.[98] The combined information suggests that the Wuffingas centre was in Suffolk, and in particular in the south-east coastal area of the Wicklaw hundreds which contained Sutton Hoo, Snape, Rendlesham, Ipswich, Burrow Hill and Iken and preserved a certain administrative distinctiveness in later centuries. It is possible that their control of Norfolk was a secondary development.

We do not know anything of male members of the royal house who did not become kings, and references to the nobility as a whole are little better and do not go far beyond such observations as the endowment of *Cnobheresburg* by Anna and his nobles with stately buildings and gifts.[99] Bede does, however, refer in passing to Owine, a monk of Lastingham, who had come to Northumbria with Queen Æthelthryth as *primus minstrorum et princeps domus eius*.[100] Another thegn of Æthelthryth's, Imma, became a thegn of the Northumbrian kings, but he may not have been of East Anglian birth.[101]

East Anglian princesses, like those of other kingdoms, were important for the marriage connections they could bring. Alliances with Kent and Northumbria were strengthened in this way, and Æthelthryth's marriage to Tondbert of the South Gyrwe seems to have been particularly significant as it may have eased the absorption of the South Gyrwe into the East Anglian kingdom.[102] The founding of a double monastery by Æthelthryth at Ely, which may have been an administrative centre of the South Gyrwe, may have eased the transfer and have been a diplomatic way of transferring land to East Anglian control.[103] The fact that Æthelthryth apparently remained a virgin throughout two marriages indicates that the symbolic nature of such unions could be more significant than the sexual dimension.

Ely may have been the first double monastery founded in East Anglia as other East Anglian princesses who wished to live as nuns had gone to Francia. Æthelthryth was succeeded as its abbess by her sister Seaxburh and she in turn was probably followed by her daughter Eormenhild.[104] King Ælfwald's sister Ecgburh was an abbess and Ely is most likely to have been her monastery as it was clearly the dominant female royal proprietary house and perhaps exceptionally well-endowed.[105] There may also have been a royal double monastery at East Dereham in Norfolk where Saint Wihtburh was buried until her bones were shamelessly purloined in the late tenth century by the monks of Ely.[106] According to one tradition Wihtburh was the youngest daughter of King Anna,[107] but if this was the case it is surprising Bede does not mention her when he was so well-informed about her sisters. The traditional date for her death of 743[108] is also rather late for a daughter of Anna and it may be that we do not know her true identity. Ely traditions about its East Anglian princess-saints are very unreliable and in general the monks of Ely, like other reformed houses of Bishop Æthelwold, seem to have had little compunction about distorting earlier history to suit their needs.[109]

The East Anglian kings also did their duty by the church and Bede singled out Sigebert and Anna for particular praise. Sigebert founded the see at *Dommoc* and the monastery at *Cnobheresburg* and possibly a third house to which he retreated; in the tenth century this monastic retreat was believed to be *Betrichesworde* (Bury St Edmunds).[110] Anna is associated with Blythburgh where he was apparently buried[111] and Iken, which was founded in the year he was killed, may have had a particular commemorative function.[112] King Ælfwald in a letter to Boniface refers to seven monasteries at which prayers were offered for Boniface and his mission.[113] The second see at North Elmham and the double monasteries of Ely and East Dereham can be added to those mentioned above, but there may have been other monasteries which have not found their way into any written records, and it is possible that the recently excavated sites at Burrow Hill and Brandon in Suffolk could have been religious communities.[114] The *Life of St Guthlac* and the letter to Boniface, both from the reign of Ælfwald, show that the East Anglian church was in good heart in the first half of the eighth century, and it still possessed its two bishops on the eve of the Danish conquest, though the shortage of sources does not permit any more detailed appraisal of its condition at this time.[115]

Conclusion

We have frequently had to regret the loss of early East Anglian records which prevent a full appraisal of many aspects of East Anglian kingship. However, the ability of the kingdom to recover from a period of Mercian conquest in the late eighth and early ninth centuries and to survive until the period of the Danish conquests suggests that it was a kingdom in which an effective royal administration and control of royal resources existed. Many aspects which we have been able to look at suggest parallels with the kingdom of Kent; these include overlordship in the early seventh century, an early link with Francia, signs of above average wealth expressed in imported goods, early trading bases, and the confinement of the succession to a narrow group of royal kin (until the mid-eighth century at least). Such parallels are probably not so much the result of conscious borrowing from the one kingdom to the other, but to be explained by exploitation of similar opportunities. Both kingdoms had exceptionally powerful and wealthy royal houses at the beginning of the seventh century which had probably established themselves 50 to 75 years before. Both kingdoms only expanded modestly from their original powerbases, perhaps checked by natural barriers and the ambitions of other rulers, though ruthless expansion in the Mercian mould does not seem to have been one of the aims of their kings. The advantages provided by their extensive seaboards with easy contact with the Continent may have made westward expansion less imperative.

Chapter Five

NORTHUMBRIA

Sources

The chronology and many of the main events in the history of Northumbria during the seventh and eighth centuries are relatively well recorded thanks to the endeavours of Bede and to other Northumbrians who maintained an annalistic tradition. Only when we get to the ninth century do narrative and annalistic sources fail us so that the last years of the Anglo-Saxon kingdom of Northumbria are obscure.

Bede's *Ecclesiastical History* is, of course, a history of the whole 'English' church and people, but Bede's natural interest in the history of Northumbria, the greater ease in gathering material from his own province and the overlordship which some Northumbrian kings imposed south of the Humber for much of the seventh century mean that the Northumbrian rulers play a particularly important part in Bede's narrative. Bede's work is not entirely straightforward. A good deal of his material came from oral sources and so needs careful evaluation. Naturally much of his information on Northumbria came from the Northumbrian monasteries, but Canterbury was also a major source for Northumbrian affairs and an important influence on the form of the *Ecclesiastical History*.[1] Bede's belief in the use of history as a moral exemplar and his desire to influence contemporary society affected the way he selected and presented incidents from Northumbria's past, though Bede was also concerned to establish as accurate a picture as possible of events so that the pattern of God's relationship with man would emerge clearly. The basis of Bede's narrative was a secure chronology, and in the reconciliation of several disparate systems of dating to produce *anno Domini* dates he must have faced a formidable task. Doubts have been expressed about whether Bede was fully successful in overcoming all the difficulties, and various schemes for emending Bede's Northumbrian dates have been proposed.[2] However, although Bede's sources may sometimes have posed him insurmountable problems – the dating clauses of the synods of Hertford and Hatfield being prime examples – his own methods of calculation were sound and consistently imposed so that no major system of redating seems necessary.[3] Bede's dates for the reigns of the Northumbrian kings may be accepted as they stand.

Bede concentrated on events of the seventh century and has comparatively little to say about the kings who ruled during his own lifetime. Fortunately some other writers of the eighth century were not so reticent and historians are particularly grateful to Stephanus, the biographer of St Wilfrid, for his de-tailed discussions of the political problems in Northumbria in the late seventh and early eighth centuries in which Wilfrid himself was frequently a protago-nist.[4] For instance, whereas Bede simply records that Osred succeeded his father Aldfrith in 705, Stephanus reveals that there was a disputed succession on Aldfrith's death which his hero, Wilfrid, endeavoured to exploit.[5] Step-hanus judges events and people by the way they affected Wilfrid and it is not hard to detect how his aim – the justification of Wilfrid's actions and the presentation of his sanctity – has influenced his approach to Northumbrian history. We also get a different view of Northumbria's early Anglo-Saxon history from the British compilation of the early ninth century known as the *Historia Brittonum* and traditionally ascribed to Nennius.[6] The work draws upon a variety of sources including British traditions concerning events of the seventh century. The northern recension of the *Anglo-Saxon Chronicle* (MSS D and E) also seems to have had access to early annals which may have had a Celtic source.[7]

The last chapter of the *Ecclesiastical History* contains a series of annals summarizing the most important events in the history of Britain from the conquest by the Romans to 731 when Bede's history was completed. The annals were probably compiled by Bede himself and seem to have been an important spur to chronicle writing in Northumbria. Several manuscripts of the *Ecclesiastical History* contain a continuation of Bede's annals to 766,[8] but the most important source for the history of Northumbria in the eighth cen-tury is a Northumbrian chronicle which is most fully preserved in a twelfth-century compilation known as the *Historia Regum* and attributed to Symeon of Durham.[9] Recent research has established that the Northumbrian chronicle to 887 was reworked at the turn of the tenth century by Byrhtferth of Ramsey abbey.[10] The style of the work as it survives is Byrhtferth's, but the historical content up to 802 derives from a chronicle written at a Northumbrian religious house, most probably in York, and which was also the source of Northumbrian entries in the northern recension of the *Anglo-Saxon Chronicle* (to 806). Unfor-tunately this source ends in the first decade of the ninth century and we have only a few dates for the Northumbrian kings of the ninth century which were taken from an unknown source and incorporated in the *Historia Regum* and in another post-Conquest compilation, the *Flores Historiarum* of Roger of Wen-dover. The coinage provides an opportunity to reach an independent assess-ment of the dates of the ninth-century kings and some numismatists have proposed a radical redating of the reigns.[11] However, although the coinage can provide a relative chronology of reigns it cannot, as yet, furnish us with absolute dates. There are many controversial elements in the interpretation of the Northumbrian styca coinage and for the time being historians are continu-ing to make the best they can of the chronology provided by the surviving written works.

The high cultural profile of the early Northumbrian church means that Northumbria has the fullest range of ecclesiastical sources surviving of any early Anglo-Saxon kingdom. Such sources include hagiographies, histories of individual monastic communities and works of ecclesiastical legislation such as the Penitential and *Dialogus Ecclesiasticae Institutionis* of Archbishop Egbert of York (734-66). Many of these sources survive because, thanks to the work of Northumbrian missionaries, they found a safe haven in Continental religious houses; for the Viking raids and subsequent settlements have meant the loss of most of the monastic archives of the pre-Viking Northumbrian church. One result of this is that no Northumbrian charters survive in their entirety, although it is clear from Bede and other writers that they once existed and summaries of the landed possessions of the Durham community seem to draw upon charters of the monastery of Lindisfarne, though not all of these can be genuine.[12] The lack of charters hinders the study of the administration of the Northumbrian kings and details of internal divisions within the kingdom can only be deduced from later sources.

The royal houses of Bernicia and Deira and the origins of Northumbria
The kingdom of Northumbria was formed by the amalgamation of the two Anglo-Saxon kingdoms of Bernicia and Deira and from the absorption of a number of small Celtic kingdoms. The Celtic provinces are only mentioned incidentally in the *Ecclesiastical History* and will be examined in greater detail later. In contrast, the history of the rival Anglo-Saxon dynasties received considerable attention from Bede and provides some of his passages which are closest in spirit to traditional heroic verse; no doubt much of his information came from oral sources and so was presented to him in that way. The final absorption of Deira into Bernicia occurred in Bede's lifetime and he obviously wanted his Northumbrian audience to feel themselves heirs to the traditions of both provinces. Even the name 'Northumbria' may have been coined by Bede and popularized through the *Ecclesiastical History*.[13]

Bede does not discuss the early history of either kingdom. The original nucleus of Deira was the East Riding of Yorkshire and that of Bernicia was probably in the Tyne area; the Tees valley seems to have formed the boundary between the provinces in the seventh century. Both kingdoms have British names and were surrounded by Celtic kingdoms; it is possible that both were in origin British kingdoms or tribal territories which were taken over by Anglo-Saxon warbands.[14] The *Historia Brittonum* links Anglo-Saxon settlement of the north with the Kentish foundation legend by having Hengist despatch his son Octha and nephew Ebissa to fight in the vicinity of Hadrian's Wall, but such claims are as ephemeral as Hengist and Horsa themselves.[15] The specific origins of the two royal houses which dominated Northumbria in the seventh century are also obscure. A note in the *Historia Brittonum* says that Sœmil the great-great-great-grandfather of Ælle of Deira (ruling in 597) was the first to separate Deira from Bernicia by which it presumably means that he detached Deira from British control, an event that would have taken place (if the notice has any historical validity) in the first half of the fifth century.[16] A fragment of a Northumbrian chronicle based on the annals with which Bede closed the *Ecclesiastical History* records that Oessa, the grandfather of King Ida of Bernicia (who reputedly ruled 547-59) was the first of the dynasty to come to Britain, though Ida seems to have been the first of the line to rule.[17]

Information from the *Historia Brittonum*, the *Anglo-Saxon Chronicle* and a regnal list in an eighth-century manuscript of the *Ecclesiastical History* ('Moore MS') seems to indicate that there were English kings ruling Northumbria in the late sixth century who were not related to Ida's dynasty and were not infrequently in opposition to it.[18] Bede used a version of the regnal list to produce the date of 547 for the beginning of the reign of Ida on the assumption

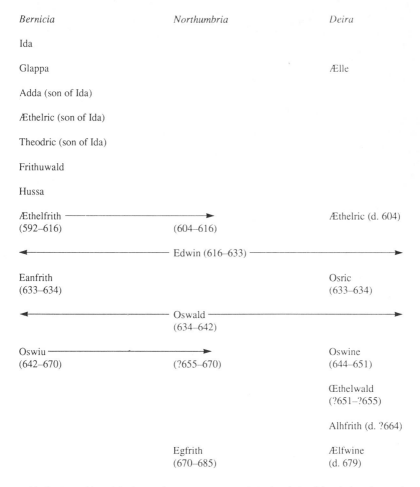

Bernicia	Northumbria	Deira
Ida		
Glappa		Ælle
Adda (son of Ida)		
Æthelric (son of Ida)		
Theodric (son of Ida)		
Frithuwald		
Hussa		
Æthelfrith (592–616) ⟶	(604–616)	Æthelric (d. 604)
⟵ Edwin (616–633) ⟶		
Eanfrith (633–634)		Osric (633–634)
⟵ Oswald (634–642) ⟶		
Oswiu (642–670) ⟶	(?655–670)	Oswine (644–651)
		Œthelwald (?651–?655)
		Alhfrith (d. ?664)
	Egfrith (670–685)	Ælfwine (d. 679)

Table 8: Regnal list of the kings of Bernicia, Deira and Northumbria of the sixth and seventh centuries

The Bernician kings down to Æthelfrith are those named in the Moore Memoranda. There is reason to believe that several of these kings in fact ruled concurrently (perhaps in different parts of Bernicia)

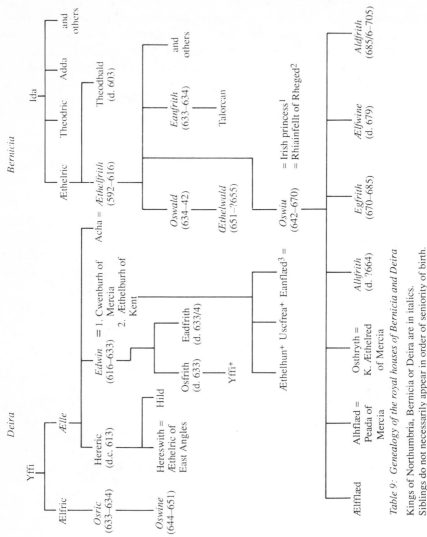

Table 9: Genealogy of the royal houses of Bernicia and Deira

Kings of Northumbria, Bernicia or Deira are in italics.

Siblings do not necessarily appear in order of seniority of birth.

that all the kings in the list ruled successively, but other sources suggest that some of them may have been ruling contemporaneously which means that Ida's reign would have begun later.[19] The brief and often enigmatic records we possess for Bernicia in the late sixth century seem to indicate a period in which rival Anglo-Saxon warleaders battled for supremacy with the house of Ida eventually emerging as triumphant. The contests between the Anglo-Saxons were complicated by opposition from neighbouring British communities. Landmarks in the struggle are hard to find. The *Historia Brittonum* credits Ida with the conquest of the Bamburgh area and his son Theodric was besieged by British rulers on Lindisfarne, but it is hard to produce a continuous narrative of these early stages of Bernician expansion.[20] Detailed Bernician history begins with Æthelfrith, a grandson of Ida (592-616) whose reign is the first to be reliably dated.

It is usually assumed that the Deiran kingdom was established earlier than Bernicia and the province certainly seems from the cemetery evidence to have been more intensively settled by Germanic immigrants than Bernicia, with settlement beginning in the fifth century.[21] But in spite of the brief reference to Soemil we know very little about the Deiran dynasty before the seventh century. Sixth-century Deiran history has been unnecessarily confused because a compiler of the *Anglo-Saxon Chronicle* took unwarranted liberties with a Deiran king-list and wrongly assumed that Æthelric of Deira was the same person as a King Æthelric of Bernicia, hopelessly muddling their chronology as a result.[22] The first Deiran king of whose existence we can be satisfied is Ælle whom Bede tells us, in another of his historical works, was ruling at the time of the arrival of the Augustine mission in 597.[23] Ælle was the father of Edwin (616-33) who is the first of the Deiran kings to be securely dated; if the *Anglo-Saxon Chronicle* can be trusted, a king called Æthelric ruled briefly between Ælle and Edwin, but his relationship to them is unknown.

Bede begins his narrative account with the reign of Æthelfrith of Bernicia who was the first to rule in both Bernicia and Deira (592-616). It appears that Æthelfrith invaded Deira in 604, killing its king (presumably Æthelric), sending Ælle's son Edwin into exile and marrying Ælle's daughter Acha.[24] Bede saw Æthelfrith's intervention as providential for Edwin's exile took him to the southern kingdoms of the Anglo-Saxons and was ultimately to result in his conversion. The turning-point for Edwin came at the court of King Rædwald of the East Angles in a scene redolent of heroic verse.[25] According to Bede's vivid account, Æthelfrith tried to persuade Rædwald to do away with Edwin by promising large rewards if he did so and threatening war if he did not. Rædwald had just come round to Æthelfrith's point of view when his wife (filling the traditional role of queens in such situations) reminded him of his true obligations to one who had placed himself under his protection. Rædwald did the more honourable thing and in 616 defeated and killed Æthelfrith in the battle of the river Idle, thus helping Edwin to take over Æthelfrith's position as ruler of both Bernicia and Deira. The tables were well and truly reversed as now Æthelfrith's sons had to go into exile and fled to Ireland and the Celtic kingdoms of Scotland.[26]

To Bede it was evident that Divine providence lay behind these events for King Edwin maintained his links with the southern kingdoms and married a Christian Kentish princess. His own conversion seems to have been delayed until after the death of Rædwald which also enabled Edwin to take over Rædwald's position of overlordship over other Anglo-Saxon kingdoms.[27] Edwin's very successful reign was ended when he was killed on Hatfield Chase in 633 fighting against the joint forces of Cadwallon of Gwynedd and Penda of Mercia.[28] This battle also temporarily ended the union of Bernicia and Deira for the throne of Bernicia passed to Eanfrith, son of Æthelfrith, and that of Deira to Edwin's cousin Osric. Both these pagan kings fell within the year to Cadwallon of Gwynedd and, according to Bede, it was later decided to expunge them from the official king-lists.[29]

The successor in both kingdoms was Oswald (634-42). Oswald was another son of Æthelfrith, but he was also the son of Acha of Deira and so apparently acceptable as king to the nobility of both provinces.[30] Oswald was a particular hero to Bede. He had been converted to Christianity while in exile in the Irish kingdom of Dalriada in south-west Scotland and reintroduced Christianity to both Northumbrian provinces after his accession though he looked to the Dalriadic centre of Iona for missionaries rather than to Canterbury.[31] After his death in 642 Oswald was venerated as a saint, partly for his services to the church, but chiefly because he fell in battle against the pagan Penda of Mercia and so could be seen as a Christian martyr.[32] Oswald was therefore an ideal model king for Bede to present to his eighth-century audience. Much is made of Oswald's care of the church and his willingness to follow the advice of Bishop Aidan. But Bede's Oswald is an insipid saint-king and we get little flavour of the formidable warrior king who like Edwin was overlord of many Anglo-Saxon and Celtic kingdoms. We see glimpses of the other side of Oswald when Edwin's widow hastily packs her infant sons and step-grandson off to France for fear that Oswald will have them murdered or when the monks of Bardney in Lindsey who have suffered Oswald's overlordship refuse to temporarily house his body because of their resentment towards him.[33]

Oswald was succeeded by his brother Oswiu (642-70) who was apparently acceptable to the Bernicians, but not to the Deirans. The Deiran throne passed back to the original Deiran house in the person of Oswine (644-51), son of the last independent Deiran king Osric, but as he does not appear to have begun ruling until 644 it is likely Oswiu attempted to take both kingdoms. When Oswiu failed to get rid of Oswine by comparatively legitimate means he had him murdered.[34] Although Oswiu had attempted to make himself more acceptable to the Deirans by marrying Edwin of Deira's daughter Eanflæd, he did not take direct control of Deira on Oswine's death and it was ruled instead by Œthelwald, Oswiu's nephew and the son of King Oswald. Œthelwald may have begun ruling as a subking under his uncle, but Bede's references suggest that he was soon following an independent line and recognized the authority of

Penda of Mercia on whose side he fought at the battle of the river *Winwæd* in 655.[35] Bede says that Œthelwald's withdrawal from the battle at a strategic point was one reason for Oswiu's success, but if Œthelwald hoped to curry favour with his uncle by such a manoeuvre he was probably to be disappointed for he is never heard of again and it is likely that Oswiu removed him from office. When we next hear of Deira it is ruled by Oswiu's son Alhfrith as subking to his father, but Alhfrith too seems to have attempted to use Deiran separatism to try and gain independence from Oswiu. Bede hints that this was the case, and he and Stephanus demonstrate how in the early 660s Alhfrith began following a different religious policy from his father through rejecting the customs of the Ionan church in favour of those of Canterbury which were still followed by some in Deira and by Oswiu's queen who had been brought up in Kent. After the synod of Whitby in 664 at which these matters came to a head, Alhfrith too disappears suddenly and silently from the written record.[36]

Oswiu is the one ruler from Bede's gallery of early Northumbrian kings who displays clearly those qualities of ruthlessness which must have been an essential prerequisite of early medieval kingship. A cousin, nephew and son all seem to have suffered at Oswiu's hands when they threatened to thwart his power or his ambitions, and Oswiu was prepared to risk the life of a second son in his battle for dominance with the Mercian kings. For at the time of the battle of the river *Winwæd* Oswiu's son Egfrith was a hostage at the Mercian court as a guarantor of Oswiu's recognition of Penda's superiority and could have forfeited his life if Oswiu had not defeated Penda.[37] In the event Egfrith (670-85) lived to benefit from his father's efforts to bring Deira under his control. For the first part of Egfrith's reign (670-79) Deira was probably a subkingdom for Ælfwine, a third son of Oswiu, but after Ælfwine was killed fighting against the Mercians at the battle of the river Trent, Egfrith united the two provinces.[38] 679 is the true beginning of the united kingdom of Northumbria and there is no recorded division of kingship after this time. From the succession of Aldfrith (685-705), Egfrith's half-brother, kings of Northumbria succeeded to the control of both provinces, though for administrative purposes the division into Bernicia and Deira seems to have remained significant.[39]

Bede's account shows that the conquest of Deira by Bernicia was not achieved either quickly or easily and the Bernicians were not assured of success until the reign of Oswiu. Even when Deira became a Bernician subkingdom it retained a tendency towards separatism and tempted its Bernician rulers to rebellion. The Bernician royal house had to work hard to get itself accepted by the Deiran nobility. Males of the Deiran royal house were naturally suspect, but Deiran princesses were wooed for their traditional peace-weaving qualities. Æthelfrith's union with Acha apparently made their son Oswald acceptable to the Deiran nobility. Oswiu, who seems to have been particularly unwelcome to the Deiran aristocracy, repeated the prescription and married Eanflæd, the daughter of King Edwin. Eanflæd passed the Deiran royal blood on to her sons and thus helped Egfrith gain control of both provinces.

Oswiu's murder of Oswine was obviously a potential threat to such harmony; Oswine was Eanflæd's second cousin and she was in that unenviable position that so interested the writers of Germanic verse of only being able to revenge her relative by attacking her husband. However, Eanflæd was also in the position to end the potential feud by accepting compensation for the murder and this she did in the form of an estate based on Gilling where Oswine had been killed and which was used to found a monastery. Its first abbot Trumhere was also a close relative of the murdered king.[40] The murder of Oswine opened the way to a means of reconciliation between Oswiu and surviving members of the Deiran royal house who by entering the family monastery of Gilling could have a place in the hierarchy of Northumbria without threatening the secular power of the Bernician royal house.

Another member of the Deiran royal house who took high office in the church under Oswiu was Hild the daughter of Hereric, a nephew of King Edwin. Hild's sister Hereswith had married into the East Anglian royal house and when widowed had entered a nunnery in Francia. Hild proposed to follow her but in c. 647 was persuaded by Bishop Aidan to take up the monastic life in Northumbria instead. At the time of the battle of the river Winwaed Hild was abbess of a foundation at Hartlepool. Oswiu had been so anxious to win the battle that he had vowed to give his infant daughter Ælfflæd to the church if he was successful. Hild was an obvious choice to take charge of the infant princess because she and Queen Eanflæd, the child's mother, were, of course, both Deiran princesses, but the decision made sound political sense as well. Whitby, the monastery to which Hild and Ælfflæd soon moved, became a monument to the new unity of Bernicia and Deira.[41] The body of King Edwin was moved to Whitby and his cult was fostered there;[42] it was possibly at Whitby that the names of the members of the Deiran royal house who became Christian were preserved and passed on to Bede.[43] But Whitby was also the chosen burial place of Oswiu and so preserved memory of his deeds as well.[44] It became one of the leading religious houses of Northumbria, a major training ground of future bishops (for like most Anglo-Saxon abbesses Hild ruled a mixed community of monks and nuns) and the venue for the famous synod of 664 when Oswiu put an end to any separatist tendencies in the Deiran church by deciding that the whole of the Northumbrian church would recognize the authority of Canterbury. The abbesses of Whitby – Hild, Eanflæd, who retired there on the death of Oswiu, and Ælfflæd – became personages of great influence not only in the Northumbrian church, but in the political sphere as well. Ælfflæd, for instance, seems to have played an important part in arranging the succession of Aldfrith, half-brother of King Egfrith, and of Aldfrith's son Osred on his father's death.[45]

Through the church we can see how the kingdom of Northumbria was founded on Bernician dominance, but also depended upon reconciling and uniting elements of the Deiran royal house with the Bernician ascendancy. If we had the relevant evidence, we would no doubt discover that various important Deirans also took on significant secular administrative roles as well. By such means a new Northumbrian kingdom gradually emerged from the union of the provinces of Bernicia and Deira.

The early Northumbrian kings and the kingdoms of southern England
It was the province of Deira which initially had the closest contacts with the kingdoms of southern England as one would expect from its geographical position. We first become aware of these contacts during the period of Edwin's exile, though it is, of course, possible that they existed before. Edwin apparently visited a number of southern kingdoms before his arrival at King Rædwald's court, including that of King Cearl of Mercia whose daughter he married.[46] Rædwald's decision to help his guest against his Bernician enemies guaranteed that the Northumbrians would be brought into closer contact with the southern provinces. Edwin's obligations to Rædwald meant that Northumbria joined the kingdoms forced to acknowledge Rædwald's overlordship, but once Rædwald was dead Edwin used the formidable fighting forces of Northumbria to take over his position of dominance. Oswald, Oswiu and Egfrith all also collected tributes from the southern kingdoms for parts of their reign at least.[47] Dominance achieved through warfare was reinforced by other forms of alliance and those sealed by marriages are most clearly observable in the historical record. Edwin's marriage to a daughter of Æthelbert of Kent is one of the first of these recorded foreign alliances, and the retreat of his widow, daughter and other infant descendants to Kent on his death ensured continued contact and bargaining between the two kingdoms.[48] Links with East Anglia seem to have been particularly significant. Edwin's kinswoman Hereswith married a prince of the royal house and their son was King Aldwulf;[49] Hereswith's niece, Æthelthryth subsequently married King Egfrith – one of the least successful recorded royal marriages for the bride was rather older than the groom and, in spite of having been married once before, maintained a vow of chastity.[50] The West Saxons had resented Northumbrian overlordship to the extent that they sent an assassin to attempt the murder of Edwin,[51] but subsequently the families were linked by various marriages. Oswald and Aldfrith both married West Saxon princesses, and the incorporation of part of the prehistoric part of the Bernician genealogy into that of the West Saxon royal house may underline the strength of the relationship between the two kingdoms.[52]

But the southern kingdom with which the Northumbrian rulers were most frequently in contact was Mercia. Most of this contact was hostile for Mercia vied with the Northumbrian kings for dominance of the other southern kingdoms – Oswiu, for instance, only achieved this position for part of his reign because at other times it was held first by Penda and then by Wulfhere of Mercia. Mercia and Northumbria were in direct competition for permanent conquest of smaller kingdoms with which they had a common border, especially the kingdom of Lindsey on whose borders two of the major battles between the Mercians and the Northumbrians (Hatfield and Trent) were fought.[53] The Mercians may even have had hopes of detaching Deira from

Bernicia and bringing it more fully into their own sphere of influence. Certainly Œthelwald of Deira entered the battle of the river *Winwæd* on the side of Penda of Mercia. The survival of males of the Deiran royal house was not only threatened by the dynastic ambitions of the Bernicians, but by those of the Mercians as well. Bede records that Eadfrith, one of Edwin's sons, was forced to desert to King Penda after the battle of Hatfield, but that the latter had him murdered in spite of an oath to the contrary.[54] But Northumbria was equally hostile towards Mercia. After his success at the battle of the river *Winwæd* Oswiu ruled Mercia directly for three years, though allowing Penda's son Peada (who was also Oswiu's son-in-law) to rule the southern part as his subking – until his murder also was arranged. Bede seems to have felt that Oswiu's treatment of Mercia was excessively highhanded.[55]

One of the commonest causes of death amongst early Northumbrian princes was battle against the Mercians. Penda was a protagonist at the battles in which Edwin and Oswald were killed and was himself killed in battle against Oswiu. Other males of the Northumbrian royal house, of course, also fell in such engagements and so the conditions for a mighty feud existed between the two kingdoms throughout the seventh century. However, there were also frequent attempts to heal the breach through treaties and marriage settlements. Relations between the two royal houses were therefore complicated by these intermarital ties. In the 650s Oswiu's son Alhfrith was married to a daughter of King Penda, while Penda's son Peada was married to Alhfrith's sister.[56] Subsequently a second daughter of Oswiu, Osthryth, was married to another son of Penda, Æthelred.[57] This must have been an ill-omened marriage from the start because in addition to the carnage already mentioned Osthryth's sister was suspected of having connived in the murder of Æthelred's brother Peada! The unfortunate Osthryth had to live through the battle of the river Trent in which her husband's forces slew one of her brothers (Ælfwine). Bede records that Ælfwine had in fact been a much loved figure at both royal courts so that the archbishop of Canterbury was able to intervene and make a firmer truce than was usually the case in which 'no further lives were demanded for the death of the king's brother, but only the usual money compensation which was paid to the king to whom the duty of vengeance belonged'.[58] However, there was no happy ending for Osthryth; she was murdered by the Mercian nobility in 697.[59]

Thus the Northumbrian kings up to the end of Egfrith's reign were fully involved in the affairs of the Anglo-Saxon kingdoms to the south. They had intermarried with them and played an active role in their system of overlordship. Oswiu's decision at the synod of Whitby showed a willingness to be more fully integrated with the southern kingdoms and recognize the authority of Canterbury. Northumbrian missionaries worked in pagan southern kingdoms that came under Northumbrian overlordship and numerous links with religious houses south of the Humber are attested. There were other areas as well in which the Northumbrian and the southern kingdoms had common interests such as trading links across the North Sea.[60] However, the political involvement of Northumbria in affairs south of the Humber markedly declined after the disastrous defeat of Egfrith at Nechtansmere. Egfrith's successor and half-brother, Aldfrith (685/6-705), made some attempt to keep up the traditional links with the southern kingdoms and, for instance, seems to have produced a fine series of sceattas which mirrored the production of coinage in the eastern kingdoms of southern England.[61] But a major change took place in the orientation of Northumbria after his death. The severity of the change is rather concealed in the *Ecclesiastical History* as Bede stresses the unity of the Anglo-Saxon church. But Northumbrian kings no longer concerned themselves with Southumbrian politics in the way that they had done before and although Mercian and West Saxon kings did attempt to get some recognition of their supremacy from Northumbrian rulers this never seems to have amounted to anything substantial in the period up to the time that much of Northumbria became a Viking kingdom.

Northumbria and the Celtic kingdoms in the seventh century
Although the Northumbrian kings devoted much time and energy to pursuing overlordship south of the Humber, they were equally active against their Celtic neighbours to the west and north. Map 2 (p. 14) shows the principal Celtic kingdoms of northern Britain with which the Northumbrians had dealings, and there may have been additional smaller kingdoms of which little is known like the kingdom of Craven in the north-west corner of the former West Riding whose existence has been suggested from later administrative evidence.[62] The only permanent gains of territory by Northumbrian kings between 600 and 700 were at the expense of the British kingdoms of Elmet, Rheged and Gododdin.[63] Western Scotland also contained an extension of the northern Irish kingdom of Dalriada which was drawn into the complex alliances and hostilities of the British and Northumbrian kingdoms. Bernician exiles were to be found in Scottish Dalriada before the end of the sixth century and the link was ultimately to draw Northumbrians to the Irish mainland as well.[64] Relations with the Celtic kingdoms are not nearly so well recorded by Bede as those with the Anglo-Saxons and he gives contradictory statements about the extent of overlordship achieved by individual Northumbrian rulers. Celtic sources provide the only record of some of the major Northumbrian campaigns such as that of Oswald which resulted in the acquisition of the Edinburgh area.[65] However, the Celtic sources are not easy to use and are of varied historical reliability.[66] It is clear that campaigns against the Celtic kingdoms were just as important – if not more important – to the kings of the Bernician dynasty as their relations with other Anglo-Saxon kingdoms, but this is concealed in the *Ecclesiastical History* because of Bede's concern with the achievement of a united Anglo-Saxon church.

In tracing the history of the Northumbrian and Celtic kingdoms it is important to draw a distinction between temporary overlordship and permanent acquisition. Æthelfrith's battle at Chester in 616 does not mean that Æthelfrith had permanently conquered the lands west of the Pennines, but merely that he was enforcing overlordship of the area.[67] The *Life of St Wilfrid* implies that it was Egfrith who really conquered this area for Northumbria in the 670s.[68] As the history of Bernicia and Deira indicated, the permanent annexation of one substantial kingdom by another was frequently a long drawn out process in which there might be several reversals of fortune. The history of the British kingdom of Elmet in western Yorkshire is a case in point. The end of the independent history of this British kingdom has traditionally been dated to 616 when it is recorded in the *Historia Brittonum* that Edwin expelled its king. However, Elmet appears as an independent unit in the *Tribal Hidage* which suggests that it had detached itself from Northumbria by the second half of the seventh century and had moved, for a time at least, into the Mercian sphere of influence. Its permanent acquisition by Northumbria must have been subsequent to the compilation of the *Tribal Hidage* and may have occurred in the reign of Egfrith who granted land to Wilfrid at Yeadon (W. Yorks) which would have been in Elmet.[69]

By the time our study begins in 600 both Bernicia and Deira had already enjoyed successes at the expense of British kingdoms. In 600 Æthelfrith controlled the coastal lowlands between the Tweed and the Tees and his aggressive policy against the British, of which Bede writes approvingly, brought counterattacks which he successfully parried.[70] An ill-fated expedition sent by the king of the Gododdin (based in Lothian) to the Catterick area is the subject of the celebrated British poem *Gododdin*.[71] Æthelfrith also won decisive victories against the Irish king of Dalriada (Argyll and adjacent islands) and against western British enemies at Chester in 616.[72] No doubt the defeated enemies were required to pay tribute. Edwin of Deira was able to extend Northumbrian overlordship to the islands of Man and Anglesey though he was not in a position to stop Æthelfrith's sons seeking exile in the northern Celtic kingdoms.[73] However, the formidable combination of English and Welsh enemies under Penda of Mercia and Cadwallon of Gwynedd put a brake on Northumbrian expansion.[74]

Bede says (rather vaguely) that Oswald enjoyed overlordship of all the English, British, Irish and Pictish kingdoms in Britain.[75] But in the long run his most significant achievement seem to have been the extension of Northumbria to the river Forth through the annexation of the former British kingdom of the Gododdin based in Lothian.[76] Northumbrian control of south-east Scotland was consolidated in the reigns of Oswald and Oswiu by Anglo-Saxon immigration into the area which included the foundation of the monasteries of Melrose and Coldingham; the latter was ruled by Æbbe, sister to Oswald and Oswiu.[77] It is probably Oswiu to whom the credit should go for strengthening Northumbrian overlordship over the Picts. Between 653 and 657 Oswiu's nephew Talorcan, who had a Pictish mother, was king of the Picts and presumably subordinate to his uncle. Oswiu's exact relations with the Picts after Talorcan's death are hard to establish, but Drest (665/6-72) may also have been under the control of Oswiu for Wilfrid was described as being bishop of the Northumbrians and the Picts in 669.[78] In

681 a bishopric was established at Abercorn with jurisdiction over the Picts.[79]

Expansion west of the Pennines was made at the expense of the British kingdom of Rheged. The main advances here seems to have been achieved by Egfrith though we are dependent on veiled allusions in the *Life of St Wilfrid* whose hero benefited from grants of substantial estates that had supported British religious communities in the kingdom.[80] Egfrith had even greater ambitions for the expansion of Northumbrian power over the Celtic world. He sent an army to ravage in Ireland, presumably to exact tribute, even though many at his court felt this to be a foolish and unnecessary expedition.[81] This was not the first contact between the Bernician royal house and mainland Ireland for Oswiu seems to have spent part of his period of exile in Ireland and Egfrith's half-brother Aldfrith was the result of Oswiu's union with a princess of the Cenél nEogain branch of the Ui Neill dynasty. Desire to forestall any claims Aldfrith might have had to the Northumbrian throne could have been one reason for Egfrith's raid.[82] There were also strong links between the Irish and Northumbrian churches and some Anglo-Saxon monks who were unwilling to accept the decision of the synod of Whitby had retreated to Ireland.[83] In 685 Egfrith overreached himself, as some of those around him had feared. In an attempt to consolidate Northumbrian power over the Picts Egfrith journeyed far beyond his bases on the Forth. The Picts lured Egfrith and his army into a narrow mountain pass at Nechtansmere (near Forfar) and slaughtered the king and the greater part of his army. As Bede realized the death of Egfrith marked a turning-point in Northumbrian history:

> From this time the hopes and strength of the English kingdom began to 'ebb and fall away'. For the Picts recovered their own land which the English had formerly held, while the Irish who lived in Britain and some part of the British nation recovered their independence, which they have now enjoyed for about forty-six years.[84]

The Northumbrian northern boundary now lay on the south bank of the river Forth, though Egfrith's successes west of the Pennines seem to have been permanent.

Military superiority lay at the heart of Northumbrian advances to the west and north, but, as with the Bernician annexation of Deira, military might was backed up by other manoeuvres. Strategic marriages and links made during periods of exile helped pave the way to more permanent conquests. Æthelfrith's son Eanfrith apparently married a Pictish princess when in exile after his father's death and Oswiu seems to have been able to insinuate Talorcan, the son of this union, on to the Pictish throne where presumably he ruled in subordination to his uncle Oswiu.[85] Oswiu himself, according to British sources, took as one of his wives Rhiainfellt, a princess of the house of Rheged,[86] and the union was presumably connected with Northumbrian ambitions against Rheged which came to fruition in the reign of his son. When the Northumbrian rulers fought against Celtic leaders they were likely to be fighting their own kinsmen as frequently was the case in their battles with other

Anglo-Saxon kingdoms. Egfrith's main Anglo-Saxon opponent was Æthelred of Mercia who was his brother-in-law, while his chief Celtic protagonist, King Bridei of the Picts, was his cousin.[87]

Whether British or Pictish notables were integrated into the Bernician regime in the way that Deirans were is harder to demonstrate, but once again the church is likely to have been an important mediator. Oswald's choice of missionaries from Iona in the kingdom of Dalriada, where he had spent his period of exile during the reign of Edwin, must have made the integration of other Celtic Christian communities into the Northumbrian kingdom easier.[88] St Cuthbert visited the Picts in the 660s at a time when Oswiu was trying to strengthen Northumbrian control of the province and in 681 the Picts were provided with their own Northumbrian bishop.[89] The establishment of religious houses in Lothian (formerly the British kingdom of Gododdin) would have provided opportunities for the local British to be integrated with the Northumbrian establishment.

Finds of Anglo-Saxon cultural material and of place-names of Old English origin are concentrated in the eastern part of Northumbria.[90] Solid archaeological evidence for Anglo-Saxon settlement further west is hard to find; for instance, the archaeological evidence for Anglo-Saxons in the West Riding of Yorkshire, originally part of the kingdom of Elmet, but firmly in Northumbria by the latter part of the seventh century, so far consists of three beads and a handful of graves![91] It follows that a large proportion of the population of Northumbria must have been Celtic and that the Celtic foundations of the province must be far more substantial than the written sources indicate.[92] As Northumbria expanded the proportion of Celtic to Anglo-Saxon inhabitants must have increased. Similarities between the organization of Northumbrian estates and those of Wales have been deduced,[93] and there has been a vivid demonstration of the Celtic infrastructure of the kingdom in excavations at Yeavering.[94] Here a British cult site and seat of secular power was taken over by the new Anglo-Saxon regime to become, as Bede indicates, a *villa regalis*, a royal estate centre.[95] The buildings erected for the Anglo-Saxon rulers drew upon Roman and British building traditions and the Anglo-Saxons seem to have been scrupulous in preserving aspects of the site which had a ritual significance and allowed these to affect the alignment of buildings, for instance (see Fig. 8). One hardly receives any consciousness of this British heritage in the pages of the *Ecclesiastical History* or in other Anglo-Saxon sources, but it must have been of considerable importance in shaping the nature of the Northumbrian kingdom and the interests of its rulers.

Northumbrian kingship in the eighth century
Bede and the West Saxon missionary Bishop Boniface both considered that abuses in Northumbria of their own day had begun in the reign of King Osred (705/6-16), the son of King Aldfrith.[96] One irregularity that is immediately apparent is that Osred came to the throne as a minor and his reign is the only certain minority recorded for Anglo-Saxon England pre-900. His position was

only achieved after a major struggle within Northumbria for, as Stephanus reveals in the *Life of St Wilfrid*, the throne was held briefly on Aldfrith's death by one Eadwulf, whose ancestry is not given, but who is likely to have been a member of a rival branch of the royal house.[97] The elevation of a boy king to the throne represents a desperate attempt to retain power by those whose fortunes were bound up with the continuing success of the house of Oswiu. Successive deaths in battle or as a result of family rivalries had left the line bereft of adult male heirs and the young sons of Aldfrith were apparently the

Aldfrith 685/6–705	
Eadwulf 705/6	
Osred I 705/6–716	murdered 'south of the border'
Cenred 716–718	
Osric 718–729	
Ceolwulf 729–737	abdicated to enter religious house
Eadbert 737–758	abdicated to enter religious house
Oswulf 758	murdered by household
Æthelwold Moll 758–765	deposed
Alhred 765–774	deposed and exiled
Æthelred I (1) 774–779	exiled
Ælfwold I 779–788	murdered
Osred II 788–790	tonsured and exiled
Æthelred I (2) 790–796	murdered
Osbald 796	exiled
Eardwulf 796–806	exiled
Ælfwold II 806–808	
Eanred c. 808–840/1	
Æthelred II (1) 840/1–844	
Rædwulf 844	
Æthelred II (2) 844–848/9	murdered
Osbert 848/9–867	expelled
Ælle 867	

Table 10: Regnal list of the kings of Northumbria of the eighth and ninth centuries

only male survivors. According to Stephanus Osred was enabled to rule through the support of such notables as Abbess Ælfflæd of Whitby, daughter of King Oswiu, and Bishop Wilfrid, but the murder of the young king in 716 was an indication that the family of Æthelfrith of Bernicia were not going to be able to dominate eighth-century Northumbria in the same way that they had been able to do during the seventh century.[98]

The pattern of kingship in the eighth century in Northumbria was different from what had gone before. Instead of dominance by one family the throne was regularly disputed between a number of contenders, none of whom was able to establish an ascendancy. The feuding between the rival families and their supporters is recorded in some detail in the continuation of the *Ecclesiastical History* and in the Northumbrian chronicle incorporated in the *Historia Regum* (see Table 11). Osred was murdered in 716 and succeeded by Cenred (716-18) who, according to the genealogy of his brother Ceolwulf, claimed descent from Ida, the traditional founder of the Bernician dynasty, but can only have been distantly related to Osred.[99] Cenred only ruled two years and was then replaced by Osred's brother Osric (718-29), who apparently appointed Cenred's brother Ceolwulf (729-37) as his successor.[100] Ceolwulf was the king to whom Bede dedicated the *Ecclesiastical History* and it is clear that Bede was very alarmed by the rivalries within the Northumbrian royal house and apprehensive about the future which is one reason why he looked back nostalgically to the apparently stable kingship of the seventh century.[101] In the year after Bede completed his great historical work Ceolwulf was overthrown by rivals, forcibly tonsured and immured in Lindisfarne monastery, but was then brought out again by his own supporters to continue his reign for another six years until he (apparently) voluntarily resigned the throne to his cousin Eadbert in order to enter the Lindisfarne community.

Eadbert (737-58) seems to have been the type of strong leader which Bede believed Northumbria needed. He continued Northumbria's expansion to the north, warded off threats from Mercia and reformed the currency.[102] With Eadbert's aid his brother Egbert, archbishop of York from 735, was able to tackle some of the problems of the Northumbrian church which had so troubled Bede, Egbert's former tutor.[103] After a reign of twenty years Eadbert resigned the throne to his son Oswulf who was murdered soon after. New dynasties now emerged to claim the throne. The ancestry of the next ruler Æthelwold Moll (758-65) is not known. Æthelwold was deposed in favour of Alhred (765-74) for whom a genealogy claiming descent from Ida survives.[104] Alhred was in turn replaced by Æthelwold's son, Æthelred (774-79). Æthelred was eventually forced into exile, allowing the throne to return to the family of Eadbert in the person of his grandson Ælfwold (779-88). Ælfwold was murdered in 788 and his successor Osred II (788-90) was the son of former King Alhred. Osred was forcibly tonsured and sent into exile in 790 and was replaced by King Æthelred (790-96), son of Æthelwold Moll, who had ruled previously but been forced into exile. After Æthelred's murder Osbald, whom Alcuin seems to imply was descended from former Northumbrian kings,[105] ruled a few months but was replaced within the same year by Eardwulf (796-808). An attempt had been made to murder Eardwulf in 790, while he was an ealdorman, and he had been left for dead outside the monastery of Ripon.

This bald summary does not do justice to the details of the many conspiracies of the period nor give the full flavour of the violence of the times.[106] Violent attacks were not only made against reigning kings, but also against æthelings, the sons of kings who were potential candidates for the throne. King Eadbert, for instance, besieged the church of Lindisfarne in 750 in order to extract Offa, the last surviving son of King Aldfrith, and King Æthelred murdered Ælf and Ælfwine, the sons of King Ælfwold, in 791. Table 11 is an attempt to present in schematic form the feuding of the rival candidates; the arrows indicate who was killing whom. Five main families seem to have been providing candidates for the throne in the eighth century: those of Aldfrith, Ceolwulf and his cousin Eadbert,[107] Æthelwold Moll, Alhred and Eardwulf. There is a hypothetical element in the family tree of King Eardwulf as presented in Table 11 where it is proposed that King Eardwulf and his father ealdorman Eardwulf may have been descended from Eadwulf, who ruled briefly on the death of Aldfrith, and his son Eanwine who was murdered in 740. King Osbald is not known to fit into any of the groups (which is not to say that he was not a member of one of them). The families of Aldfrith, Ceolwulf/Eadbert and Alhred all claimed descent from Ida and Alcuin seems to indicate that Osbald was of royal descent. It is not known whether the families of Æthelwold Moll and Eardwulf also claimed to be Idings.

There were fourteen reigns between those of Osred and Eardwulf (see Table 10). The fate of two rulers, Cenred and Osric, is obscure but their reigns are suspiciously short; six rulers were deposed and forced into exile or into religious houses; four were murdered; and two apparently resigned voluntarily to enter religious houses and secure the succession of relatives. This contrasts with the previous century when there were seven reigns between those of Æthelfrith and Aldfrith (if the contemporary rulers Eanfrith and Osric are counted together and subkings are ignored). The commonest cause of death was battle with foreign rulers, though Oswiu and Aldfrith apparently died of natural causes. It would be wrong to turn the seventh century into an oasis of peace and quiet compared to the eighth century. There was much conflict between the rival dynasties of Bernicia and Deira, and the reign of Oswiu shows that kings were murdered then as well and that relatives could conspire against one another.[108] However, internal conflicts took up much more of the eighth-century kings' time and none of them died in battle with kings of other kingdoms.

In the seventh century the descendants of Æthelfrith were apparently unchallenged as Bernician claimants of the Northumbrian throne. In the eighth century not only did this dynasty fall from power, but also none of the rival claimants was able to establish a monopoly of the throne. In order to reach a better understanding of such changes we must take account of a major shift in

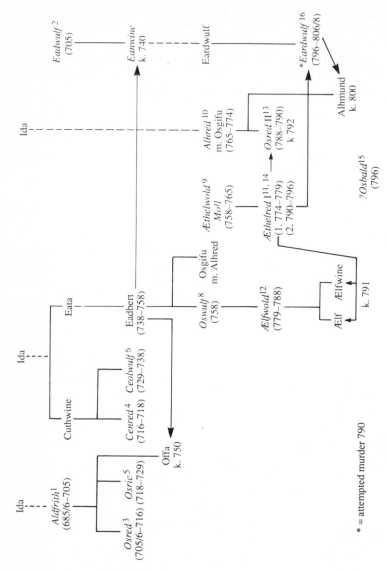

* = attempted murder 790

Table 11: The rival families of eighth-century Northumbria
Kings are in italics and numbered in order of ruling. The arrows indicate the vicitims of individual kings as recorded in the *Historia Regum*.

Fig. 1 *The Benty Grange helmet.* The helmet was discovered during excavation of a barrow burial in a barrow at Benty Grange (Derbs) in 1848 and probably dates to the second half of the seventh century. The nose-guard is decorated with a cross suggesting that its owner was Christian, though boar-crested helmets are mentioned in *Beowulf* and the idea of the boar having a protective function is presumably pagan. For a reconstruction of the helmet, see the front cover. (© *Sheffield City Museums*)

Fig 2. *The Sutton Hoo helmet,* recovered in fragmentary state from Mound 1. The main body of the helmet was covered with figural panels, which, like the dragon which forms the 'nose' and 'eyebrows', have strong Swedish parallels, though the helmet was probably manufactured in England. 'Protective' boar's heads form the terminals of the eyebrows. (*British Museum*)

These are the only two helmets recovered from burials of the Anglo-Saxon period (the Coppergate helmet from York was found in a pit on its own). As can be seen they represent two distinct types of helmet manufactured by the Germanic peoples in the early medieval period, though these examples are presumably for display rather than protection in battle and would be appropriate symbols of warrior kingship.

Fig 3. *The Sutton Hoo 'sceptre'.* This object from the Sutton Hoo ship-burial is in effect a large whetstone, decorated with four human faces at each end and surmounted by a bronze stag. It would appear to be of symbolic rather than practical use, hence the suggestion that it was a sceptre or symbol of royal authority. No exact parallel is known for this piece from either the Germanic or Celtic worlds. *(British Museum)*

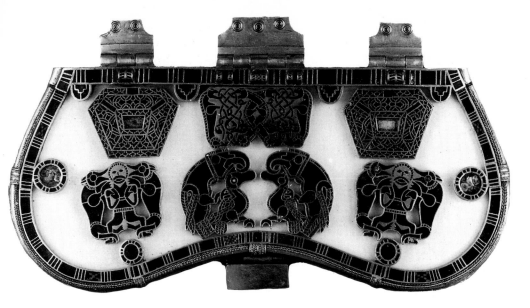

Fig 4. *The Sutton Hoo purselid.* The purse contained thirty-seven Merovingian gold coins, three gold blanks and two gold ingots. The latest coin to be minted probably dates to 620-25 and provides a *terminus post quem* for the Mound 1 burial. The purse was probably worn on a belt and is remarkable for its decorative work in gold and garnets, the work of the master craftsman responsible for most of the jewellery in the Mound 1 burial. The motifs of the man among two beasts and the bird of prey seizing a duck occur on other high status metalwork of the early Middle Ages. *(British Museum)*

Fig 5. *The Alfred Jewel.* The jewel carries the inscription *Alfred mec heht gewyrcan* ('Alfred ordered me to be made') and is usually assumed to have been commissioned by King Alfred of Wessex (871-99). The main framework is gold and it encloses an enamelled figure surmounted by rock crystal. The Jewel may have been a book pointer, in which case the figure could be a personification of sight and the stylized boar's head which forms the terminal piece would have held a pointer in its mouth. *(Ashmolean Museum)*

These two works of different, but equally skilled, craftsmanship are separated by some 250 years and serve to emphasize the continuing importance of kings as patrons of craftsmen and distributors of wealth.

Fig 7. *Hamwic.* An artist's reconstruction of how the port of Hamwic might have appeared at the height of its prosperity in the mid eighth century. Note the regular layout of the streets and the density of housing. A variety of excavated evidence supports the contention that the settlement was founded during the reign of King Ine of Wessex (688–726). *(Southampton City Museums)*

Fig 6. *Offa's Dyke.* King Alfred's biographer Asser, writing at the end of the ninth century, attributes the building of the great earthwork between Mercia and the Welsh kingdoms to King Offa of Mercia (757–96). It would have appeared more impressive originally when it was probably surmounted by a wooden palisade. *(The Clwyd-Powys Archaeological Trust. Photographer: C.R. Musson)*

Offa's Dyke and Hamwic are both examples of how early Anglo-Saxon kings could undertake public building works with the aid of services they could demand from their subjects. The imposition of the economic position of the Northumbrian rulers. The Northumbrian kings of the seventh century were immensely successful in battle and so immensely rich on the proceeds. The eighth-century kings were not necessarily any less aggressive, but there is reason to believe that individually none of them was nearly so wealthy. The defeat of Egfrith at Nechtansmere was one of the reasons for the contrast between the two centuries. Egfrith and the greater part of his army perished in the battle, and as a result of it the Northumbrian kings lost some lands in the north and the ability to collect tribute from their Celtic and Anglo-Saxon neighbours.[109] The loss of tribute must have been a severe financial blow and was exacerbated, as Bede indicates, by the introduction of new concepts of land law ('bookland') in the aftermath of the synod of Whitby.[110] Bookland had been introduced to provide suitable endowments for the church. The demands of the Irish missionaries in Northumbria in this respect had been modest and Oswiu had been able to found monasteries with an endowment of only ten hides.[111] But when Northumbrian churchmen travelled abroad or even to other parts of England they realized that Northumbrian religious establishments were unduly modest. Urged on by Bishop Wilfrid, kings made grants of several hundred hides of land to the church.[112] While they were conquering new areas the kings could afford it, but after Nechtansmere the grants appeared more foolhardy, but proved difficult to revoke as King Eadbert and Archbishop Egbert found when the pope intervened to forbid a transfer of land from ecclesiastical to secular hands.[113] What made matters worse was that the secular nobility had come to expect to be rewarded with similar grants of land.

Such changes seem to be reflected in the narrative sources. In the early pages of the *Ecclesiastical History* individual nobles appear in the context of the royal court as when Edwin is shown consulting his leading nobles about the adoption of Christianity or when his life is saved by a loyal thegn who takes the full thrust of an assassin's dagger intended for the king.[114] But by the latter part of the seventh century we are presented with nobles living on country estates who invite bishops such as John of Hexham to dedicate churches they have founded.[115] Some of these may be representatives of the nobles Bede castigated in his *Letter to Egbert* for acquiring land from the kings under the pretext of founding monasteries so that they too could enjoy the privileged tenure of bookland. One of the attractions of bookland was that the gift of it was permanent whereas previously, it would appear from what Bede says, that grants to laymen in royal service had been for life only.[116] There seems to have been a belief that the family had an interest in land granted to one of its members irrespective of whether they were laymen or churchmen. It is clear that Benedict Biscop's brother, even though he was not in holy orders, expected to inherit the monasteries of Wearmouth and Jarrow which Benedict had founded and that he would have done so if Benedict had not protected his foundations with royal and papal privileges.[117]

From the latter part of the seventh century there was a rapid transfer of land from the royal fisc to churches and leading nobles. At the same time we find the leading nobles playing an increasingly important role in royal government (though it must also be noted that we do not possess the necessary sources to really study the nobility before the reign of Egfrith). Stephanus' description of the dedication of the church at Ripon (which would have occurred between 671 and 678) includes the attendance of King Egfrith and his brother Ælfwine and their *praefecti* and *subreguli*.[118] Other chapters in the *Life of St Wilfrid* enable us to see representatives of these groups at work. When Wilfrid was imprisoned in Dunbar, in former British territory, he was under the care of a *praefectus* called Tydlin.[119] The highest ranking of the nobles referred to in the *Life* is the *subregulus* Beornhæth who in joint command with Egfrith won an important victory over the Picts at the beginning of the king's reign.[120] A large kingdom like Northumbria could only be managed by effective delegation of royal power to members of the nobility, particularly of territories which had formerly been self-governing units. By the eighth century, in spite of some uncertainties about terminology because the Northumbrian chronicle is only preserved through the edition of Byrhthferth and the translation of the northern recension of the *Anglo-Saxon Chronicle*, the subdivisions seem to have been regularized into a series of ealdormanries each with their own *dux*. In 867, when Northumbria was conquered by the Vikings, there were apparently at least eight of these.[121]

Not infrequently one of the leading nobles seems to have been more significant than the rest and to have acted on occasion as the king's deputy. At the beginning of Egfrith's reign *subregulus* Beornhæth seems to have been in this position and it was subsequently filled by two other members of his family who like Beornhæth seem to have held a major military command. Beornhæth's son Berhtred (*dux regius*) on two occasions led the Northumbrian army, first in a raid on Ireland and then, in the reign of Aldfrith, against the Picts who killed him in battle in 698. His position seems to have been inherited by Berhtfrith who was responsible for the Northumbrian victory of 711 and may be presumed from his name to be a close relative of Beornhæth and Berhtred.[122] In addition Berhtred played a major role in establishing the minority of Osred according to Stephanus who calls him *secundus a rege princeps* ('second in rank to the king'). It was Berhtred who led the forces loyal to Osred at the siege of Bamburgh and who worked in favour of an alliance with Bishop Wilfrid to help consolidate the minority.[123] The normal title for these royal deputies in the Northumbrian chronicles of the eighth century seems to have been *patricius*.[124]

It was presumably also Berhtred and his successor Berhtfrith whom Bede had in mind when he criticized those who had ruled on behalf of Osred during his minority for granting themselves estates from the royal fisc and seriously undermining royal financial resources.[125] It would also appear that Berhtred and his faction took revenge against those who had opposed them. An anonymous poem called *De Abbatibus* describes a religious community founded by a former ealdorman who had been forced to retire from active service during the reign of Osred.[126] An Anglo-Saxon king had to keep a delicate balance of power between different noble families. Aldfrith, who apparently had spent much of his life in Ireland, may have been forced to rely on the established power of Berhtred and the minority of Osred tipped the balance even further in the favour of this particular family. Inevitably those who were not enjoying the fruits of power would form rival factions who would be on the look out for opportunities to reverse the balance of power in their favour.

The result of the tensions inherent in the power structure of Northumbria in the reigns of Aldfrith and Osred was the faction fighting of the eighth century so vividly portrayed in the Northumbrian chronicle. Ealdormen and *patricii* are repeatedly portrayed fomenting plots or falling prey to the manoeuvrings of others. The *patricius* Sicga, for instance, is held responsible for the successful rebellion against King Ælfwold in 788, while in 780 two ealdormen had raised an army and 'burnt' a *patricius*. A number of those who became king in the eighth century had held the office of ealdorman or patrician. Eardwulf had been an ealdorman before he became king, and his father had also been an ealdorman.[127] Æthelwold Moll and Osbald are both described as *patricius* before their accessions.[128]

Leading churchmen who had considerable resources at their disposal were actively involved in the power struggles of the eighth century and might be related to the leading protagonists. Egbert's long period as bishop and then archbishop of York coincided with the rule of a number of his relatives, including his cousin Ceolwulf and his brother Eadbert. Æthelwold Moll's brother Forhtred was an abbot[129] and other rulers seem to have had links with particular religious houses. Hexham promoted the cult of the murdered King Ælfwold, whereas the patrician who murdered him was buried at Lindisfarne which also gave protection to the banished patrician Osbald who later became king;[130] an earlier bishop of Lindisfarne had been imprisoned in Bamburgh in 750 because he would not hand over the ætheling Offa to King Eadbert. Alcuin's letters to Archbishop Eanbald II of York (796–808x837) reveal that the latter was a major political force who gained the enmity of King Eardwulf by harbouring various political enemies of the king together with their armed followings in his very substantial secular household.[131] The partisanship of religious houses is only to be expected not only because leading ecclesiastics came from the major noble families, but because many of the inmates of monasteries and other ecclesiastical institutions were former ealdormen or kings who had been forced to retire from active life and be tonsured.

Bede had been concerned with the worldliness of the Northumbrian church in 734 in his *Letter to Egbert* and in the *Ecclesiastical History* looked back nostalgically to the time of Bishop Aidan of Lindisfarne who had not been interested in acquiring land or money.[132] Alcuin was inclined to believe that many of the Bernician monasteries had brought the Viking raids upon themselves because the inhabitants tended to prefer feasting and hunting to God's work and he deplored the political involvements of churchmen like his contemporary Archbishop Eanbald.[133] But it should not be forgotten that some of the wealth that the family of Æthelfrith passed on to the church was put to good effect and that its by-products included the outstanding literary and artistic achievements in which the Northumbrian church outclassed the other kingdoms of England in the eighth century, its 'golden age'.[134]

The failure of the family of Æthelfrith to adequately husband their resources helps to explain the unsettled position in eighth-century Northumbria when wealth and power seem to have been shared between various leading families in such a way that it was hard for any one family to establish a monopoly of power. Many of the leading nobles who became wealthy ealdormen are likely to have been collaterals of the royal house. We do not know whether Beornhæth whose family was so powerful in the late seventh and early eighth centuries was related to the royal house, but some of those who became king in the eighth century were apparently both of royal descent and held the position of ealdorman or *patricius*. It is in fact a moot point whether all those who became king in the eighth century were of royal descent or if circumstances were sufficiently flexible for anyone who could establish a sufficient following to become king. It can, for instance, be neither proved or disproved that Æthelwold Moll or Eardwulf were collaterals of the royal house. In spite of the relative wealth of information we have for the politics of eighth-century Northumbria there are many things we do not know enough about. We cannot, for instance, fully understand the many alliances of varied interest groups which must have occurred. Osric's nomination of his distant kinsman Cenred as his successor hints at an arrangement between these rival kindreds. Alhred's marriage to Osgifu, the sister of King Ælfwold, may have helped the accession of their son Osred on the death of his uncle in 789.[135] But in spite of such alliances no ruler was able to satisfy all the rival factions for long.

Eighth-century Northumbrian kings and the other kingdoms of Britain
Although the eighth century was not a period of great expansion and wide ranging overlordship like the seventh century, there were modest territorial gains and the continuation of links with Celtic and Anglo-Saxon neighbours. One of Bede's fears about the economic problems of the eighth-century kings was that the rulers would be too impoverished to provide an adequate defence against 'barbarians' by whom he presumably meant the Picts.[136] But some of the eighth-century Northumbrian kings did pay attention to the consolidation of their north-western border. By the time Bede had completed the *Ecclesiastical History* in 731 a see had been founded at Whithorn,[137] and in 750 Eadbert conquered the plain of Kyle from the Britons of Strathclyde, though he suffered a severe defeat in 756 when he joined King Oengus of the Picts on a campaign against the British capital of Dumbarton.[138] However, even if there were few gains for Northumbria there were few losses either and the follow-up Bede feared to the major battles between Northumbria and the Picts in 698 and 711 did not materialize, perhaps because the Picts had their own internal troubles.[139] Looser links with the Celtic neighbours continued. King Alhred

and King Osbald both went into exile among the Picts, while King Osred sought refuge on the Isle of Man.

But there were also potential dangers to Northumbria from the south through the expansionist policies of Æthelbald, Offa and Cenwulf of Mercia. In 740, for instance, Æthelbald took advantage of Eadbert's absence on campaign in the north to ravage part of Northumbria.[140] The rivalries between the royal branches of Northumbria provided opportunities for Mercian intervention. Æthelred I seems to have had Mercian backing during his second reign (790-96) and married one of Offa's daughters in 792. Cenwulf's harbouring of Northumbrian exiles led to an outbreak of hostilities between Eardwulf and the Mercian king in 801. Matters were solved by a negotiated agreement in which each side recognized the sovereignty of the other.[141] Cenwulf's involvement in Northumbrian politics is also suggested by the development in Mercia of the cult of Alhmund son of King Alhred whom Eardwulf had murdered in 800.[142] Alhmund was buried at Derby where the remains of what may have been his sarcophagus still exist.[143] Cenwulf was suspected in Francia of being involved in the plot which unseated Eardwulf (probably) in 806.[144]

Links between the Northumbrian and Frankish royal houses are also attested. From the late seventh century Northumbrian churchmen not only travelled extensively on the Continent in search of Christian culture, but worked in some numbers as missionaries in pagan Germanic areas on the borders of Francia.[145] Their missionary activities coincided with the rise of the Carolingian house and their ambitions to conquer the same areas. Not surprisingly links formed as a result between the royal houses of Northumbria and Francia. Eadbert exchanged gifts with King Pepin and King Alhred, an active supporter of Northumbrian missions overseas, sent an embassy to Francia after the accession of Pepin's son Charlemagne.[146] When Alcuin left the school of York to join the palace school of Charlemagne in the 780s Northumbria was drawn even closer into the Frankish orbit. To Charlemagne the kings of Northumbria and Mercia were the two great powers in Anglo-Saxon England and the papal legates who came to England in 786 held separate synods in Northumbria and Mercia.[147] Alcuin, from the safety of Charlemagne's court, took it upon himself to harangue Northumbrian kings for their moral shortcomings and reported that Charlemagne, who seems to have become increasingly convinced that he had a duty to supervise affairs in other kingdoms in western Christendom, was also concerned by the political instability of the province.[148] King Eardwulf (796-806/8) was reported to have married a daughter of Charlemagne, but, if so, his bride can at best have been only an illegitimate daughter as all Charlemagne's legitimate daughters are otherwise accounted for.[149]

Northumbria in the ninth century
Unfortunately the written evidence for Northumbria in the ninth century is extremely poor and only the barest narrative can be provided with most dates

being problematical. The Northumbrian chronicle upon which Byrhtferth and the northern recensions of the *Anglo-Saxon Chronicle* drew apparently ended in 802. Some record of the kings who ruled in the ninth century was kept, and was utilized by the post-Conquest authors Roger of Wendover and Symeon of Durham.[150] Such writers, when they can be checked against reliable pre-Conquest material, are often found to be extremely careless and cavalier with dates and so it comes as no surprise that the two writers, although apparently drawing on the same source, provide different dates, and it is sometimes impossible to choose between them.

At the beginning of the ninth century Eardwulf was on the throne of Northumbria, but was expelled probably in 806 and took refuge at Charlemagne's court. The Royal Frankish Annals record how envoys of the pope and Charlemagne escorted Eardwulf back to Northumbria in 808, but none of the English sources indicate that he ruled for a second time.[151] Roger of Wendover records a two-year reign of Ælfwold, about whom nothing else is known, and then the succession of Eanred who was Eardwulf's son. Possibly Charlemagne's intervention helped to remove Ælfwold, but in the event it was Eardwulf's son, rather than Eardwulf himself, who was chosen to replace him. Eanred had a substantial reign of at least thirty years ending in 840 or 841. It would have been Eanred who met with Egbert of Wessex and his army at the river Dore in 829. The *Anglo-Saxon Chronicle* makes as much as it can of this event and speaks of the Northumbrian's submission to Egbert, but there is more likely to have been a mutual recognition of sovereignty similar to that between Eardwulf and Cenwulf in 801. Eanred was succeeded by his son Æthelred II who probably ruled until 848 or 849.[152] Roger of Wendover records that Æthelred was expelled in 844 and replaced by a king called Rædwulf who fell in the same year in battle against the Vikings, thus allowing Æthelred to return. The brief reign of Rædwulf is confirmed by the numismatic evidence.[153] Æthelred was killed in 848 or 849 and succeeded by Osbert whose ancestry is not known.[154]

All of these ninth-century kings must have faced the problem of increasingly ambitious Viking attacks on the coasts of Northumbria. The first raid on Northumbria was the sack of Lindisfarne in 793 which seems to have come as a complete shock to the Northumbrian establishment and was seen by Alcuin as divine judgement for the sins of the Northumbrian rulers and weaknesses in their churches.[155] The impression that Alcuin gives of the raids being momentous and serious is reinforced by the temporary collapse of the Northumbrian coinage.[156] We cannot reconstruct the full course of the attacks on Northumbria in the ninth century though we do know of a major engagement in 844 when King Rædwulf and many leading nobles were killed. But it was Northumbria which was to be the first target of the Great Heathen Army which arrived in England in 865 with the intention of conquest.[157] The events which led up to the end of the Anglo-Saxon kingdom of Northumbria in 867 are relatively well recorded albeit from a West Saxon viewpoint that was less than complimentary to the Northumbrian leaders.[158] The Great Heathen

Army began its assault with a raid on York, catching the town unawares on All Saints' Day 866. The attack was also well timed as King Osbert was disputing the throne with a rival claimant, Ælle, specifically said in Symeon's *History of the Church of Durham* not to be of royal descent. Although the rivals joined forces against the common enemy both were defeated and killed, with eight ealdormen, on Palm Sunday 867. With this battle the Deiran province of Northumbria passed under Scandinavian rule until 954, but the Vikings left Bernicia under native rulers whom southern chroniclers generally regarded as ealdormen, but who seem to be seen as kings in Northumbria itself. Aldred, the last of them to be described as king, formally submitted to Athelstan in 927, but the ealdormen of Bamburgh (as they were known) remained a formidable power after this date and it would be true to say that the Anglo-Saxon kings never found a satisfactory way to control this most northerly Anglo-Saxon province and to integrate it with the rest of England.[159]

There is a tendency to assume that the shortage on information on Northumbria in the ninth century, coupled with the ultimate failure of conquest by the Vikings, must indicate a province undergoing severe decline. We can see disputes between rival claimants to the throne continuing, but should not underestimate the domination in this period of the family of Eardwulf and the long reign of Eanred in particular. The Northumbrian coinage of the ninth century has been seen as typifying a decline. Unlike other provinces in England the Northumbrians did not adopt the new 'penny' coinage, but, after a gap in minting in the reigns of Eardwulf and Ælfwold (perhaps connected with the Viking attacks in the 790s), King Eanred produced a debased form of sceatta coinage usually known as stycas. The silver content of these coins was undoubtedly less than that of the sceattas and they became increasingly debased as the century progressed; by the reign of Æthelred II it becomes appropriate to talk of a brass coinage in Northumbria. A variety of findspots show that the stycas may have been used for exchange outside Northumbria and inside the province they circulated much more widely than the sceattas had done and were produced in some volume.[160] The stycas could be seen as evidence of efficient royal control of the economy and a sensitive response to changing circumstances rather than as evidence of decline. Nor must the Northumbrian church be written off in the ninth century. The library of York was still regarded as one of the best in contemporary Europe and this is not the only sign of vigour in the ninth-century Northumbrian church.[161] The church of Lindisfarne weathered any temporary setbacks from Viking raids to become a major political and economic force in Scandinavian Northumbria from its new base at Chester-le-Street.[162]

Conclusion

The relatively full narrative records available for Northumbria have enabled us to study some aspects of kingship in the province in detail. Of particular interest has been the evidence for the merger of Bernicia and Deira and the efforts made by the Bernician royal house to reconcile surviving members of the Deiran royal family. We have also been able to study the problems the royal house encountered in making the transition from a very wide-ranging military overlordship to rule of a consolidated kingdom within narrower bounds. As we have seen the branch of the royal house that was dominant in the seventh century failed to make the transition successfully and was unable to find a satisfactory solution to the necessary delegation of power to other members of the royal house and to the demands of these relatives and other members of the nobility for grants of land on privileged terms. The result was a very different pattern of kingship in the eighth century from that of the seventh with the throne frequently passing between distant collaterals rather than to much closer relatives as it had done before. There was also a marked change within the same period in Northumbria's relations with both Celtic and other Anglo-Saxon kingdoms leading ultimately in the ninth century to an apparent isolation from other provinces within Britain although when necessary the Northumbrian army could still see off attacks from Mercia and Wessex.

The history of Northumbria thus seems to fall into three main periods – expansion and military overlordship in the first three-quarters of the seventh century under the family of Æthelfrith; consolidation in the late seventh and eighth centuries with the throne disputed between several royal branches; a final phase in the ninth century dominated (though not exclusively) by the family of Eardwulf. Although these periods do seem to mark significant stages in the history of Northumbria they are also phases dictated by the surviving written sources. The period up to the death of Egfrith is the period covered in detail by the *Ecclesiastical History* in which Bede's dominant approach is one of praise for successful kings. Bede has relatively little to say about the royal house after the accession of Aldfrith and the sources we use from this time such as the *Life of St Wilfrid*, the Northumbrian chronicle and Bede's own *Letter to Egbert* encourage us to look more critically at the kings and to stress their civil wars and failures rather than their successes. The darkness into which we are plunged by the cessation of the Nothumbrian chronicle at the beginning of the ninth century means that many comments on the period are drawn *a silentio* and one of the few well-recorded events, the conquest by the Vikings, colours our perception of this final phase.

There is therefore a danger that in trying to categorize Northumbrian history we will erect artificial barriers that are pre-selected by the surviving written evidence. A case can be made for seeing a king like Eadbert as ruling very much in the tradition of Oswald and Oswiu and carrying to a logical conclusion policies which they had begun. In partnership with his brother Egbert, the archbishop of York, Eadbert was able to tackle some of the problems in the relationship of church and state which had troubled Bede. However, no writer was concerned to provide an *encomium* for Eadbert in the way that Bede had pointed out the successes of seventh-century rulers, so inevitably Eadbert is a less rounded figure for the modern historian. Perhaps the severest barrier thrown up by the selectivity of surviving sources is that between the eighth and the ninth century. The temptation is to see the lack of written sources in the ninth century as symptomatic of a further decline in the province and in the calibre of its kings, but such subjective interpretations may be inappropriate. After the power struggles of the eighth century the thirty-year reign of Eanred stands out as a major achievement which could only have occurred if he had solved some of the problems which had defeated his eighth-century predecessors.

Chapter Six

MERCIA

Sources

In spite of Mercia's dominant political position in the late seventh and early eighth centuries, remarkably few Mercian primary sources have survived. No Mercian chronicle or other narrative source exists, with the result that we have to study much of Mercian history through sources written in kingdoms such as Northumbria and Wessex which were frequently the victims of Mercian aggression. This tangential approach begins with Bede's *Ecclesiastical History* for rather surprisingly Bede was not in contact with any of the major Mercian religious houses and his main sources for Mercia were the Deiran monastery of Lastingham, which had supplied an early Mercian bishop, and various communities in Lindsey, a province disputed between Mercia and Northumbria in the late seventh century.[1] As a result Bede's treatment of Mercian political and ecclesiastical history was far from comprehensive. He apparently did not know, for instance, about the division of the Mercian diocese during the archepiscopate of Theodore which is recorded in the surviving versions of the Mercian episcopal lists.[2] Bede's Northumbrian sympathies have also affected his treatment of Mercian history and one example of this is his reticence about the extent of Mercian overlordship in the second half of the seventh century. Nevertheless Bede is our most important source for the early history of Mercia and the chronology of its kings.

The practice of Mercian kingship can best be studied through the charters issued by its kings, but the majority of those that have survived are grants to religious communities in Kent and the kingdom of the Hwicce rather than in the main Mercian province. This uneven representation is presumably the result of the disruption caused by the Viking settlement and the West Saxon reconquest of Mercia. The bishoprics and many of the major religious communities of Mercia and the former Middle Anglian province disappeared altogether and with them went their archives. Survivals like the memoranda from *Medeshamstede* (Peterborough) are rare,[3] and so we are left in the curious position of knowing more about the Mercian patronage of churches in subsidiary provinces than in Mercia itself. Few Mercian administrative documents other than charters and allied memoranda survive though a copy of a Mercian regnal list was preserved at Worcester and two versions of it survive, one of which has some important additions which are not in the version in the Anglian collection.[4] The Tribal Hidage has generally been interpreted as a

Mercian tribute list and is key evidence for the political structure of the Midlands.[5]

One aspect of the Mercian past which did survive the disappearance of the kingdom was its saints' cults.[6] Many of the major religious houses disappeared, but lesser minsters continued to exist and to honour their native saints, many of whom seem to have been of royal birth. The traditions surrounding these saints are of varying reliability, and most only survive in texts written after the Norman Conquest. A good, if rather extreme, example of the problems these saint cults can pose is the *Life of St Rumwold*. It is extremely improbable that Rumwold was really an infant prodigy who died three days after his birth having first preached a sermon on the Trinity, as his *Life* records. Yet his cult undoubtedly existed and is well-attested at three places which may originally have been part of the same large royal estate. It is even possible that Rumwold was a grandson of Penda as his *Life* claims, but on this there can be no certainty.[7] Of a rather different order are the *Lives* of Kenelm (Cynehelm)[8] and Wigstan,[9] two ninth-century Mercian princes who were murdered in the course of dynastic disputes. Although the hagiographies of these two princes only survive in post-Conquest versions, there is reason to believe that they are based on pre-Conquest accounts and can be used to help us understand the political situation in Mercia in the early ninth century.

There is clearly a danger that the achievements of Mercia and its kings are inadequately represented in the surviving written sources, but other sources of evidence can help to redress the balance. Archaeology can reveal something of what was happening in places within the main Mercian kingdom about which the written sources are silent. Northampton, for instance, is first mentioned in the *Anglo-Saxon Chronicle* for 913, but aspects of its earlier history have been recovered during excavations which revealed a series of timber and stone halls from the period when it was a Mercian administrative centre.[10] Surviving churches like Repton and Brixworth can help to rectify the lack of direct information about patronage of the church in the main Mercian province and allow us to see the influence of the Carolingian Renaissance on the Mercian church which is hinted at in the letters between the courts of Offa and Charlemagne (see Figs 10 and 13).[11]

The origins of Mercia

No Mercian origin legend survives comparable to those from Kent or Wessex, though the Mercian kings apparently claimed descent from legendary kings of Continental Angeln.[12] We learn from the *Life of St Guthlac* that Icel was regarded as the founder of the dynasty,[13] and in the genealogy of Æthelred in the Anglian collection he appears five generations above Penda,[14] the first Mercian ruler for whom reliable dates survive. However, the earliest common ancestor in the four genealogies of Mercian kings in the Anglian collection (Æthelred, Æthelbald, Egfrith and Cenwulf) is Pybba, the father of Penda. The first Mercian king mentioned by Bede is Cearl who does not appear in any of the surviving genealogies.[15] Edwin of Deira was married to his daughter and Bede says that their children were born while Edwin was in exile from Northumbria (604-16). A group of post-Conquest annals claims that Creoda (father of Pybba) founded the kingdom of Mercia in 585 and also provides succession dates for Pybba, Cearl and Penda.[16] Although it is possible that some kind of regnal list could be the source of the information (though the Worcester lists begin with Penda), these entries could be nothing more than intelligent guesswork based on names derived from Bede and the genealogy of Æthelred, while the dates seem to be influenced by an entry in the *Anglo-Saxon Chronicle* for the death of a West Saxon Creoda.[17] The post-Conquest annals' date of 610 (or earlier) for the accession of Penda seems too early. The surviving sources allow us to say with confidence little more than that the kingdom of Mercia was in existence by the end of the sixth century.

It is not as clear as it is for many of the other kingdoms where the original focus of the kingdom of Mercia lay. Bede, describing the arrangements for Mercia following Penda's death in 655, speaks of a division between Northern and Southern Mercians separated by the river Trent.[18] The site of the Mercian bishopric, from 669 at least, was Lichfield on the south bank of the Middle Trent, and two other key early centres of the Mercian kings – the royal vill of Tamworth and the monastery of Repton – were in the vicinity. Later charters define all three centres as being in the territory of the Tomsæte and it is possible that the Mercian royal line began as the leaders of these people, 'the dwellers by the river Tame' (a tributary of the Trent).[19] It is likely that much complex manoeuvring and amalgamation of peoples had occurred before the Mercians came to pre-eminence under Penda and there are occasional glimpses of what may have been earlier folk groupings in charters; for instance, the Tomsæte seem to have been bordered on the west by the Pencersæte. We cannot hope to reconstruct the earlier arrangements with precision, though archaeology can help identify the earliest centres of settlement and provides some support for the idea that the Trent valley was originally settled by disparate groups of Anglo-Saxons who had moved westwards from the earlier settlements in eastern England.[20]

By the second quarter of the seventh century the family of Penda had emerged as the leaders of these people centred on the Trent valley. They were known as the Mercians – 'the borderers' or 'dwellers on the march'. It has often been assumed that the people they 'bordered' were the Northumbrians,[21] but although Mercia and Northumbria shared a common border in the eighth century, in the seventh century they were separated by peoples such as the Pecsæte and the Elmetsæte who are listed separately from the main Mercian province in the Tribal Hidage. In the early seventh century the Mercians must have been pioneers living on the edge of the territories already controlled by Anglo-Saxon rulers and engaged in pushing back the frontiers of British rule. It is more likely to have been their position on the borders of British territory which gave rise to their name.[22]

Mercia in the seventh century

Mercia truly enters the field of the historian with the reign of Penda. Although Penda's death can be securely dated to the battle of the river *Winwæd* in 655,[23] there is greater uncertainty about his accession.[24] The writers of different kingdoms have varied views perhaps depending on when their particular provinces came into contact with Penda. According to the *Anglo-Saxon Chronicle* Penda came to the throne in 626 and 'held his throne for 30 years and he was 50 years old when he succeeded to the kingdom'. The last part of the

Penda d. 655

Oswiu of Northumbria 655–658 (Peada subking of S. Mercians 655–656)

Wulfhere 658–675

Æthelred I 675–704

Cenred 704–709

Ceolred 709–716

Ceolwald 716

Æthelbald 716–757

Beornred 757

Offa 757–796

Egfrith 796

Cenwulf 796–821

Ceolwulf I 821–823

Beornwulf 823–826

Ludeca 826–827

Wiglaf (1) 827–829

Egbert of Wessex 829–830

Wiglaf (2) 830–840

Berhtwulf 840–852

Burgred 852–874

Ceolwulf II 874–?879

Æthelred II ?879–911

Table 12: Regnal list of the Kings of Mercia

statement is highly unlikely, and, as Professor Brooks has suggested, it is more probable that what the chronicler should have said was that Penda ruled for 30 years and was 50 years old when he died.[25] For Bede Penda's reign began in 633 as a result of his role in the defeat of King Edwin at the battle of Hatfield Chase.[26] The *Historia Brittonum* placed Penda's accession even later, after the battle of *Maserfelth/Cocboy* of 642 in which Oswald was slain, and believed that he succeeded his brother Eowa who had also been killed in the battle.[27]

Bede characterized Penda as a *vir strenuissimus*, 'a man exceptionally gifted as a warrior'.[28] Bede's commendation is particularly significant because from his point of view he had every reason to vilify Penda who lived and died a pagan and was responsible for the deaths of at least two Northumbrian kings and several princes. Although we cannot present a comprehensive view of Penda's career it is clear that he was active over a wide geographical area.[29] He sought to extend Mercian control in all directions and fought battles to the north, south and east of his territory with the Northumbrians, West Saxons and East Angles respectively. To his west lay British kingdoms and Penda's early success against the Northumbrians was the result of an alliance with Cadwallon of Gwynedd. Other Welsh princes seem to have fought on Penda's behalf on other occasions including at his final battle at the river *Winwæd*. However, by the end of the seventh century Mercian expansion westward was at the expense of the British kingdom of Powys, and from this time the Welsh are more often found as enemies than as allies of Mercia.[30] Although Penda undoubtedly was very successful, Bede comments that he ruled with 'varying

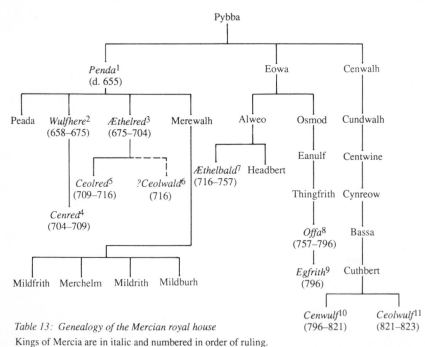

Table 13: Genealogy of the Mercian royal house
Kings of Mercia are in italic and numbered in order of ruling.

fortune' and there were powerful rulers like Oswald of Northumbria and Anna of the East Angles to curb his ambitions.

Although Penda does not appear in Bede's list of great overlords it would appear from what Bede says elsewhere that he was dominant over the southern kingdoms at the time of the battle of the river *Winwæd* when thirty *duces regii* fought on his behalf.[31] Oswiu too seems to have had to recognize Penda's overlordship; his son Egfrith was a hostage at the Mercian court and Oswiu had apparently been obliged to pay a large amount of tribute and return earlier tributes exacted from Penda and his British allies.[32] Bede claims that Oswiu had no option but to challenge Penda who would otherwise have destroyed the Northumbrian people, but this is a very partial view of what was evidently a Northumbrian bid for Penda's position. Penda and his allies were decisively defeated and Penda himself killed. Oswiu tried to take over the Mercian province. At first Penda's son Peada, who was Oswiu's son-in-law, was allowed to rule the southern Mercians, but within the year he had been murdered. Three years later the Mercian *duces* rebelled against Oswiu and placed Penda's son Wulfhere on the Mercian throne.

Wulfhere (658-75) seems to have reasserted his father's control of the other kingdoms south of the Humber and Bede provides scattered references to his ability to intervene in the affairs of a number of the southern kingdoms.[33] Stephanus portrays Wulfhere riding against Egfrith of Northumbria c. 674 with an army drawn from all the southern kingdoms though in the event Wulfhere was defeated and forced to pay tribute to the Northumbrians.[34] Unlike his father, Wulfhere was a Christian and oversaw the conversion of Mercia and a number of her subject areas. Wulfhere's successor was his brother Æthelred (675-704) who, in spite of his later career as a monk, seems to have come from the same mould as his brother and father. His victory against Egfrith of Northumbria at the battle of the river Trent in 679 ended Northumbrian overlordship south of the Humber and saw the province of Lindsey pass permanently into the Mercian sphere of influence.[35] Stenton's judgement that the southern kingdoms were largely free from Mercian over-lordship during Æthelred's reign reflects the fact that Æthelred had to con-tend with the rising power of Wessex under Cædwalla and Ine.[36] Mercia and Wessex competed for spoils from the other southern kingdoms and, for in-stance, in the 680s both tried to establish their own subkings within Kent.[37]

Although there are many gaps in our knowledge it is clear that these seventh-century Mercian kings were formidable rulers who were able to exercise a wide-ranging overlordship from their Midland base. Military success seems to lie at the basis of their power, as it no doubt did for the other great overlords, though it may be significant that it is only the Mercian kings who are depicted as drawing military contingents from their subject kingdoms.[38] The thirty royal *duces* who fought on Penda's behalf at the battle of the *Winwæd* should presumably be interpreted in this way and we know that Penda's army included sections led by Æthelhere of East Anglia, Œthel-wald of Deira and probably several British princes. Mercian military power succeeded not only by winning setpiece battles, but by ruthlessly ravaging any province foolish enough to withhold tribute. There are a number of casual references scattered through the *Ecclesiastical History* to this aspect of Mercian military policy. At some point in Aidan's episcopate Penda is found ravaging Northumbria as far north as Bamburgh and only a miraculous intervention from the bishop prevented the complete destruction of the settlement.[39] In 676 Æthelred conducted a similar ravaging in Kent and caused such damage in the Rochester diocese that two successive bishops gave up their position because of lack of funds.[40] In these accounts we get a rare glimpse of the realities of early Anglo-Saxon overlordship and how a widespread overlordship could be established in a relatively short period.

A reconstruction of the political map of the latter half of the seventh century enables us to reach a further understanding of the nature of Mercian power at the time (see map 1, p. 12). The Tribal Hidage is a key document here in spite of the formidable obstacles in the way of its interpretation.[41] The list begins with 30,000 hides of the Mercians which is specified as that 'which is called the first (land) of the Mercians'. This presumably means that the 30,000 hides constituted the main Mercian province. All the other peoples listed in the Tribal Hidage must have been regarded as separate entities for the paying of tribute, or whatever other purposes lay behind the hidage assessment. The 30,000 hides allotted to Mercia contrasts with the 12,000 hides which Bede says was the assessment of the North and South Mercians in 655. The extra 18,000 hides for Mercia in the Tribal Hidage can either be interpreted as an assessment of the same area which has been made on a different basis,[42] or as an indication that additional lands had been absorbed into the main area of Mercia between 655 and the time when the Tribal Hidage was compiled.[43] Such problems in interpretation make it difficult to allocate exact territories on the basis of the Tribal Hidage entries. Nevertheless the approximate locations of many of the peoples listed in the document can be suggested from place-name or charter evidence, though there is a residue which cannot be located at all.[44]

From the map we can see that the main Mercian province centred on the river Trent was completely surrounded by other provinces which thus acted as a buffer between Mercia proper and the other major Anglo-Saxon and British kingdoms. The Pecsæte, Elmetsæte and Lindsey (with Hatfield land) lay between Mercia and Northumbria while at least twenty small provinces of between 300–1200 hides, which seem to have been known collectively as the Middle Angles, separated the Mercians from the East Angles and the East Saxons. On the southern side the provinces of the Hwicce (Hwinca), Chilternsæte and possibly the Hendrica (or one or more of the other tribes which cannot be securely located) bordered the West Saxons. To the west the main rivals were British rather than Saxon. The most formidable of these British kingdoms was Powys and between it and Mercia lay the substantial provinces of the Wreocensæte and the Westerna (more commonly known as the Magonsæte). The origins of these provinces are frequently obscure, but

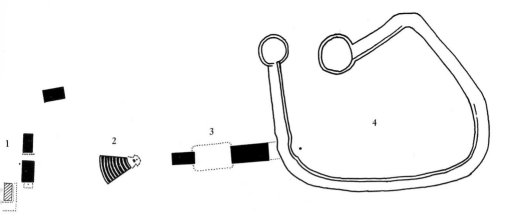

Fig 8. *Yeavering.* A plan of the royal vill site of Yeavering in Northumbria as it appeared in the early seventh century, based on the excavations of Brian Hope-Taylor. The plan shows: (1) a possible temple complex; (2) the 'amphitheatre'; (3) the main hall complex; (4) the fort.

Fig 9. *Cowderys Down.* A reconstruction of one of the early seventh-century timber halls from Cowdery's Down (Hants) by Simon James. Only the ground plan was revealed through excavation, but the foundations were massive and carried various implications for the missing superstructure, even though many elements are naturally speculative. *(The Royal Archaeological Institute)*

Although the range of buildings was different at Yeavering and Cowdery's Down both sites centred around massive timber-framed halls which would have housed the king and his itinerant court and been the scene of various public transactions as depicted in *Beowulf* and Bede's *Ecclesiastical History.*

Fig 10. *Repton church*. The Anglo-Saxon crypt at Repton (Derbs) showing the pillars which supported the roof and the stairs giving access to the main body of the church. Repton is known to have been the burial place of several members of the Mercian royal house. The crypt seems to have originated as a freestanding mausoleum, which may have been the burial-place of Æthelbald of Mercia (d. 757), and to have been adapted to form a crypt in the ninth century, perhaps to house the body of prince Wigstan who was murdered in 849 and later venerated as a saint. *(Frank Rogers)*

Fig 11. *The Repton sculpture*, discovered during recent excavations at the church. The sculpture depicts a moustachioed horseman, apparently wearing a mail shirt and a pleated skirt, with a seax at his waist and with a shield in his left hand. The sculpture was probably part of a cross or other memorial to one of the Mercian royal house buried at Repton and may be an unique sculptural portrayal of an early Anglo-Saxon ruler. *(Photograph:*

The adoption of Christianity gave the royal houses new opportunities for privileged burial and conspicuous royal

Fig 13. *Brixworth, Northants: All Saints.* There has been considerable controversy about the date of the main fabric of Brixworth church, though there is general agreement that it dates to before 900. The church has undergone considerable alteration in later centuries and the round stair-turret and upper storey of the tower are later Saxon additions. The arcade containing the present lower windows of the nave originally provided access from the main body of the church to side-chapels which have since been removed. (*A. F. Kersting*)

Fig 12. *Bradwell-on-sea, Essex: St Peter's.* Bede described the foundation of a church inside the former Roman fort at Bradwell by the Northumbrian missionary Cedd during the reign of the East Saxon king Sigebert 'Sanctus' (dead by 664). The surviving church is either of the time of Cedd or not long after and shares many characteristics with the early churches of Kent (a province with which the East Saxons had close contacts). Although it has suffered during its later use as a barn, the church's fine stone coursing and a number of windows with heads constructed in brick are still visible. (*The Royal Commission on the Historical Monuments of England*)

Fig 14. *Seven coins of the early Anglo-Saxon period.* (1) A primary series sceatta from Kent c. 680-700, showing (obverse) a (royal?) bust and (reverse) a military standard surmounted by a cross; (2) A series H sceatta (type 49) probably manufactured in Hamwic. Its date is debated, but a good case has been made recently for placing this type in the second half of the eighth century. It shows (obverse) a bearded head surrounded by roundels and (reverse) a stylized bird; (3) A penny of King Beonna of East Angles c. 760 (obverse) *Beonna Rex* in Latin and runic letters and (reverse) a military standard and *Efe* (moneyer's name); (4) A penny of King Egbert II of Kent (c. 764- c. 785), reading (obverse) *Egcberht r(e)x* and (reverse) Udd; (5) Obverse of a penny of King Offa of Mercia (757-96) with a bust of the king; (6) Obverse of a penny of Queen Cynethryth of Mercia, wife of Offa, with a bust of the queen and the moneyer's name (Eoba); (7) Obverse of a penny of King Alfred of Wessex (871-899) with a bust of the king.

many of the more westerly provinces in particular are likely to have been predominantly British creations. Elmet originally had its own British dynasty and there may have been others which we do not know about.

Although these 'buffer' provinces were not part of the Mercian kingdom as such it can be shown that many of them were satellites of Mercia in the late seventh century. Some of them were ruled by members of the royal house. Bede records that Penda made his son Peada *princeps* of the Middle Angles in 653.[45] It is to be regretted that Bede did not provide more information about the extent of the Middle Angles at this time and on whether the Middle Angles had existed as a political unit before they were assigned to Peada to govern.[46] The issue is complicated by the fact that the Middle Angles do not appear as such in the Tribal Hidage, though some of the smaller provinces in the document are described elsewhere as being Middle Anglian. But at the moment the solid core of Middle Anglia, the later counties of Leicestershire and Northamptonshire, cannot be equated with any of the entries in the Tribal Hidage. Either they are to be found among some of the indecipherable peoples or they constitute the bulk of the extra 18,000 hides assigned to Mercia.[47] Such are the problems with which the historians of Middle Anglia have to wrestle. For our purposes we can simply note that Bede seems to have thought of the Middle Angles as a distinct *gens* and that they were ruled as a separate province by Peada.[48] Their history after this time is obscure, but they were carefully preserved as a people distinct from the Mercians by having their own bishopric based on Leicester. In the reign of Æthelred a royal kinsman, Penwalh the father of St Guthlac, was based among the Middle Angles, perhaps, taking Guthlac's area of activities into account, in the fenland area which was disputed with the East Angles.[49] In the same period a *princeps* called Frithuric was active among the more northerly Middle Angles. It is possible that Frithuric was also a member of the royal house as he seems to have been involved in the foundation of religious houses in Mercia.[50] He may be related to Frithuwold who was subking of Surrey under Wulfhere.[51]

Penda's action in placing his son Peada as a subordinate ruler over the Middle Angles can be paralleled on Mercia's western border where another son Merewalh was created ruler of the Magonsæte (or Westerna). There has been some reluctance to accept Merewalh as Penda's son as the attribution only occurs in the 'Testament of St Mildburh' (daughter of Merewalh), which Goscelin included as part of his *Life of St Mildburh* (c. 1080-90).[52] However, the Testament appears to draw on reliable pre-Conquest materials and in it Mildburh describes King Æthelred of Mercia as her uncle. Merewalh's membership of the Mercian royal house can receive some support through his naming of one of his sons Merchelm 'helmet of the Mercians' and by the tradition of Merewalh's burial at Repton where a number of members of the Mercian royal house were buried.[53] Merewalh married the Kentish princess Eormenburh, a sister of the murdered Kentish princes Æthelred and Æthelbert, and their daughter Mildrith became abbess of Minster-in-Thanet and the focus of the series of texts concerning the saints of Minster known as the 'Mildrith Legend' which contains additional information about the Magonsætan royal family.[54] Merewalh seems to have had two successors as rulers of the Magonsæte, Merchelm and Mildfrith, both of whom were probably his sons.

Other members of the Mercian royal house can be identified as assisting in the Mercian control of satellite provinces in the seventh century. Berhtwald, a nephew of King Æthelred (perhaps a son of Wulfhere) seems to have been a *subregulus* on the borders of the Hwicce and the West Saxons and able to grant an estate in Wiltshire to Aldhelm, abbot of Malmesbury.[55] Aldhelm also received land in Gloucestershire from a relative of Æthelred called Cenfrith described as *comes* and *patricius*.[56] Among possible subrulers of royal birth can be included Penda's brother Eowa. According to the *Historia Brittonum* Eowa was a Mercian ruler who was killed at the battle of *Maserfelth/Cocboy* which is usually identified with Old Oswestry in Shropshire and may have been part of the province of the Wreocensæte.[57] The author of the *Historia Brittonum* apparently believed that Penda only became king after Eowa's death, but this goes against the evidence of other sources and the entry may merely be an indication that Eowa was the Mercian ruler in charge of the western march with the British kingdoms until his death in battle when Penda took over command of forces in the area.[58] There is some evidence, as we have seen, to suggest that Frithuwold who was subking of Surrey under Wulfhere could have been a member of the royal house.[59] Frithuwold's Chertsey charter was witnessed by three *subreguli*, Wigheard, Æthelwold and Osric.

Some other satellite provinces seem to have had rulers who were not members of the Mercian royal house, but in most instances we do not known much about them. An independent royal line in Lindsey has been assumed from the genealogy of a king of Lindsey in the Anglian collection, but no other Lindsey rulers are definitely known unless the *praefectus* of Lincoln who was the first of the province to be converted by Paulinus should be so interpreted.[60] The South Gyrwe had their own ruler, the *princeps* Tondbert, around the middle of seventh century, but we do not know whether any of the other small Middle Anglian people had individual rulers.[61] The South Gyrwe were on the borders of Middle Anglia and the East Anglian kingdom and seem to have been absorbed into the latter after Tondbert's marriage with the East Anglian princess Æthelthryth. A separate dynasty among the Pecsæte might be assumed from the series of rich burials in barrows, including that at Benty Grange which produced the only other helmet found in an Anglo-Saxon burial besides that of Sutton Hoo, but the archaeological remains cannot be supplemented by any written records which would clarify their significance.[62] In fact, the only satellite kingdom in this category for which adequate written records exist is the kingdom of the Hwicce.

The Hwicce had their own dynasty who ruled for five generations.[63] The origins of the dynasty are obscure and arguments that their founders may have been junior members of the Bernician royal house are not conclusive.[64]

Although the royal house continued into the second half of the eighth century, the Hwiccian rulers frequently appear in their charters to have been under the supervision of the Mercian kings whose permission generally seems to have been needed before a grant could be made. In addition the Mercian kings seem to have been able to grant land in their own right in the Hwiccian territory, apart that is from within the shire of Winchcombe (later absorbed into Gloucestershire) which seems to have been the preserve of the Hwiccian kings.[65] In the *Anglo-Saxon Chronicle* it is Penda who is presented as successfully contesting with West Saxon rulers in 628 for control of the Cirencester area which, unlike Worcestershire and northern Gloucestershire, had been settled by Saxon rather than Anglian colonists.[66] A concentration in the West Midlands of place-names incorporating the names of early Mercian rulers may also support the idea that Mercian kings – and perhaps Penda in particular – played a major role in the creation of the Hwiccian kingdom.[67] The circumstances in which the kingdom came into existence may have enabled the Mercian kings to keep an unusually firm control of the Hwiccian rulers who from the start had to acknowledge that they were subordinate to the main province.

A similar pattern can be found in the seventh-century Mercian kings' relations with royal families who were rather more distant from the Mercian heartlands. The Mercians began to cultivate links with the East Saxons in the second half of the seventh century. Æthelred seems to have supported Sæbbi's and Swæfheard's conquest of west Kent and probably helped to ensure that the East Saxons kept a controlling interest in London once they had dispensed with Kentish supervision. In the late seventh century the East Saxon kings are found controlling lands in Hertfordshire and the province of the Middle Saxons whose earlier history is obscure, but which may well not have been part of the original East Saxon province. It is possible that the Mercians entrusted these areas to the East Saxons to rule for, parallelling what happened in the Hwiccian province, Mercian rulers were able to grant lands in the conceded territories (but not in the East Saxon homelands).[68] They also seem to have imposed a Mercian official (*comes*) to protect their interests.[69]

Wulfhere seems to have followed a similar policy with the South Saxons. He arranged for King Æthelwalh of the South Saxons to assume control of the Isle of Wight and part of the Hampshire mainland, areas which the West Saxon kings were also interested in taking over.[70] The Isle of Wight still had its own royal house at this time who presumably had to accept Æthelwalh's overlordship. Æthelwalh's reception into the Mercian sphere of influence was also sealed by his marriage to a Hwiccian princess. There is also evidence for intermarriage between the East Saxon and Hwiccian royal houses, and one of the East Saxon princes seems to have possessed a substantial estate in the Hwiccian province.[71]

Mercian management of the satellite provinces and client kingdoms can also be studied through Mercian involvement with religious communities in these areas. Although only a handful of Mercian charters datable to the seventh century survive they show a striking degree of patronage to religious houses outside the main Mercian province. Among the Middle Angles *Medeshamstede* (Peterborough) seems to have been particularly favoured and to have been used as a base from which other areas of Mercian influence could be missionized including the main Mercian province itself (the Middle Angles had been converted to Christianity before the Mercians).[72] Seventh-century Mercian kings were patrons of the Magonsætan double monastery of Much Wenlock where their kinswoman Mildburh presided and of a number of houses in the territory of the Hwicce.[73] Chertsey, Barking, Abingdon and Malmesbury all benefited from Mercian rulers' interest in expanding the southern borders of their area of influence.[74] These last four monasteries all seem to have been founded by rulers from other kingdoms and were controlled by major aristocrats, probably themselves of royal birth, including Aldhelm at Malmesbury, Eorcenwald at Chertsey and his sister Æthelburh at Barking. It was people of this rank whom the Mercians needed to conciliate if they were to be successful in their conquest of outlying areas. No doubt their relatives in the secular sphere received similar handouts, but the evidence does not survive.

It is entirely in keeping with this policy that when Æthelred decided in 704 to retire to become a monk he chose to enter not a Mercian monastery, but the monastery of Bardney in Lindsey, the province which he had decisively detached from Northumbrian control by his victory at the battle of the Trent in 679.[75] Subsequently both Æthelred and his wife Osthryth, a Northumbrian princess, were revered as saints at Bardney, and such encouragement of Mercian royal saints' cults outside the main area of Mercia also seems to have been part of Mercian policy.[76] As mentioned above many of the cults are poorly recorded or have late and historically worthless *Lives*, but their incidence is still remarkable. Mildburh, granddaughter of Penda, was revered at Much Wenlock where she had been abbess. Two daughters of Penda, Cyneburh and Cyneswith, had a cult at Castor by Peterborough, and an even more dubious grandson of Penda called Rumwold was revered elsewhere in Middle Anglia. Aylesbury, in one of the Mercian satellite provinces whose name is uncertain, preserved traditions about three more of Penda's supposed descendants, two further daughters and a granddaughter.[77] There are also a number of saints associated with the '*Frith*' family who may have been members of the royal house, including St Frideswide of Oxford.[78] The number of Penda's daughters appears to be legion and no historian would wish to go to his or her death defending all these attributions as historically accurate, but their cumulative effect is to suggest that the promotion of the cults of members of the royal house was part of the Mercian policy for strengthening control of the satellite provinces.

A variety of sources enable us to study in some detail the kingdom of Mercia at a crucial stage in its development in the late seventh century. At this time Mercia itself seems to have been a substantial kingdom centred on the Middle Trent, but surrounded on all sides by buffer provinces separating Mercia from its main rivals, the kingdoms of Powys, the Northumbrians, the West Saxons and the East Angles. These buffer provinces had a variety of different origins as British or Saxon communities, but although retaining individual identities in some respects, they were in others subordinate to the main Mercian province. A number of them were controlled by members of the Mercian royal house. In others there were non-Mercian rulers, but these were likely to be beholden to the rulers of the main province. Signs of Mercian control of the satellite provinces include Mercian kings possessing estates within them, imposing officials, dispensing patronage to monasteries and promoting members of their families as saints. Parallels for many of these activities can be found in other kingdoms, but the thoroughness of Mercian statecraft is impressive and it can be seen extending these policies to small provinces beyond its immediate borders before the end of the seventh century.

Mercia in the eighth century

In 704 Æthelred abdicated to enter the monastery of Bardney and appointed his nephew Cenred (704-709), the son of Wulfhere, to rule in his place. Æthelred did not necessarily give up all his responsibilities and Bede portrays Æthelred summoning Cenred to meet him and advising him to make amends with Bishop Wilfrid.[79] In 709 Cenred also abdicated to become a monk and left for Rome with Offa, one of the junior kings of the East Saxons; it is not clear whether they went willingly or under pressure.[80] Cenred's abdication freed the way for the succession of his cousin Ceolred (709-16), the son of Æthelred. Ceolred died in 716, having fallen into a frenzied fit when 'feasting in splendour among his companions', according to Bishop Boniface.[81] One version of the Worcester regnal list has Ceolred succeeded by an otherwise unknown Ceolwald, perhaps his brother,[82] but Ceolwald's reign can only have been brief as Æthelbald (716-57) came to the throne in the same year. The obscure Ceolwald was probably the last of Penda's descendants to rule as with the accession of Æthelbald a new branch of the royal house came to power.

It is tempting to equate the fall of the house of Penda with the decline of the house of Æthelfrith in Northumbria which also occurred in the early years of the eighth century. Ceolred of Mercia died in the same year that Osred of Northumbria was murdered and both deaths opened up the throne to new branches of the royal house. Boniface castigated both Osred and Ceolred for personal immorality and violation of church privileges.[83] However, there is not such clear evidence for a decline in the wealth and power of the Pendings as there is for the house of Æthelfrith. It is true that the reigns of Cenred and Ceolred were not particularly distinguished and they certainly did not enjoy such wide-ranging overlordships as Penda or Wulfhere. But their grip on the Mercian satellite provinces seems to have been secure and both kings can be found granting land outside the Mercian homelands and confirming the charters of rulers of the Hwicce, Magonsæte and the East Saxons, though the Middle Anglian fens seem to have been under East Anglian control.[84] Cenred suffered from attacks from the Welsh and Ceolred fought an engagement with

Ine of Wessex in northern Wiltshire, though with what result we do not know.[85]

However, there are indications that other branches of the royal house were discontented during the reign of Ceolred. Æthelbald, who was to succeed to the throne in 716, was sent into exile by Ceolred and was comforted during his sojourn in the fens by another member of the royal house, Guthlac, who prophesied that Æthelbald would succeed to the Mercian throne and generally provided him with moral encouragement.[86] A monk in the Magonsætan royal monastery of Much Wenlock had a vision while Ceolred was still alive of the terrible punishments which awaited the king on his death.[87] Abbess Mildburh herself may have been responsible for disseminating an account of the vision which sounds very much like covert criticism of her cousin. These are faint murmurings, but they suggest that in Mercia, as in Northumbria, a downturn in the fortunes of the royal house and a feeling that the kings were not conducting themselves in an appropriate manner eased the way for a new royal lineage to come to power.

Æthelbald was descended from Eowa, the brother of Penda, who seems to have held some position of authority during Penda's reign. Æthelbald's successor Offa (757-96) was also descended from Eowa and according to the genealogies of the Anglian collection, the two kings were first cousins twice removed.[88] It is possible that both men should be understood as coming from the same broad family grouping and we can find instances of mutual co-operation. Offa's grandfather Eanulf (Æthelbald's first cousin) was given substantial grants of land by Æthelbald, some of which he used to establish a proprietary monastery at Bredon (Worcs) in the province of the Hwicce.[89] One of the most important of the nobility during Æthelbald's reign,[90] from charter evidence, was his own brother Headbert who seems to have continued in a dominant position in the early years of Offa's reign. In one of his charters Offa tried to reclaim lands which he described as 'the inheritance of his kinsman, King Æthelbald'.[91] The dominance of one branch in the seventh century seems to have been replaced by that of another branch in the eighth century, though the position of Æthelbald and Offa's family did not go entirely unchallenged. In 757 Æthelbald was murdered by members of his household and the throne went briefly to a certain Beornred whose accession is recorded in the *Anglo-Saxon Chronicle* and one of the Worcester lists.[92] Beornred was driven out by Offa before the year was out. Beornred's ancestry is not given, but he may have been connected with the kings whose names alliterate on 'B' who came to power in Mercia in the ninth century. Æthelbald's murder by men of his household, which probably included royal kinsmen, and the elevation of a man probably from a rival lineage recalls the coups of Northumbria in this period.

Both Æthelbald and Offa were dominant over the other kingdoms of southern England. In summing up the political situation in 731 when he completed the *Ecclesiastical History* Bede recorded that all the kingdoms south of the Humber with their various kings were subject to King Æthelbald, and Offa seems to have exercised a similar authority.[93] But what was more significant, both to the rulers themselves and to modern historians' assessment of their power, was the growth in size of Mercia itself. Most of the kingdoms peripheral to Mercia in the seventh century were absorbed into the kingdom of Mercia in the eighth century. The last independent ruler of the Magonsæte, Mildfrith, had ceased to rule by 740 and his place seems to have been taken by an ealdorman.[94] The Hwiccian royal family survived until almost the end of the century, but both Æthelbald and Offa frequently granted land within their province and the titles of the Hwiccian rulers acknowledged their subordinate position. Offa referred to one of the Hwiccian rulers as 'my under-king, ealdorman, that is, of his own people of the Hwicce'.[95] The Middle Anglian peoples became fully part of Mercia, but as no eighth-century charters survive from their province little can be said about its history during the period. It used to be thought that a king of Lindsey was still in power towards the end of Offa's reign as King Aldfrith of Lindsey, whose genealogy appears in the Anglian collection, was identified with one of the witnesses of a South Saxon charter of Offa. However, this identification has now been discounted and the Lindsey dynasty had probably disappeared some time before.[96]

Other kingdoms of southern England were also affected by Mercian expansionism. The East Saxons seem to have lost control of London, Middlesex and Hertfordshire to Æthelbald, though, as we have seen, these were probably fairly recent acquisitions over which the Mercian kings had previously claimed some rights. The East Saxon homelands do not seem to have been affected, and the East Saxon dynasty continued into the ninth century.[97]

The common border shared by Mercia and the West Saxons had been the subject of disputes between the two kingdoms for some time and during the eighth century the Mercian kings pressed their claims to the more northerly areas of West Saxon territory. The two powers seem to have been evenly matched for victories are recorded on both sides, and lands in the upper Thames, north Wiltshire and Somerset seem to have changed hands with some frequency. The varying fortunes of the monastery of Cookham in Berkshire, as recorded at the synod of Clovesho in 798, give the flavour of life in the disputed border areas.[98] In the late seventh century this area of Berkshire seems to have been a West Saxon preserve, but Æthelbald took control of it and granted the monastery of Cookham to Christ Church, Canterbury. On his death Cynewulf seems to have taken back the upper Thames region and with it the monastery of Cookham, for which he was given the title deeds by two well-wishers who had stolen them from Canterbury. Cynewulf and Offa fought a major battle at Bensington (Oxon) in 779 which Offa won. Then, in the words of the synod proceedings, Offa 'seized from King Cynewulf the oft-mentioned monastery, Cookham, and many other towns and brought them under Mercian rule'. But Offa's victory at Bensington must not lead us to exaggerate Offa's powers over Wessex during the reign of Cynewulf. The meeting of the southern provinces which the papal legates attended in 787 met under the joint presidency of Offa and Cynewulf.[99] Offa may have enjoyed greater authority over Cynewulf's successor Beorhtric who came to the throne in 786 and married Offa's daughter Eadburh three years later. Eadburh was remembered with great dislike in Wessex in the reign of Alfred for her tyrannical ways; perhaps she was an active representative of Mercian power in Wessex.[100]

Offa's most impressive conquests were the kingdoms of Kent and the South Saxons. Offa seems to have invaded Kent in 764 and at first allowed local kings to rule under his authority. King Egbert II put up a spirited resistance and Offa may have lost control in Kent between 776 and 784. But from 785 Offa seems to have resumed control of the province which he ruled directly (through ealdormen) for the rest of his reign.[101] His main campaigns against the South Saxons took place in 770 and 771. Offa seems to have treated the South Saxons in much the same way as the Mercians had previously treated the Hwiccians and which he seems to have originally intended for Kent. Local South Saxon rulers were allowed to continue providing they recognized Offa's overriding authority and some estates seem to have come into his direct possession.[102] However, there are no known signs of native South Saxon rulers after the end of Offa's reign. Offa also expanded Mercian authority over the East Angles. In the 790s he seems to have been minting coins at the East Anglian mint and he had the East Anglian ruler Æthelbert put to death in 794.[103]

By the end of Offa's reign Mercia had moved from being a confederation of peoples under Mercian overlordship to a vast kingdom comprising most of the English areas between the Thames and the Humber. Kent was ruled directly from Mercia and all the other southern kingdoms were satellite provinces in one sense or another, though native dynasties survived, or had suffered only temporary setbacks, among the West Saxons, East Saxons and East Angles.[104] As in the seventh century, the eighth-century Mercian kings were not necessarily in any hurry to remove native dynasties if they co-operated, though such co-operation involved recognition of the Mercian rulers' superior status and probably concession of land as well as payment of tribute. But although dominant south of the Humber, the Mercian rulers had little influence north of the river in spite of some meddling in northern affairs and the marriage of King Æthelred to a daughter of Offa.[105]

Æthelbald and Offa seem to have been very conscious of their position as the dominant kings of southern England and, in addition to having subordinate kings recognize their superior status in charters, experimented with new royal titles.[106] Æthelbald was styled *rex Britanniae* in one Hwiccian charter and there is some evidence that Offa occasionally used the form *decus Britanniae* ('glory of Britain'). A more accurate description of the real extent of Æthelbald's powers was his *rex Suthanglorum* and *rex non solum Mercensium sed etiam in circuitu populorum*. Offa may on occasion have used the title *rex Anglorum*,[107] but in spite of these experimentations the commonest form of address for both Æthelbald and Offa was *rex Merciorum* which was appropriate enough as what both rulers was really doing was extending the borders of Mercia outwards.

The expansion to London and Kent gave the Mercians ports and well-developed trading links with Francia which the Mercians were quick to exploit. The profits of trade were clearly of great interest to the Mercian kings. Æthelbald controlled the tolls at London,[108] and a surviving letter from the Frankish king Charlemagne to Offa concerns trading problems between the two countries.[109] Desire to acquire the lucrative trading interests of Kent may have been one of the factors which encouraged Offa to get rid of the native Kentish dynasty. With the ports came mints. Æthelbald may have been the first of the Mercian kings to mint coins, perhaps at London,[110] but Offa's was the first named Mercian coinage.[111] By the end of his reign Offa was minting the new penny coinage at Canterbury, Rochester, London and in East Anglia, perhaps at Ipswich, but Canterbury was his most productive mint (see Fig. 14.5). The acquisition of mints provided new opportunities for royal aggrandizement. Æthelbald may have produced a sceatta coinage at the London mint showing himself as a standing figure holding two crosses.[112] Offa adopted the new named penny coinages which the Canterbury and East Anglian mints had introduced in response to King Pepin's reform of the Frankish coinage. Offa's mints not only produced coins bearing his name and portrait, but coins for his wife Cynethryth with the title *regina Merciorum* (see Fig. 14.6). Cynethryth's coinage is un-paralleled in England or elsewhere in western Europe and may have been inspired by that of the Byzantine empress Irene.[113] Cynethryth's coins are part of the evidence that Offa had an enhanced sense of the importance of his own dynasty which is also revealed in the efforts he made to make sure that his son Egfrith succeeded him. These efforts culminated in the unprecedented corona-tion of Egfrith as king in 787 while his father was still alive.[114]

The coronation of Egfrith and many of Offa's other attempts to find new ways in which to express the dignity of Mercian kingship owed much to the example of the contemporary Frankish court of Charlemagne. Offa was in correspondence with Charlemagne and his Northumbrian adviser Alcuin, and received gifts from the great hoard of Avar treasure which Charlemagne cap-tured in 795.[115] Offa was equal to any condescension from Charlemagne. When Charlemagne proposed a marriage between one of Offa's daughters and one of his sons, Offa replied with a request for a Carolingian princess for Egfrith; Charlemagne angrily broke off negotiations.[116] Offa had reason to be suspicious of Charlemagne who had Mercian and other exiles at his court, including Egbert who was later to become king of Wessex and, probably, Eadbert Præn who took the throne of Kent on Offa's death.[117]

The reigns of both Æthelbald and Offa were affected by the contemporary renaissance in the Frankish church. In 747 Æthelbald received a letter from Bishop Boniface and seven other missionary bishops urging him to reform his personal morality and that of his subjects, and making specific complaints about the exorbitant demands the king made on ecclesiastical estates.[118] One result was the synod of Gumley in 749 in which it was agreed that Mercian monasteries and other holders of bookland could be exempted from all royal services with the exception of the building of bridges and defences; exemption clauses from the reign of Offa add military service to the 'common burdens' which all landowners had to perform. The Mercian common burdens seem to have been very similar to the rights the Frankish rulers claimed from lands held by the church.[119]

Offa was responsive to what was expected of a Christian ruler in the climate of the Carolingian Renaissance and drew praise from Alcuin for his efforts on behalf of his kingdom.[120] Offa cultivated the papacy. He showed a personal devotion to St Peter in whose name he built a number of churches and promised a yearly payment of 365 mancuses to Rome, one of which survives.[121] The papal legates who visited England in 786 were the first papal representatives to visit the Anglo-Saxons since the days of the Gregorian mission.[122] Their recommendations to the English church reveal the concern for uniformity within the western church which was an important element of the Carolingian renaissance. Presumably there were cultural influences as well, but unfortunately few manuscripts or buildings survive which can be definitely dated to the reigns of Æthelbald and Offa though the churches of Repton and Brixworth and the sculptures of Breedon-on-the-Hill may show us something of royal patronage at the time (see Figs 10 and 13).[123] A recent discovery at Repton of a sculptured stone depicting a Germanic horseman in a classical victorious pose has been tentatively identified by Martin and Birthe Biddle as part of a memorial cross to Æthelbald who is known to have been buried in the royal monastery there (see Fig. 11).[124]

However, such interest in the church was not purely altruistic. It was also part of the spirit of the times that monasteries were seen as personal possessions of rulers who had founded them and one of the ways of providing for members of their family. Offa obtained a papal privilege for the many monasteries he had founded or acquired so that they could remain the possessions of him, his wife and his offspring.[125] In keeping with Offa's devotion to the Holy See the religious houses were consecrated in the name of St Peter. In addition to the monastery at Bredon which his grandfather had founded, a number of other proprietary monasteries in the kingdom of the Hwicce were in Offa's hands, including Bath of which a kinswoman, Eanburh, was abbess, and Winchcombe.[126] This was in spite of the bishop of Worcester's objection to religious communities being under lay control, though Offa did agree to surrender some minsters.[127] The monastery of Cookham which Offa won in 779 was the possession of Queen Cynethryth after Offa's death,[128] and Offa may have founded houses at Westminster and Bedford where he was buried.[129] The list could probably be extended. Although Offa was affected by the Carolingian concept of rulership, like the Carolingians he also saw the church as an adjunct of his power and that of his family.

But just as Æthelbald and Offa had a heightened awareness of their role as Christian kings, so were their bishops more alive to the responsibilities of office and their duty to oppose kings who did not act in accordance with God's will. In Kent Offa discovered a formidable opponent in Archbishop Jænbert, a Kentishman from a prominent noble family who opposed Offa's removal of the native dynasty.[130] Major causes of discord seem to have been Offa's rescinding grants to Canterbury made by Egbert II of Kent and his possession of properties like the monastery of Cookham which the archbishop claimed. Matters seem to have come to a head over the coronation of Offa's son Egfrith which Jænbert refused to perform. A further benefit from Offa's cultivation of the papacy can now be seen for, in spite of an apparent attempt by Jænbert to persuade the pope that Offa was plotting with Charlemagne against him, the pope agreed that a third archbishopric should be established in the Mercian bishopric of Lichfield. Jænbert lost a sizeable area which had been under his jurisdiction and Offa had his new archbishop crown Egfrith as king. When Jænbert died in 792 Offa was careful to have a more compliant individual installed as his successor and was able to impose the common burdens on Kentish churchlands.

The main gap in our assessment of Æthelbald and Offa is of their government of Mercia itself and the shortage of charters from the Mercian province is keenly felt. However, some tangible signs do remain of the imposition of the common burdens through which Æthelbald and Offa were able to counteract some of the effects of the introduction of bookland and to establish important principles on the rights of kings to exact public services. Perhaps the most impressive memorials to the kings' power in Mercia are Offa's and Wat's dykes.[131] Attacks from the Welsh became an increasing problem in the eighth century and the solution seems to have been to establish a patrolled frontier along the 150-mile western border of Mercia from the Irish Sea to the Bristol Channel. The defences included at least 80 miles of earthwork defences with a rampart 24 feet high and a six foot ditch and associated forts.[132] Even today the dykes are impressive monuments (see Fig. 6), but they do not survive in their entirety and may originally have carried stone fortifications on top. Thousands of labourers must have been conscripted from different parts of Mercia to build them and a substantial force would have been needed if the frontier was to be fully patrolled. The Mercian rulers may have been responsible for building other defences as well, such as the earliest phase of the ramparts at Hereford.[133] By the end of his reign Offa was organizing defences against the Vikings in both Mercia and Kent. Jeremy Haslam has suggested that not only was Offa responsible for a defensive network of burhs at important bridgeheads in eastern England, but that he may also have established a series of 'urban' markets to stimulate the Mercian economy.[134] Some caution is necessary here for Offa does not seem to have been sufficiently aware on economic matters to encourage the use of coin throughout Mercia or establish Mercian mints. But, even if we do not know as much about Mercian administration as we would like, we can see that Offa, like Charlemagne, had the ability to exact substantial services from his subjects and organize major campaigns of public building works.

Mercia in the ninth century
Offa was succeeded by his son Egfrith as he intended, but Egfrith died after ruling for only 141 days. Alcuin was not surprised:

For truly, as I think, that most noble young man has not died for his own sins, but the vengeance for the blood shed by the father has reached the son. For you know very well how much blood his father shed to secure his kingdom on his son. This was not a strengthening of his kingdom, but its ruin.[135]

Offa seems to have got rid of various rival candidates for the throne to ease Egfrith's way. As we shall see it is likely that there were still a number of distant royal kinsmen living at the end of Offa's reign, but no close male kinsmen other than Egfrith are known, and Offa's wife and daughters were his main heirs on Egfrith's death. It may therefore have been members of Offa's own kingroup who were purged to ensure Egfrith's succession. The experiment of having a designated heir crowned as king was not repeated either in Mercia or elsewhere in Anglo-Saxon England, although it did become the practice for kings to be anointed on their accessions.[136]

The death of Egfrith enabled more distant collaterals to lay claim to the throne, and Mercia in the ninth century was characterized, like Northumbria in the eighth century, by fighting between rival claimants and their supporters. Egfrith's successor was Cenwulf (796-821), a very distant cousin descended, according to his genealogy in the Anglian collection, from a brother of Penda called Cenwalh who is otherwise unknown (see Table 14).[137] Cenwulf's father Cuthbert may have been the ealdorman of that name who lived during the reign of Offa.[138] After his accession Cenwulf appointed various relatives to positions of pre-eminence. One of Cenwulf's brothers, Cuthred, ruled as king of Kent (800/1-7) with considerable delegated powers including the right to mint coin in his own name, and another brother, Ceolwulf, who was eventually to succeed Cenwulf (821-23), was an ealdorman. Cenwulf's son Cynehelm (Kenelm) seems to have been an ealdorman, and Cuthred's two sons, Cynebert and Cenwald, were prominent witnesses in some of their father's charters. There were in addition during Cenwulf's reign four ealdormen with names whose first element was 'Ceol' who could also have been close relatives though they cannot be fitted into the family tree.[139] Other relatives held positions in the church. A kinsman called Cunred was abbot of St Augustine's, Canterbury (802-23) and Cenwulf's daughter Cwenthryth was abbess of Minster-in-Thanet, the richest of the Kentish royal nunneries.[140] The Kentish monastery of Reculver was also regarded as a possession of Cenwulf's family and the monastery of Glastonbury was assigned by Cenwulf to his son Cynehelm.[141] The recently conquered areas outside the main Mercian province were thus used as a means of enriching Cenwulf and his close relatives. The former kingdom of the Hwicce was also plundered and Cenwulf drew particularly on the shire of Winchcombe (Gloucs) which seems to have been the particular preserve of the Hwiccian royal house and so had only recently come into Mercian hands. Cenwulf set out to establish a major proprietary monastery for himself and his immediate heirs at Winchcombe, and obtained a papal privilege to secure his rights over it, which recalls Offa's attempts to safeguard his family monasteries.[142] When Cenwulf's son Cynehelm/ Kenelm was murdered, probably in 811, he was buried at Winchcombe and was honoured there as a saint.[143] On Cenwulf's death the rights over the monastery passed to his immediate heir his daughter Cwenthryth and from her they passed to her cousin Ælfflæd, the daughter of Ceolwulf. Ceolwulf II (874-?79) who was the last of the native Mercian kings to rule could also have been a member of Cenwulf's lineage.

There appear to be two other family groups who provided Mercian kings in the ninth century and who like the family of Cenwulf favoured alliterative names and assiduously promoted their kinsfolk when they had the opportunity. There were three rulers in the ninth century who had names beginning with 'B' – Beornwulf (823-26), Berhtwulf (840-52) and Burgred (852-74) – and although it cannot be proved that they were related it seems a likely possibility because of the alliteration not only of their names, but also of those of kinsmen who were prominent during their reign. During Beornwulf's reign Baldred who is likely to have been a kinsman ruled in Kent. Berhtwulf had a brother called Bynna and two sons called Berhtfrith and Berhtric.[144] Witnesses to charters of Burgred include two significant pairs of names, Berhtic and Beornwulf and Berhtfrith and Berhtric. Possibly Beornred who ruled briefly on Æthelbald's death belonged to the same family.

A third family who contested for the throne in the ninth century was that of Wiglaf (827-29 and 830-40). Wiglaf was the only member of the family to rule, but we learn of other members and their relationship with the 'B' group from the *Life of St Wigstan*.[145] The *Life* tells the story of the murder of prince

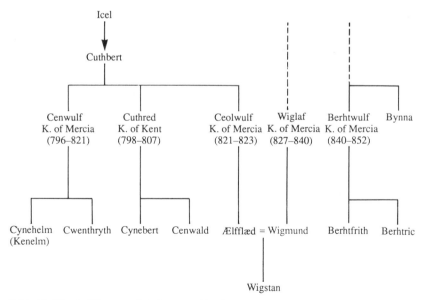

Table 14: The rival lineages of ninth-century Mercia

Wigstan in 849 during the reign of King Berhtwulf (840-52) who had succeeded Wigstan's grandfather Wiglaf as king of Mercia. Wigstan was the son
of Wigmund, son of Wiglaf, and Ælfflæd, the daughter of King Ceolwulf and
heiress of much of the family wealth in succession to her cousin Cwenthryth
(see Table 14). Ælfflæd was clearly a desirable match for any upwardly mobile
male of the royal house and when Wigmund died Berhtfrith, son of King
Berhtwulf, sought to marry her. Her son Wigstan opposed the marriage on the
grounds that Berhtfrith was his father's kinsman and his own godfather – but
presumably also because the marriage could weaken his own chances of becoming king of Mercia. Berhtfrith's response was to lure Wigstan to a meeting
and to kill him. The body of Wigstan was buried in the mausoleum of Wiglaf
at Repton – also the burial place of King Æthelbald and other princes of the
royal house – and a cult quickly developed around it. The remains of
Wigstan's shrine can still be seen in the crypt at Repton (see Fig. 10).[146]
Wigstan's family seem to have been quick to win what mileage they could from
the circumstances of his death to claim a family saint who could enhance the
claims of their lineage, in the same way that Cenwulf had promoted the cult of
the murdered Cynehelm at Winchcombe.

The family of Cenwulf is the only one for which a genealogy claiming royal
descent survives, but it is, of course, possible that the 'B' and 'Wig' families
were also collaterals of the royal house and the *Life of St Wigstan* claims that
the two families were related. It would not be surprising to find several royal
lineages in existence in the ninth century in view of the policy of Penda and his
sons of placing provinces which they conquered under the control of royal
kinsmen. A parallel could be found with Penda's son Merewalh who became a
subregulus of the Magonsæte and began to found a dynasty all of whose names
also began with 'M'. Merewalh's line seems to have died out in the early eighth
century, but there is no reason why other members of the royal house should
not have founded similar lines which lasted into the ninth century. We can in
fact find putative representatives for the 'B', 'C' and 'Wig' groups in the late
seventh century in the persons of Berhtwald, the nephew of King Æthelred,
Cenfrith, the *propinquus* of Æthelred, and Wigheard who has the title *subregulus* in the witness list of Frithuwold's Chertsey charter.[147]

In the eighth century most of the subkingdoms became ealdormanries and
although some of the families who had previously ruled subkingdoms probably
died out, like that of Merewalh, others could have continued with members
holding the lesser office of ealdorman. The witness lists of the charters of
Æthelbald and Offa contain numerous individuals among the ealdormen and
other attesting nobility with the name-elements 'Beorn', 'Berht', 'Cen', 'Ceol',
'Cuth' and 'Wig' which were used by the ninth-century kings and their relatives. Cenwulf's father Cuthbert may have been an ealdorman and Cenwulf,
Ceolwulf, Beornwulf, Ludeca and Burgred all appear in charters as ealdormen
before they became king.[148]

It is against this background of rivalry between different kin-groups that we
have to view the history of Mercia in the ninth century. There is a danger of

bringing down the curtain too soon on Mercia and of seeing the ninth century purely as a period of decline in contrast to the achievements of the eighth century. In fact, Cenwulf (796–821) who succeeded on the death of Egfrith was just as successful and as powerful as Offa. Offa's death and Egfrith's brief reign had given the kingdoms of Kent and the East Angles the opportunity to recover their independence, but it was shortlived. Eadwald of East Anglia only ruled for a very short time, judging from the number of his coins, and Cenwulf then regained control of the East Anglian mint and presumably of East Anglia itself.[149] In 798 Cenwulf recaptured Kent and the unfortunate native claimant, Eadbert Præn, had his eyes torn out and his hands cut off. Cenwulf received some support for his actions from the pope on the grounds that Eadbert was 'an apostate cleric'.[150] In 798 Cenwulf appointed his brother Cuthred as king in Kent, though on his death in 807 Cenwulf resumed direct control of the province.[151] Kings of the East Saxons sometimes appear in Cenwulf's charters though always acknowledging their inferiority to the Mercian ruler with the titles of *subregulus* or *dux*.[152] The exact relationship of Mercia and Wessex is hard to define. The Hwicce under their ealdormen lost an engagement with the men of Wiltshire in 802 when Egbert succeeded Beorhtric as king, but all Egbert's significant achievements came after Cenwulf's death. Like Offa Cenwulf dabbled in Northumbrian politics and was able to make a treaty with King Eardwulf.[153] Also like Offa, Cenwulf paid considerable attention to his western border and campaigned west of Offa's dyke. He was probably preparing another campaign against the Welsh when he died at Basingwerk in Flintshire in 821.[154]

Cenwulf therefore seems to have maintained the gains of Offa and to have enjoyed for nearly all of his reign command of the kingdoms of Kent and East Anglia of which Offa only acquired full control in the latter part of his reign. At the beginning of his reign Cenwulf seems to have been anxious to reconcile the Kentish province to Mercian rule; he provided the province with its own sub-king and restored lands to Canterbury which Offa had taken over as part of his own patrimony. He also agreed to the dismantling of the third bishopric which Offa had created at Lichfield and placed the Mercian province once again under the control of Canterbury, though he failed to persuade the pope to transfer the see from Canterbury to the Mercian city of London (which was where Pope Gregory had originally intended that it should be).[155] However, by the end of his reign Cenwulf's relations with the archbishop of Canterbury were as bad, if not worse, than Offa's had been, and for much the same reasons. Cenwulf, like Offa, claimed to be the heir of the Kentish kings and on these grounds took control of the royal monasteries of Reculver and Minster-in-Thanet. Archbishop Wulfred (805–32), who was anxious to reform his diocese on Carolingian lines, took a stand against lay ownership of religious houses and said that they should come under his jurisdiction. Matters became so bad that Cenwulf suspended Wulfred from office for the last years of his reign, and he was not restored until September 822 when Cenwulf's brother Ceolwulf was obliged to come to terms with the archbishop so that he could be anointed as king.[156]

Ceolwulf I (821-23) was thus left with a certain amount of unfinished business on his brother's death. He decisively completed Cenwulf's Welsh campaign and according to the *Annales Cambriae* brought the kingdom of Powys under his control.[157] As we have seen, Ceolwulf reached an accommodation with the archbishop of Canterbury and looked set fair to continue Mercian dominance in southern England when he was deposed, presumably by a coup in Mercia which brought Beornwulf (823-26) to the throne. Beornwulf won acceptance from Archbishop Wulfred by finding in favour of the archbishop in his disputes with Cwenthryth, the daughter and heir of Cenwulf, over the ownership of Kentish monasteries.[158] Baldred who ruled as king of Kent during Beornwulf's reign is probably best interpreted as a kinsman of Beornwulf who exercised the same kind of delegated authority that Cuthred had held under Cenwulf.[159] However, the success of the line was shortlived and the more powerful of the southern kingdoms took the opportunity of the new political changes in Mercia to reclaim their independence. Egbert of Wessex decisively defeated Beornwulf in battle at *Ellandun* near Wroughton (Wilts) in 825 and the West Saxons followed up the success by sending an army to Kent which expelled Baldred and ensured that Kent together with the South Saxons and Surrey passed from Mercian to West Saxon control. Essex may also have come under West Saxon control at the same time.[160] The East Anglians took the opportunity to regain their independence, chiefly recorded for us by the resumption of coinage in the names of native kings, and Beornwulf was killed when he invaded their province in 826.[161] His successor Ludeca (826-27), of whom little is known except that he had previously been an ealdorman, was also killed by the East Anglians.

The throne then passed to Wiglaf (827-40) whose reign falls into two parts. In 829 Egbert of Wessex expelled Wiglaf and attempted to rule as king of Mercia; the Worcester lists gives him a reign of one year, but Egbert's attempted takeover was premature[162] and Wiglaf was able to resume his reign. The West Saxons may have replaced the Mercians as rulers of the south-eastern provinces, but the Mercians under Wiglaf and his successor Berhtwulf (840-52) were secure in their control of their Midland heartlands and still held land south of the Thames in Berkshire.[163] In the west the Welsh were a perennial problem and Mercian resources were stretched further by increasingly severe Viking attacks.[164] The cumulative effect of these threats led the next Mercian king, Burgred (852-74) to reach an accommodation with Æthelwulf of Wessex which was sealed by Burgred's marriage to Æthelwulf's daughter Æthelswith. Part of the agreement between the two provinces was that Berkshire should become part of Wessex though it continued to be controlled by its Mercian ealdorman.[165] Possibly the area was settled on Æthelswith as part of her marriage settlement as she granted land in her own right in the shire.[166] The two kings issued a compatible coinage and campaigned together with some success against the Welsh.[167] However, as Burgred's reign progressed it became clear that the Mercian defences and army were not able to contain the increasingly powerful Viking armies which were able to winter in Nottingham in 868, London in 872 and Lindsey in 873 and had to be repeatedly bought off.[168] In 874 they wintered in Repton, the burial place of several Mercian kings and princes, and a place at the heart of Mercia. Burgred was expelled and sought refuge in Rome for the rest of his life.[169]

The Vikings were content with the eastern provinces of Mercia and the western half of Mercia, principally the diocese of Worcester, was entrusted to Ceolwulf II (874-79). The *Anglo-Saxon Chronicle* dismisses him as 'a foolish king's thegn', but his name suggests that he could have been a member of the lineage of Cenwulf and Ceolwulf. He is recorded as king in the Worcester regnal list and issued charters in western Mercia with the same authority as earlier Mercian rulers and issued a joint coinage with Alfred.[170] According to the Worcester list Ceolwulf was succeeded after five years by Æthelred whose origins are unknown. He seems to have closely associated himself with King Alfred of Wessex who by 879 was the only other ruler of Anglo-Saxon birth south of the Humber. In 886/7 Æthelred married Alfred's daughter Æthelflæd and in West Saxon sources appears as subordinate to Alfred.[171] Mercian sources suggest that Æthelred had rather more independence than the West Saxon sources wished to imply, but the variety of titles which he is given in his Mercian charters indicate some difficulty in defining his exact position which seems to have been less than fully regal but more than that of an ealdorman.[172] These difficulties in Mercian documents could suggest that Æthelred was not of royal birth. When Æthelred died in 911, his widow Æthelflæd administered the province with the title of 'Lady of the Mercians' and as commander of the Mercian army co-operated with her brother King Edward the Elder to win back the Mercian areas which had been conquered by the Danes.[173] Æthelflæd died in 918 and seems to have intended that her daughter Ælfwyn should occupy a similar position. But not long after Ælfwyn was, in the words of the B and C texts of the *Anglo-Saxon Chronicle*, 'deprived of all authority in Mercia and taken into Wessex' by her uncle, Edward the Elder.[174] From this time western Mercia was adminstered directly from Wessex, though the distinctiveness of Mercian laws and customs was recognized for some time to come.[175]

The conquest of Mercia by Wessex was not inevitable and it is unlikely that the West Saxons could have ended the independence of Mercia in the early years of the tenth century if it had not been for the Viking invasions. In spite of Egbert's year as king of Mercia, the West Saxons made little impact on the Mercian kingdom itself. The lands Wessex detached from Mercia had only come under Mercian control relatively recently. Kent, the South Saxons and the East Angles had been under direct Mercian rule for less than half a century, and the lands on both banks of the Thames had been disputed between Wessex and Mercia since the seventh century. The East Saxon province was still an independent kingdom in the ninth century when much of it was transferred to Wessex and not fully part of Mercia. The East Saxon kings had a tradition of long co-operation with the Mercian rulers and were still to be found in attendance at the Mercian court after Essex had apparently passed to the West Saxons.[176] These shifts in control of areas on the periphery of Mercia are not particularly remarkable given the nature of Anglo-Saxon over-lordship and, had the Vikings not intervened, the Mercians might well have spread south again. The disputes between the rival lineages of the Mercian royal house may have given the West Saxons their opening, but did not necessarily damage the authority of these rulers as kings of Mercia.

Nor should the ninth century be seen as a period of decline for the Mercian church or at least not for the bishopric of Worcester which is easily the best recorded of the Mercian dioceses. The bishops of Worcester were eventually able to lay claim to most of the proprietary minsters founded by the Hwiccian royal house, though, like the archbishops of Canterbury, the bishops had to defeat claims from the Mercian rulers. The desire of the rival lineages to receive official recognition seems to have given the bishops of Worcester, again like the archbishops of Canterbury, a powerful bargaining point.[177] The vitality of the church of Worcester at this time is demonstrated by the way Alfred turned to it to provide assistance in rejuvenating the West Saxon church.[178] The success of Alfred's ventures has tended to obscure the achievements of the church in western Mercia at a time when standards of literacy and culture had reached a low point south of the Thames.[179]

Conclusion: the evolution of the Mercian state

Mercian prosperity depended upon the successful conversion of a hegemony over a variety of Midland provinces in the seventh century into a unified kingdom in the eighth century. The seventh-century satellite provinces had a variety of origins and were governed by rulers of different status, some of whom were related to the seventh-century Mercian kings, while those who were not were bound to them in varying degrees of dependence. During the eighth century the satellite provinces, in the instances we can study them, ceased to be described as separate kingdoms and instead became ealdormanries of Mercia. Although we can trace the evolution of some provinces like that of the Magonsæte from subkingdom to ealdormanry, the shortage of charters from the Midlands and the confusion caused to earlier subgroupings by the Viking settlements and subsequent reorganization under a shire system by the West Saxon kings means that we have an imperfect knowledge of the evolution of most of the subdivisions in Mercia.[180] When a group called the Tomsæte appear in a ninth-century charter with their own ealdorman and with information that helps define their boundaries, it is usually assumed that the ninth-century Tomsæte represent an earlier subdivision within Mercia (perhaps even the original Mercian homelands) whose bounds had been carefully preserved over the intervening couple of centuries.[181] However, as we do not have any information on them before the ninth century, we cannot be certain that they really represent an original Mercian 'folkgroup'. The reality may have been more complex and we must allow for the possibility of administrative subdivisions being reorganized or created to meet changing needs and political circumstances. Areas like the Thames valley which were on the fringes of Mercia had a particularly complex history as overlordship might change from reign to reign and the earliest administrative arrangements are correspondingly hard to detect.[182] The boundaries of the province of the Hwicce, for which relatively good topographical evidence survives, do not seem to have been finally determined until the ninth century.[183]

One thing which did unite the different Mercian provinces was the rights which the Mercian kings could claim within them. As far as we can see these were considerable and the introduction of bookland does not seem to have caused the problems which it did in Northumbria. The claims the Mercian kings made on churchlands were notorious in the eighth century and led to a plea for moderation from Bishop Boniface and other missionary bishops. Although concessions were apparently made at the synod of Gumley, royal claims on monasteries were still substantial in the ninth century. Some idea of what Mercian rulers could demand is provided by the exemptions granted to the monastery of Breedon-on-the-Hill by King Berhtwulf in return for a considerable sum of money.[184] Without its exemption the monastery would have been required to house and feed a constant stream of royal officials and animals, including 'the royal hawks, huntsmen, horses, and their attendants', and even with the exemption they still had to put up overseas ambassadors and messengers from the kingdoms of Wessex and Northumbria. Similar demands were made in the Hwiccian province.[185] Any exemptions granted in the ninth century did not, of course, include remission from the three 'common burdens' of military service, upkeep of roads and bridges and fortresswork which were compulsory for the whole Mercian people.[186]

But although the Mercian kings could demand impressive rights and services they were dependent on delegating their authority to the ealdormen who controlled the different subdivisions of Mercia. The ealdormen appear in charters with increasing regularity from the middle of the eighth century. It is never entirely clear how many ealdormen were in existence at any one time as the number witnessing charters is erratic and presumably they were rarely all at the royal court together. As many as twelve *duces* can be found in charters of the ninth century, but, if later Wessex can provide a reliable guide, the numbers would not necessarily have remained constant. Frequently we can distinguish one among the ealdormen who seems to have been more important than the others in that he regularly witnesses before other ealdormen and may have a distinctive title. Such individuals may have been comparable to the Frankish mayors of the palace.[187] Æthelbald's brother Headbert seems to have filled this role at the end of Æthelbald's reign and the beginning of Offa's. In the 770s the *patricius* Brorda may have held a similar office and seems to have retained his position when Cenwulf came to power. His death in 799 was noted in the northern annals and he is probably to be identified with the recipient of a letter from Alcuin which speaks of his great influence at both the Mercian and Northumbrian courts and of the range of his temporal and ecclesiastical possessions.[188] Alcuin implies that the 'patrician' to whom he wrote was a person of considerable influence in Mercia, but the sources do not allow us to see how such individuals influenced events and policies within the Mercian kingdom.

The ealdormen were clearly powerful individuals. When the abbot of Breedon bought exemption from King Berhtwulf he also had to compensate the local ealdorman, Humbert *princeps* of the Tomsæte, who could normally exact his own dues from the monastery's estates.[189] The power of the ealdormen would have been all the greater if, as seems likely, a number of the ealdormen were collaterals of the royal house perhaps with hereditary claims to the ealdormanries of various provinces. Even Offa who tried hard to emulate the Carolingians and establish through such means as the coronation ceremony that his direct descendants were the only ones who could provide kings of the Mercians does not seem to have been able to suppress the claims of collaterals which would probably have surfaced even if Egfrith had not died so suddenly. Æthelbald and Offa enjoyed particularly long and successful reigns, but there are still signs in the eighth century, in the brief reign of Beornred and in Alcuin's hints of a purge by Offa of relatives, of the rivalry between different branches of the royal house which we can see clearly in the ninth century.

There appears to be a contrast between the successful expansion of Mercia south of the Thames in the reigns of Æthelbald, Offa and Cenwulf, which continued the work which Penda had begun, and the retraction of the ninth century. Although Æthelbald, Offa and Cenwulf employed means similar to those of the seventh-century rulers to convert previously independent kingdoms into Mercian provinces – the reduction in status of native rulers, the use of relatives as subkings, and the patronage of religious houses in subject provinces – the new conquests of the eighth century did not become permanent Mercian possessions. It is hard to say exactly why eighth-century colonization was less successful than that of the seventh century, but it would probably be a mistake to put all the blame on the ninth-century kings. Like Charlemagne Offa was superficially a very successful king who amassed great personal wealth, but there is reason to suspect that, like the Frankish king, he left a legacy of major problems to his successors. His determined conquest of Kent and the suppression of its royal house (and those of other kingdoms) contrasts with the apparently more gradual encroachment on the rights of native dynasties in the previous century. Offa's and Cenwulf's blatant annexing of Kentish and Hwiccian monasteries for the personal benefit of their families can hardly have endeared them to the native aristocracy and led to conflict with the bishops.

Although royal rights were successfully asserted in the eighth century, there may have been limits to the area Mercia could effectively control without some reorganization of its administrative system. The power of the ealdormen grew with that of the Mercian kings and although Offa and Cenwulf were able to maintain their authority the situation was an explosive one. As in eighth-century Northumbria rival lineages wanted a larger share in the power and the rewards which they were helping to create. By aggrandizing their own families Offa and Cenwulf created dangerous resentments among collaterals who were not enjoying the same advantages. Civil war in Mercia gave the West Saxon and East Anglian kings the opportunity to overthrow Mercian power, and the loss of revenues from the subject provinces would then have made it more difficult for one branch of the royal house to assert itself over its rivals in the way that Æthelbald and Offa had been able to do. The need to increase revenues may have led ninth-century kings to sell exemptions from royal services in return for ready cash which would have led to further problems for successor kings who found royal rights reduced. Mercian kingship was undoubtedly undergoing major changes in the ninth century which recall some of the problems of eighth-century Northumbria, but it is nevertheless hard to predict what would have happened if the Vikings had not intervened and drastically altered the process of evolution in the Mercian state.

Chapter Seven

THE WEST SAXONS

Sources
The most important historical source produced in Wessex itself is the *Anglo-Saxon Chronicle*. The earliest version of it that has survived 'appears to reflect an act of compilation and circulation of manuscripts round about the year 890'.[1] The *Chronicle's* annals stretch back to 60 BC, but the West Saxon entries begin with the arrival of Cerdic and Cynric in 495. The *Chronicle* compilers made use of a number of earlier West Saxon documents including genealogies, regnal lists and annals that would otherwise be lost to us. Their survival within the *Chronicle* is important, but the material is often difficult to evaluate because we only know it through the medium of a ninth-century text. The fifth- and sixth-century annals in particular should be treated circumspectly as there are various indications that they are imaginative constructs that do not accurately reflect what occurred in the West Saxons' prehistoric period.

It is usually accepted that contemporary annals began to be kept in Wessex at some point in the seventh century, and Stenton suggested that the *Chronicle* entry for 648 marked the beginning of a contemporary record of events.[2] Entries are reasonably regular from 648 until 757 when they become extremely sparse until the accession of Egbert (802). There is a limit to what can be deduced about the history of the West Saxon annals before their incorporation into the *Chronicle* and it must be appreciated that earlier annals could have been revised when the final text was produced. Material from other sources was added to the annals including entries from the recapitulary of events from Bede's *Ecclesiastical History*. A series of short genealogies for most of the seventh-century kings has also been included with the annals, though unfortunately we lack similar genealogical information for the majority of the rulers of the eighth century.

It should be noted that these short pedigrees are at variance with the genealogy of Ine in the Anglian collection which also forms the basis of an extended genealogy of Æthelwulf in the *Chronicle*.[3] There are also problems in reconciling material in the *Chronicle* with the genealogical and chronological information contained in another ninth-century work styled by David Dumville the West Saxon Genealogical Regnal List.[4] This work was probably compiled in the same circle which produced the *Chronicle*, but the history of their interrelationship is particularly complex and at the moment not fully understood. There seems to have been a substantial editing of regnal information in the ninth century which raises problems about the accuracy of the dates and pedigrees of the seventh-century West Saxon kings. The regnal dates given in this chapter follow David Dumville's reconstruction based on reconciling regnal years provided in the *Chronicle* and the Genealogical Regnal List (see Table 15), but it must be stressed that these dates do not have the same authority as, for instance, those provided for Northumbria by Bede and may in reality be in need of substantial modification. We reach a period of greater chronological reliability after the accession of Cædwalla.

There are various additional problems in establishing the exact text of the *Chronicle* of c. 890 for all the surviving versions are several removes from the original and contain many variant readings. Some of these variations are the result of miscopying and all the texts share a chronological dislocation for the eighth century which must have occurred at an early stage in the copying process.[5] The scribes of individual texts might also emend entries or provide additional information of varying historical value. The identification of the original readings is a complex matter and a major series of editions of the various manuscripts of the *Chronicle* is currently being undertaken under the general editorship of David Dumville and Simon Keynes.[6] When the work has been completed we will be in a much better position to establish a definitive version of the text as it stood in the early 890s.

The *Chronicle* is not the simple record of West Saxon history which it might at first sight appear. We do not know for certain who compiled it,[7] though more than one individual was involved and many historians would now accept the likelihood that the large-scale copying and circulation of manuscripts were initiated by King Alfred.[8] By 890 Alfred had begun his campaign to improve the literacy of the West Saxon people and to give them a clearer idea of their duties and responsibilities as a Christian people. Alfred must have known that further Viking attacks were likely and was anxious to motivate his people to continue fighting and to remain loyal to the West Saxon royal house. The *Chronicle's* record of past West Saxon successes under Alfred's predecessors could have helped serve this purpose.[9] There are other signs as well, particularly in the ninth-century entries, that the *Chronicle* was presented in a way which favoured Alfred. Little information is provided about the reigns of Alfred's three brothers who ruled before him in contrast with the full accounts of Alfred's successes against the Vikings. Also omitted is any mention of the rebellion which prevented Alfred's father Æthelwulf from resuming his position as king of the main province of Wessex on his return from Rome in 856; the last thing Alfred wanted was to remind the West Saxon people that such coups were possible. We know something of what happened in 856 from the biography of King Alfred by the Welsh ecclesiastic, Asser, whose work is an invaluable source for ninth-century Wessex.[10] Asser may have written for a Welsh rather than a West Saxon audience, but the biography was never widely circulated and may not even be complete in the form in which it is known to us.[11]

The existence of the *Anglo-Saxon Chronicle* does not lessen the importance of references to West Saxon history in sources that were produced outside Wessex, and it is when we have the opportunity to correlate different accounts that we are most likely to reach a rounded view of West Saxon history. Bede's information is particularly important and was, of course, written some 150 years before the compilation of the *Chronicle*. Bede's main West Saxon informant was Bishop Daniel of Winchester who provided Bede with a particularly full account of Cædwalla's conquest of the Jutish and South Saxon provinces.[12] Bede was principally interested in these events as they led to the permanent Christianization of Wessex and its newly conquered areas, but in relating them he throws light on many aspects of the West Saxon past and his account is one of the main reasons for questioning the picture of the origins of Wessex provided in the *Chronicle*.[13] Bishop Wilfrid of Northumbria was in Sussex at the time of Cædwalla's conquest and Stephanus' *Life* provides a third version of events during his reign.[14]

Important administrative records also survive for Wessex. The greatest range is from the reign of Alfred and includes such items as his will, the text of his treaty with the Danish leader Guthrum and the Burghal Hidage which lists the burhs or fortified centres in Wessex.[15] Lawcodes of Ine and Alfred survive, though those of Ine are only known as an appendix to the laws of Alfred and may therefore have been edited and adapted to suit conditions of the ninth century.[16] The early charters of Wessex have for some time been regarded with considerable suspicion as some, especially for lands belonging to the bishop of Winchester, are undoubtedly forgeries of the tenth century or later.[17] However, recent studies have demonstrated that a body of reliable West Saxon charters does exist from some West Saxon monasteries, the most substantial early archives to survive being those of Glastonbury and Malmesbury.[18]

The most significant scholar of the early West Saxon church was Aldhelm, abbot of Malmesbury and bishop of Sherborne (705-9/10) who has left a corpus of prose and verse writings which throw some light on the early ecclesiastical history of the province.[19] The other notable West Saxon ecclesiastic of the eighth century was Bishop Boniface whose main work was in Europe.[20] West Saxon religious are included among the correspondents of his surviving letters, and considerable numbers of West Saxon men and women went to work with him in Germany.[21] The only *Lives* of West Saxon saints are for people who worked as missionaries overseas and, apart from the *Life* of Lioba which describes her early years in the double monastery of Wimborne, they throw little light on the history of Wessex.[22]

The origins of Wessex

Although, unlike many of the Anglo-Saxon peoples, the West Saxons have left a written account of the origin of their kingdom, the interpretation of that account is far from straightforward and has been the subject of much scholarly debate. According to the *Chronicle* the founders of the West Saxon kingdom were Cerdic and his son Cynric who arrived, apparently in southern Hampshire, in 495 and subsequently conquered the Isle of Wight. Historians have been suspicious for some time of the account with its many legendary elements and repetitive entries, but not surprisingly there has been a reluctance to abandon altogether the only written account of the foundation of the West Saxon kingdom.[23] However, as more work is done, so the *Chronicle* version of events becomes increasingly suspect and can be shown to conflict with other sources of information.[24] Almost the only point which is not at variance within these sources is the claim that Cerdic was the founder of the West Saxon dynasty. Even the kings who lack a genealogy in the *Chronicle* are said to be able to trace their descent back to him in the Genealogical Regnal List. However, not all sources agree that Cynric was his son, for in the earliest recorded version of the West Saxon genealogy in the Anglian collection Cynric is given as the son of Creoda the son of Cerdic. Creoda is not mentioned at all in the annalistic version of the origins of Wessex or in the short genealogies included in the *Chronicle*.[25]

The duplication of a number of the entries for Cerdic and Cynric 19 years apart has cast doubt on the validity of 495 as a date for the beginning of Cerdic and Cynric's conquest of Wessex.[26] David Dumville's detailed study of the regnal dates given in the *Chronicle* and in the closely related West Saxon Genealogical Regnal List reached the conclusion that the fifth- and sixth-century dates were extremely unreliable and had been artificially extended to make it appear that the kingdom was founded at an earlier date than was actually the case. His calculation on the basis of the reign-lengths given in the Genealogical Regnal List was that Cerdic's reign was originally seen as beginning in 538, with the arrival of Cerdic and Cynric in 532.[27]

A further problem with the *Chronicle's* account of the origins of Wessex is that it seems to locate the origins of the kingdom in southern Hampshire and the Isle of Wight, though unfortunately not all the place-names it cites can be identified. Bede, on the basis of information supplied to him by Bishop Daniel, indicates that southern Hampshire and the Isle of Wight were independent provinces which did not become part of Wessex until after their conquest by King Cædwalla in 686-8. A number of sources, including Bede and place-name evidence, affirm that the people of southern Hampshire and the Isle of Wight were classed as Jutes and not as Saxons.[28] It seems impossible to place the origins of the kingdom of Wessex in these Jutish provinces.

Attempts have been made to use archaeology to help locate the origins of Wessex and chart its expansion, but there is a danger that arguments based on archaeological evidence will become circular, for archaeologists have frequently relied upon the framework of events in the *Chronicle* to provide a historical context for their sites and a *terminus post quem* for the dating of artefacts.[29] It is also the case that in the present state of knowledge it is impossible to distinguish archaeologically between a West Saxon and any other sort of Saxon. The discovery of sixth- or early-seventh-century artefacts in an area of southern England which was West Saxon by the end of the seventh century is no guarantee that those first Germanic settlers were serving under a West Saxon flag. The history of south-east Wiltshire provides a case in point.

There was undoubtedly sixth-century settlement in Wiltshire centred in particular on the Avon valley. Richer than average burials have been discovered in the Salisbury area, perhaps implying that it was a centre of 'princely' power.[30] But were these early settlers West Saxons either by descent or allegiance? The *Chronicle* attributes various victories in the lower reaches of the Avon to Cerdic and Cynric, but the chronology is certainly wrong, the source of information unknown and other Cerdic and Cynric entries suspect. Although there was 'Saxon' settlement in the sixth century in the Salisbury area and the Avon valley, we are not able to say when it was first controlled by West Saxons, though the area was part of Wessex by the beginning of Cædwalla's reign for Bede describes the western boundary of Jutish Hampshire (i.e. the western edge of the New Forest) as bordering West Saxon territory in 686.[31]

We can no longer speak as confidently of the origins of Wessex as historians once felt able to do, but the area which has the best claim to have been the original homeland of the West Saxons is the upper Thames valley. This is the area in which Ceawlin, son of Cynric, is shown operating in the *Chronicle*. The Ceawlin entries do not suffer from the same problems of credibility which affect the Cerdic and Cynric annals, although they do seem to have been subject to some chronological distortion and are not without difficulties in interpretation.[32] The Ceawlin annals contain more convincing circumstantial details than those for Cerdic and Cynric and, it has been suggested, could derive from an oral poetic source.[33] The upper Thames valley was a centre of Saxon settlement from early in the fifth century. The presence of 'princely' burials dating to the late sixth century and other finds of prestige or 'exotic' goods is compatible with the upper Thames being the powerbase of an emergent kingdom.[34] Further support comes from the fact that when King Cynegils was converted to Christianity in 635 Dorchester-on-Thames was chosen as the site of the first West Saxon see.[35]

Critical analysis of the accounts of the origins of Wessex suggest that Cerdic the founder of the West Saxon dynasty was establishing his position in the 530s, probably in the upper Thames valley. Little more that is reliable can be said until the reign of Ceawlin which we shall look at more closely in a moment. Before leaving this section it should be observed that although for convenience we have been referring to Cerdic's people as the West Saxons they in fact seem to have been known as the 'Geuissae' until after the reign of Cædwalla when the term 'West Saxon' begins to appear.[36]

The growth of Wessex to 802

There are two apparent high points within this period in which West Saxon rulers exercised considerable authority outside their own borders: the first was the reign of Ceawlin (late 6th cent.) and the second was during the reigns of Cædwalla (685-88) and Ine (688-726). Ceawlin appears between Ælle of the South Saxons and Æthelbert of Kent as the second overlord of the southern kingdoms in the *Ecclesiastical History*'s list.[37] In the *Chronicle* Ceawlin is depicted as defeating Æthelbert in battle in 568, but the *Chronicle* is principally

Cerdic 538–554

Cynric 554–581

Ceawlin 581–588

Ceol 588–594

Ceolwulf 594–611

Cynegils 611–642

Cenwalh 642–673

Seaxburh 673–674

Æscwine 674–676

Centwine 676–685/6

Cædwalla 685/6–688

Ine 688–726

Æthelheard 726–740

Cuthred 740–756

Sigebert 756–757

Cynewulf 757–786

Beorhtric 786–802

Egbert 802–839

Æthelwulf 839–855(8)

Æthelbald 855–860

Æthelbert 860–866

Æthelred 866–871

Alfred 871–899

The table contains only the names of rulers who appear in the main West Saxon regnal lists and shows the revised West Saxon dates proposed in Dumville 1985. Although these dates seem to have been in circulation in Wessex in the ninth century, it must be stressed that regnal dates before the reign of Cædwalla cannot be fixed with any certainty and are best seen as approximations rather than absolute dates. The reign of Ceawlin is particularly problematical. The length of his reign is given variously in the West Saxon Genealogical Regnal List as '7' and '17' years and it is not clear which was the original reading. Dumville favours '7' which is followed here, but '17' could also be correct. The period between the death of Cenwalh and accession of Cædwalla is also one for which the chronology is particularly confused and there is reason to believe that the regnal list entries for the period represent a simplification of a more complex situation (see pp.145–6).

Table 15: Regnal list of the rulers of the West Saxons

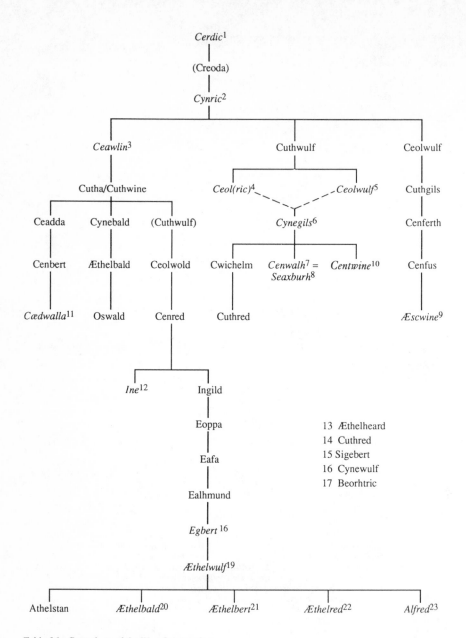

Table 16: Genealogy of the West Saxon rulers

The table is based on the short pedigrees in the *Anglo-Saxon Chronicle* with variant readings in the genealogy of Ine in the Anglian collection shown in brackets. Those who appear as rulers in the West Saxon Genealogical Regnal List are in italics and numbered in order of ruling (kings nos. 13–17 cannot be placed in the genealogy).

concerned with victories against the British. In 571 after the battle of *Biedcanford* against unidentified British Cuthwulf, who was probably Ceawlin's brother, is said to have captured Limbury, Aylesbury, Bensington and Eynsham, and in 577 Ceawlin himself is said to have defeated and killed the kings Conmail, Condidan and Fairnmail at the battle of Dyrham and to have taken Gloucester, Cirencester and Bath; the *Chronicle* writer presumably intended it to be understood that in capturing these seven important central places the West Saxons were also taking control of the areas dependent upon them.[38] It is difficult to say without knowing the exact source of the *Chronicle*'s material how reliable the information about Ceawlin's conquests is.[39] Certainly the dating of events is suspect for the West Saxon Genealogical Regnal List allotted Ceawlin a reign of either 7 or 17 years (unfortunately it is not clear which reading is correct) as opposed to the 31 or 32 years in the *Chronicle* annals.[40] Ceawlin was a direct ancestor of Alfred and his line and so there could have been reasons in the ninth century for enhancing his achievements. It seems unwise in the light of these and other uncertainties to try to construct a detailed narrative of Ceawlin's reign upon the basis of the *Chronicle* account. We must settle instead for a generalized picture of an energetic leader who sought to expand his power in all directions from his upper Thames base and who succeeded, on the testimony of the *Ecclesiastical History* list, in exacting tribute from some of the kingdoms already established in southern England.

According to the *Chronicle* Ceawlin's reign was ended in 591 by Ceol; he was the son of Ceawlin's brother Cutha (probably the Cuthwulf who fought the battle of *Biedcanford* in 571), and the throne was to remain with descendants of Cutha until 673 (see Table 16). Ceol was succeeded by his brother Ceolwulf (d. 611). The next king, Cynegils (611-42), was apparently the son of either Ceol or Ceolwulf (it is not clear which) and he was succeeded by his son Cenwalh (642-73). According to the *Chronicle*, Cenwalh's widow Seaxburh attempted to hold the throne for about a year (673-4), but was replaced by Æscwine (674-6) who was apparently descended from a second brother of Ceawlin.[41] The accession of Centwine, son of King Cynegils (676-85), saw the return of the house of Cutha. The *Chronicle* gives a hazy picture of the growth of Wessex in the period up to Cædwalla's accession. Ceolwulf, for instance, is said to have 'continually fought and contended either against the English or the Britons, or the Picts, or the Scots'.[42] It is unlikely that Ceolwulf ever met a Pict or a Scot. Various battles are recorded, but these entries are extremely uninformative and give no idea about the circumstances in which the battles took place. Location, opponents and outcome may be given, but rarely all three together, and many key place-names cannot be identified with certainty.[43] Several possible candidates exist for the sites of the battles of *Beandun* (614), *Peonnan* (658) and *Posentesbyrig* (661). It is frequently assumed that the battles mark victories in the West Saxons' westward expansion against the British, but, if the better recorded Northumbrian battles are any guide, the battles which were most memorable to the early Anglo-Saxons might include great disasters as well as great victories and be fought some distance from securely held territory. We do not know on what basis battles were recorded in the annals and we presumably have only a selection of the major engagements which occurred. For instance, Aldhelm states that King Centwine fought and won three major battles,[44] but all that is recorded in the *Chronicle* is that in 682 'Centwine put the Britons to flight as far as the sea'.

The places which can be identified where the West Saxon rulers fought battles in the seventh century are concentrated in north Wiltshire, north Somerset and southern Gloucestershire and the interest of the *Chronicle* annals seems to have been focused on this area. Sometimes the opponents were British, but many of the recorded engagements were with the Mercians who were actively expanding in all directions in the seventh century. Competition with the Mercians seems to have loomed large in West Saxon affairs and influenced West Saxon relations with other kingdoms, in so far as we can study these. In 628 Cynegils and Penda fought over control of Cirencester. Evidence from burials shows 'Saxon' settlement in south-eastern Gloucestershire which was incorporated into the Mercian satellite kingdom of the Hwicce.[45] The opposition from Penda probably encouraged the West Saxons to seek an alliance with Northumbria which was also suffering from Mercian expansion, and this was sealed by Oswald's sponsorship of Cynegils' baptism in 635 and a marriage between Oswald and a daughter of Cynegils.[46] Cynegils' son and successor Cenwalh (acc. 642) remained a pagan and was married to a sister of Penda whom he soon repudiated. Penda responded by turning him out of his kingdom and Cenwalh was forced to seek refuge with another leading opponent of Penda, King Anna of the East Angles. Cenwalh regained the throne in 648 and no further clashes with Penda are recorded. But in 661 Penda's son Wulfhere ravaged Ashdown, right in the heart of the West Saxon homelands, and it was at about the same time that a new West Saxon see was established at Winchester.[47] Bede has an unlikely story of Cenwalh growing tired of the Frankish speech of his bishop based at Dorchester-on-Thames and so deciding to divide his see, but a major factor must have been the fact that by the 660s Dorchester was dangerously close to the southern border of outer Mercia.[48] In fact, the whole length of the West Saxon's northern border was threatened by Mercian expansion and control of north Wiltshire and Somerset was frequently contested. In the early years of King Æthelred of Mercia's reign, his nephew Berhtwald commanded a province in this border area.[49] The abbey of Malmesbury seems to have lain within the disputed border area and was patronized by both sides.[50] The Mercians must also have prevented West Saxon expansion to the east when peoples such as the Chilternsæte came under their control.

The rise of Mercia must have altered the pattern of West Saxon development which had been established under Ceawlin and helped to concentrate West Saxon interests to the south and west of their original territory. The details of West Saxon expansion are imperfectly recorded in the narrative sources though some successes in British territory in north Wiltshire and Somerset can be identified in the *Chronicle* annals. We receive no guidance about exactly when and how north Hampshire, southern Wiltshire, Dorset and eastern Devon came under West Saxon control, but it would appear that their initial conquest at least had been achieved by the beginning of Cædwalla's reign. The confirming evidence comes partly from indications in the *Ecclesiastical History* of the extent of Wessex at the time of Cædwalla's accession,[51] and partly from evidence for West Saxon patronage of British monasteries. Cenwalh (642-73) was remembered as the first Saxon benefactor of Sherborne (Dorset) and Centwine (676-85) as that of Glastonbury (Somerset).[52] The West Saxons must have been in control of the Exeter area by about 680 as the young Boniface received his education in a monastery in Exeter at about that time.[53] The very large assessment for Wessex of 100,000 hides in the Tribal Hidage would imply, if it was genuine, that Wessex was a very large kingdom by the late seventh century, but the figure may well be a later emendation to reflect Wessex's subsequent success.[54] However we have already seen from study of Mercia and Northumbria that dramatic expansion could be rapidly achieved once the bandwagon of military success started to roll. With Wessex we can see that such expansion did occur, but the sources are not sufficient to provide a proper narrative or chronology of the progress of the conquest.

However, the expansion of Wessex under Cædwalla is relatively well recorded. Cædwalla was a descendant of Ceawlin and was sent into exile from Wessex early in the 680s.[55] His response was to gather an army and invade the kingdom of the South Saxons, killing their king in the process. His control of the South Saxon province was short-lived, but the experience and the forces he gathered together seem to have helped him gain the West Saxon throne in 685 when Centwine abdicated to retire to a monastery.[56] Within a couple of years Cædwalla had taken control of all the other provinces south of the Thames and established himself as ruler of the South Saxons, Surrey, and the Jutish provinces in Hampshire and the Isle of Wight.[57] He made his brother Mul king of Kent, but Mul was burnt to death by the men of Kent in 687.[58] Bede does not seek to hide the brutality which accompanied Cædwalla's conquests; the males of the royal house of Wight were hounded and put to death, and the subject provinces ravaged and made to pay a crippling tribute. What is rather more surprising is to read that Cædwalla voluntarily abdicated after a reign of less than three years in order to be baptized in Rome.[59] One may detect the influence of Bishop Wilfrid here who had been at the South Saxon court when Cædwalla had invaded and had profitably transferred his allegiance to Cædwalla. It may also have been the case that when Cædwalla abdicated he knew he did not have long to live; Bede refers to a serious wound he received during the conquest of the Isle of Wight and Cædwalla died, soon after his baptism in Rome, on 20 April 689.[60]

Cædwalla's reign may have been short, but it was significant. Previously West Saxon expansion had been in the south-west and chiefly at the expense of British rulers. Cædwalla turned attention eastwards and in the process gained control of long-established Germanic kingdoms. These south-eastern areas had probably recognized the overlordship of Ceawlin, but, as far as we know, had not otherwise been a West Saxon target though plans may have begun shortly before Cædwalla's time to conquer the Jutish province in Hampshire. The transfer of the see to Winchester in the 660s suggests an interest in the land to its south (for Winchester lay close to the northern border of the Hampshire Jutes) and the more westerly parts of the Jutish province may even have been in West Saxon hands by the beginning of Cædwalla's reign.[61] Although Cædwalla's victories helped increase the size and wealth of Wessex, the conquest of the Jutes was also important for defensive reasons. In about 661 Wulfhere of Mercia had used his power as military overlord to place the Isle of Wight and the eastern parts of Hampshire under the overlordship of his ally the South Saxon king.[62] Such a move must have seemed threatening to Wessex which had already lost territory in the north to the Mercians. Wulfhere's action helps explain Cædwalla's interest in provinces to the east of Wessex and his harshness towards them – though such behaviour was probably par for the course at times of conquest. It is from the time of Cædwalla that his people came to be known as the 'Saxons' or the 'West Saxons' instead of the earlier 'Geuissae'.[63] The change of name may reflect the fact that the West Saxon rulers now controlled other Anglo-Saxon peoples besides the Geuissae.

Cædwalla's successes were consolidated by his successor Ine (688–726) who was also a descendant of Ceawlin.[64] Ine lost control of Kent, but received appropriate compensation for the murder of Mul.[65] He was successful in retaining control of the South Saxons whom he ruled through the subking Nothhelm.[66] Ine is recorded at various times fighting with Ceolred of Mercia, with Geraint, the British king of Dumnonia, and with the East Saxons (presumably over control of Surrey).[67] However, for the most part Ine maintained his borders and consolidated earlier successes within them. Although the vagaries of survival of evidence may be deceptive, what we have suggests that Ine played an important part in developing the powers of West Saxon kingship. Ine's is the only West Saxon lawcode of which we know besides Alfred's.[68] Like all early Anglo-Saxon lawcodes Ine's seems to be so haphazardly arranged that it is hard to imagine it of being of any practical use in the form in which it is presented.[69] Nevertheless it is an important indicator of the duties expected of a West Saxon king at this time and provides invaluable insights into many areas of West Saxon society. Perhaps one of its most interesting aspects is the way it legislates for all Ine's subjects – the British as well as the Anglo-Saxon. Care is taken to equate British and Anglo-Saxon social classes and, although the British are treated less favourably than Anglo-Saxons in some respects, on the whole the laws would not hinder the integration of British and Anglo-Saxon society. The laws imply that such integration had not yet occurred within Wessex, or at least in parts of Wessex, and studies of place-names, estates and their boundaries, religious communities, and archaeological material suggest that the more westerly parts of Wessex housed relatively few settlers of Germanic origin by the end of the seventh century.[70] It is possible that control of British areas was helped by intermarriage between the families of West Saxon and British leaders. Cædwalla's name is an anglicized version of the British name Cadwallon and the element *walh* (as in Cenwalh) also points to a British connection. What is perhaps most surprising is that the name of the putative founder of the West Saxon royal house, Cerdic, is also an anglicized version of a British name.[71]

The laws of Ine also indicate that although the West Saxons were nominally Christian, many Christian practices such as infant baptism and the payment of tithes had yet to become widely established. The slow progress of Christianization revealed in the laws is not surprising. Cynegils, the first of the West Saxon rulers to be baptized, was not converted until 635. His successor Cenwalh was a pagan at the time of his accession and even after his conversion dispensed with the services of a bishop for part of his reign; there was further disruption in the 660s with the removal of the see to Winchester. Cædwalla had apparently not been baptized by the time of his accession, though, under the guidance of Bishop Wilfrid, he seems to have been assiduous in setting up a proper church structure in Surrey and the Jutish provinces.[72] Both through the laws and by other means such as the holding of synods and extensive patronage of monasteries, Ine continued the development of Christian rulership among the West Saxons.[73] The topic is also relevant to the question of integration of the British subjects, for the Britons of the west country were Christians long before the conversion of the West Saxons.[74] Two at least of the main recipients of West Saxon patronage, Glastonbury and Sherborne, seem to have been in origin British foundations.[75] In 705 a new diocese was created based on Sherborne for Wessex 'west of Selwood', that is for the predominately Celtic area of Wessex.[76] Aldhelm, abbot of Malmesbury and probably a member of the royal house, was its first bishop. Ine was also patron of Bradfield in Berkshire in the former West Saxon homelands[77] and the first West Saxon nunneries were founded during his reign by his sister Cuthburh (at Wimborne) and his kinswoman Bugga, daughter of King Centwine.[78]

Further insight into Ine's capabilities as king come from the excavations of the Middle Saxon trading settlement of Hamwic on the Southampton peninsula.[79] A body of archaeological evidence points to Ine's reign as the most likely time for the settlement to have been founded. It is easily the largest and most densely occupied settlement known from Middle Saxon England and Hamwic's population has been estimated as upwards of 5000 people at a time when few rural settlements are likely to have contained more than 50 people. Regular building plots were laid out along a grid of gravelled streets that were relaid at regular intervals (see Fig. 7). The inhabitants were engaged in specialist craft activities, including bone-working, cloth-making, smithying, metalworking and glassworking. Finds of imported goods such as pottery, quernstones and whetstones point to overseas trade taking place and this may well have been the raison d'être for the settlement. A concentration of finds of sceattas, including Frisian sceattas and types 39 and 49 which may have been minted in Hamwic, helps support this conclusion (see Fig. 14.2).[80] Hamwic was ideally situated for trade with similar Frankish bases such as Quentovic and the desire to take control of the Solent so that a trading base could be established may have helped fuel the resolve of the

West Saxons to conquer the Jutish provinces. Although there are no written sources to explain the circumstances of Hamwic's foundation it is surely correct to see it as a royal foundation. In West Saxon society of the late seventh century no one but the king could mobilize such a large group of people and arrange the complicated business of feeding and housing them. By trading agricultural surpluses and finished items such as cloth the king could acquire bullion from overseas and other essential raw materials and exotic items which his followers would expect to receive as royal gifts.[81] The Kentish kings had at one time held a virtual monopoly of such items and the establishment of Hamwic, like Ine's lawcode, shows the ability of the West Saxons in this period to benefit from what they had learnt of other kingdoms.

In contrast to the variety of sources surviving from the reign of Ine, the reigns of the other West Saxon kings who ruled in the eighth century are poorly recorded. Ine's successors, Æthelheard (726-40), Cuthred (740-56), Sigebert (756-7), Cynewulf (757-86) and Beorhtric (786-802), are all said to be descendants of Cerdic, but no more precise genealogical information has survived. The *Chronicle* pays particular attention to disputes within the royal house in the eighth century, though in fairness one must add that this was just as much a feature of Ine's reign as those of his successors. One of these interfamily feuds is described in a notable passage included under the entry for the year 757. This long piece does not seem to have been the work of the *Chronicle* compiler and must have been composed independently.[82] The entry describes the feud between King Cynewulf and Cyneheard, the brother of King Sigebert whom Cynewulf had deposed in order to take the throne. In 786 Cynewulf determined to get rid of Cyneheard as well, but before this could be achieved Cyneheard caught the king unawares when he was visiting a mistress and slew him. The king's thegns gallantly rushed to avenge him, spurning attempts by Cyneheard to buy them off, and were slain as well. The next day more of Cynewulf's entourage arrived and proved equally unwilling to come to terms with Cyneheard. On hearing that various of their kinsmen were supporting Cyneheard they replied 'that no kinsman was dearer to them than their lord, and they would never serve his slayer'. More fighting ensued and Cynewulf's loyal thegns had their revenge. The passage has clearly been composed in line with the conventions of the heroic code of behaviour, but is to be valued as one of the few detailed accounts of feuding between rival branches of a royal house.

None of the other eighth-century kings was as powerful as Ine, but before we rush to declare Wessex in a state of decline after Ine's death we must remember the strength of the opposition. Æthelheard and his successors had to contend with the Mercian expansion under Æthelbald and Offa. Æthelheard lost control of the South Saxons and part at least of Somerset and Wiltshire to the Mercians.[83] However, his successor Cuthred is said in the *Chronicle* 'to have fought stoutly against King Æthelbald' and defeated him in 752, and seems to have regained control of north Somerset and north Wiltshire even before this date.[84] The border between Wessex and Mercia was also hotly disputed by Cynewulf and Offa, with Cynewulf apparently having the upper hand at the beginning of his reign, but losing ground to Offa in Berkshire, north Wiltshire and the Bath area after he was defeated by Offa at Bensington in 779.[85] However, Cynewulf remained an independent ruler and when the papal envoys attended a synod for the diocese of Canterbury in 786 it met under the aegis of both Offa and Cynewulf.[86] Cynewulf may have produced a revised sceatta coinage analogous to that of Eadbert of Northumbria and restored the fortunes of Hamwic which seems to have suffered a recession around the middle of the eighth century perhaps because of Mercian competition.[87]

After Cynewulf was killed in 786 Offa was able to increase his control over Wessex. The new king Beorhtric either came to the throne with Offa's help or came under Offa's influence soon afterwards. In 789 he married Offa's daughter Eadburh about whom Asser heard barbed stories from King Alfred.[88] Offa helped Beorhtric to exile various troublemakers, such as the future king Egbert,[89] and may have influenced some administrative developments in Wessex. The first exemption clauses in charters of a type already known in Mercia and the first silver pennies in imitation of the Mercian coins appear in Beorhtric's reign though few examples of either are known.[90] Beorhtric apparently continued the Mercian alliance after Offa's death when Egfrith may have needed his brother-in-law's support. Beorhtric was able to persuade Egfrith to return estates which Offa had confiscated from Malmesbury, although he apparently agreed that Glastonbury could come under the control of Cynehelm of Mercia.[91]

Expansion westwards at the expense of the British continued, but the British of Cornwall seem to have resisted the West Saxon advance. Æthelbald of Mercia and Cuthred of Wessex fought together against the British in 743, though it is not clear which particular group of British is meant. A chance reference in a charter from Cynewulf to the minster of Wells refers to harassment from 'our enemies' the men of Cornwall, and the *Chronicle* records that Cynewulf 'often fought with great battles against the British'.[92] The eighth-century kings like their predecessors were also patrons of religious communities and can in particular be seen supporting foundations in the Sherborne diocese.[93] The missions to the pagan Continental Germans received substantial support and personnel from Wessex during the eighth century, and the letters to and from Boniface suggest a thriving West Saxon church.[94]

It is tempting to see lack of sources as indicating a decline in Wessex within the eighth century, but although Wessex must frequently have had to recognize Mercian overlordship its survival as an independent kingdom never seems to have been seriously in doubt. The preoccupations of the eighth-century kings seem to have been remarkably similar to those of their seventh-century predecessors and no reduction in the effectiveness of royal power can be identified. The real work of the eighth century must have been the consolidation of seventh-century gains in Hampshire, the Isle of Wight and the southwest, though this is something which we cannot study in detail. However, the large-scale replacement of British place-names by English in Devon, Dorset and Somerset gives some indication of the dominance eventually achieved by the Anglo-Saxons.[95]

The pattern of West Saxon kingship to 802

From the surviving sources it is possible to draw various general conclusions about the practice of kingship within Wessex. Although there are problems in reconciling the various West Saxon pedigrees, and one may be unwise to take them at face value, they imply the existence of rival lineages within the royal house. Three major subgroupings emerge from the genealogies as given within the *Chronicle* annals (Table 16):

(1) the descendants of Cutha/Cuthwulf (brother of Ceawlin) who include all the rulers in the regnal list between Ceol and Cenwalh (d. 673), and also King Centwine (676-85).

(2) the descendants of Ceolwulf (brother of Ceawlin) of whom the only one named in the regnal lists is Æscwine (674-76).

(3) the descendants of Ceawlin who include Cædwalla (685-88) and Ine (688-726), as well as King Egbert (802-39) and his descendants.

No genealogical information survives for the kings who ruled between Ine and Egbert, but the *Chronicle* gives a clear impression of continuing rivalry between different interest groups and the Genealogical Regnal List claims that all were descendants of Cerdic. The last pedigree to be provided in the *Chronicle* is that of Oswald ætheling who unsuccessfully contested the throne with Æthelheard on Ine's death.[96] Like Ine, Oswald was a descendant of Ceawlin, from which one might perhaps deduce that Æthelheard represented a different factional interest. It is possible that the descendants of Ceawlin did not provide another successful candidate until the accession of Egbert in 802 and that all the rulers of the eighth century were from other branches of the royal house. The fact that Cynewulf was buried in Winchester, which was not yet established as the premier place of burial of the West Saxon line, and that several of the other eighth-century kings are known to have been buried elsewhere, could suggest that Cynewulf was a descendant of Cenwalh who founded the Winchester Old Minster, but such evidence cannot be pushed too far.[97]

The genealogical information implies that any adult male who could claim descent from Cerdic was eligible for the West Saxon throne; eligible candidates are referred to as æthelings in the *Chronicle*.[98] However, the discrepancies between the genealogies have led some historians to question whether all the West Saxon rulers were really members of the same royal house sharing a common ancestor.[99] The greatest problems are caused by the genealogy of Ine in the Anglian collection which was subsequently adapted for the genealogy of Æthelwulf given under the year 855 in the *Chronicle*.[100] These versions differ from the short genealogy of Ine given in the *Chronicle* by the inclusion of two extra names (Creoda and Cuthwulf) which would make Ine two generations younger than Cædwalla, whom he succeeded, and Oswald, who tried to take the throne on Ine's death (Table 16). The longer version of Ine's genealogy is the only source to refer to Creoda as a son of Cerdic and father of Cynric; elsewhere in the *Chronicle* Cerdic is Cynric's son. Such problems have led to a suspicion that Ceawlin and his line may not have been Cerdicings at all and that the discrepancies may have arisen from trying to unite the pedigrees of disparate lineages. Certainly there has been, as we have already seen, a substantial rewriting of the West Saxon history of the sixth century and the *Chronicle* entries for Cerdic and Cynric seem to be largely fictitious. It would not be surprising in light of this to find discrepancies between pedigrees written or edited at different times. It cannot be proved that the *Chronicle*'s claim that all those who ruled in Wessex were members of the same royal house and descended from a common ancestor is correct, but equally we have no positive evidence to disprove it. In support could be cited the remarkable consistency in nomenclature displayed by the early members of the royal house. It is not until the last decades of the seventh century that we find West Saxon princes whose names do not begin with the letter 'C'.

The question of rival lineages within the royal house must be viewed in relation to the evidence for multiple kingship within Wessex. For in addition to the rulers who appear in the West Saxon regnal lists, other individuals are known from the *Chronicle*, Bede's *Ecclesiastical History* and charters who bore the title of 'king' (*rex*) or *subregulus* and its variants. Most of these additional rulers can be readily identified as kinsmen of the main West Saxon kings. They include Cynegils' son Cwichelm (d. 636), Cwichelm's son Cuthred (d. 661), Cenbert the father of Cædwalla (d. 661), Cenred the father of Ine, and Baldred, who describes himself as a kinsman of West Saxon kings in a Glastonbury charter.[101] Ceawlin's brother Cutha/Cuthwulf and son Cutha/Cuthwine should probably be considered as kings during his reign. They are not given a title, but are represented as leading the army or sharing command with Ceawlin. Ceawlin died in 593 according to the *Chronicle* which also states that Cwichelm and Crida, who are not otherwise known, died in the same year. It is not clear whether Crida and Cwichelm should be classed as kings but their names follow the 'C' alliteration favoured by West Saxon æthelings.

Not all these supplementary kings were necessarily of the same status. Some, like Baldred, are described as *subregulus*, clearly implying inferior status, but others seem to have shared power with the rulers whose names appear in the regnal lists.[102] Bede's account of the West Saxon attempt to assassinate Edwin in 626 attributes the plot solely to Cwichelm and does not refer in this context to Cwichelm's father Cynegils who was the main ruler according to the regnal lists. Of course, Bede and the Northumbrian source from which he took his information may not have known the exact situation in Wessex, but his account does open up the possibility that Cynegils and Cwichelm were sharing power in a way that it would be difficult to convey in the limited format of a regnal list. Both are named as the leaders of West Saxon forces in 614 and 628 which could support the view that they should be considered as joint rulers. A similar joint leadership is implied in the *Chronicle* notice of the victory of

Ceawlin and Cutha in 568 and of Cuthwine and Ceawlin in 577. The last possible example of joint kingship comes from the early years of Ine's reign when he seems to have shared power with his father Cenred. Cenred seems to have had a different status from the other supplementary rulers who were alive during Ine's reign. The prologue to Ine's laws states that they were promulgated with Cenred's assistance; Cenred was remembered as a co-donor with Ine at Abingdon and in a South Saxon charter is described as 'king of the West Saxons' and given precedence over Ine.[103]

It is not that surprising to find West Saxon kings sharing power with close kinsmen, but not all rulers who were contemporary with the kings of the regnal lists were closely related to the dominant West Saxon king. Cenwalh seems to have recognized his nephew Cuthred as a subking in 648, but he must also have shared power with Cenbert, the father of Cædwalla, whose death is recorded in the *Chronicle* for 661; Cenwalh and Cenbert were third cousins. Possibly it was Cenbert who ruled Wessex during Cenwalh's period of exile between 645 and 648; neither Bede nor the *Chronicle* state how the kingdom was managed during the three years and the regnal lists do not recognize the interregnum.[104] It is also possible that Ine's father Cenred was a subking before Ine's accession for he is probably the same person as the Cenred who made a grant of land in Dorset 670x676.[105] Cenred is not given any title in the charter, but it would be unusual for a layman who was not a king to be able to grant land by charter in the late seventh century. Cenred was a distant cousin of both Cenwalh and Æscwine whose reigns span the period during which the charter seems to have been issued.

Some of the additional West Saxon kings can be associated with subdivisions within Wessex. The *Chronicle* annal for 648 states that Cenwalh gave his kinsman Cuthred 3,000 hides of land near Ashdown. This is equivalent to some of the middling units of the Tribal Hidage and Cenwalh was presumably making Cuthred subking over a province within Wessex centred on the Berkshire Downs. In the reign of Ine a subking called Cissa may have controlled the same area.[106] Another of Ine's subkings was Baldred who granted land in north Somerset and Wiltshire and was presumably based there. The number of West Saxon rulers who can be definitely associated with specific provinces within Wessex is small, but subsidiary kingships are not found after 700 and so there are relatively few documents available for the period in which they existed. What we know of seventh-century Wessex suggests that it consisted of a series of provinces which had at various times come under West Saxon control, some of which at least, like the Isle of Wight, would originally have had their own rulers. Parallels with other Anglo-Saxon kingdoms support the idea that the West Saxon rulers would have appointed subkings of their own house to control these areas in the place of native rulers after conquest, and we can see traces of such a system in the subkings who appear in the *Chronicle* and in charters. Kings might prefer to appoint close relatives to such positions wherever possible, but the major branches of the royal house may have had hereditary claims to certain provinces. That could explain how Cenwalh came to be ruling with his third cousin Cenbert and how Cenred apparently held a similar position under an equally distant relative.

Although the association of rival lineages with different provinces of Wessex has been attempted, such divisions are not clearly represented in the sources for the seventh century.[107] The fullest example of an association between a particular branch of the royal house and an area of Wessex over a spread of time is that of the family of Alfred with Dorset. Ine's father Cenred granted land in Dorset for the foundation of a monastery and Ine's sister Cuthburh founded a double monastery at Wimborne.[108] Ine established the second see of Wessex in Sherborne. We lose sight of the family for the rest of the eighth century, but in the ninth century the family was evidently still strongly attached to the same area, and this can most clearly be seen in their relations with certain religious houses in which they had a proprietary interest. Two of Alfred's brothers were buried at Sherborne, and a third, Æthelred, at Wimborne;[109] Alfred founded a nunnery for one of his daughters at Shaftesbury.[110] When one of Æthelred's sons tried to take the throne on Alfred's death he launched his campaign by seizing Wimborne and asserting his control over its nunnery.[111] Alfred's family had hereditary claims over religious houses founded by their kinsmen, but these foundations may have been made in the first place because the family had rights of rulership within Dorset.

The system of rulership in early Wessex was complex. For most periods there does seem to have been a dominant king although there are several apparent instances of joint kingship for the late sixth and seventh centuries in which kings who can be found in the king-lists shared power with a close relative. The evidence for joint kingship, however, is not strong. Beneath the dominant kings were subkings controlling individual provinces; some of these subsidiary rulers were closely related to the main ruler, but others seem to have been distant cousins, perhaps with a hereditary right to control certain areas. After the deposition of Ceawlin, descendants of his brother Cutha succeeded in dominating the kingship until the death of Cenwalh in 673 when the system seems to have temporarily broken down. Bede, probably drawing on information from Bishop Daniel of Winchester, says that 'sub-kings took upon themselves the government of the kingdom, dividing it up and ruling for about ten years'.[112] According to the *Chronicle* and the West Saxon Regnal List the ten-year period (673-83) would be covered by the successive reigns of Seaxburh, Æscwine and (in part) Centwine, but Bede's words imply a more complex situation in which no one ruler was dominant and the kingdom was effectively divided into a number of subkingdoms. The situation may have been extremely complex in the 670s as this was the period in which Cenred granted land without reference to any other ruler and a variant version of the West Saxon regnal list cited by 'Florence of Worcester' implies that Cenfus, father of Æscwine, also ruled following the death of Cenwalh.[113] Bede goes on to say that during the episcopate of Hædde (676-705) 'the subkings were conquered and removed, and Cædwalla became king'. This has often been taken to mean that Cædwalla was responsible for ending the dominance of the subkings though Bede does not actually say as much and the ten-year period he cites is not compatible with Cædwalla's being responsible for their suppression. Aldhelm represents Centwine, who was apparently not known to Bede, as a particularly strong West Saxon ruler,[114] and Centwine may have begun his reign sharing power with other rulers, but succeeded in gaining full power before the end of his reign.

Subkings are not known after the reign of Ine, and it is in Ine's laws that the first references to ealdormen and shires appear.[115] Ealdormen also appear in the witness lists of the charters of Ine and his successors, generally bearing the title *patricius, princeps* or *praefectus*.[116] It would appear from the charters of Æthelheard and Cuthred that the maximum number of ealdormen was seven.[117] It is likely, as Chadwick argued at the beginning of the century, 'that the shires of Wessex owe their origin to divisions of the kingdoms between members of the royal family',[118] but as we know so little about the territories controlled by the subkings the topic cannot be studied in detail. The 3,000 hides near Ashdown which Cuthred received from Cenwalh sounds as if it would have been comparable with the later shires. It is also not clear how the shires of Ine's time equated with those of the ninth century. The first shire to be mentioned by name is *Hamtunscir* in the *Chronicle* annal for 757. It is not clear whether *Hamtumscir* of the eighth century had the same bounds as Hampshire did later or whether it was a rather smaller area, perhaps the equivalent of the former Jutish province which was centred on the Solent.[119] Some reorganization of *Hamtunscir* in the ninth century seems likely as the centre of the shire's administration was moved from *Hamtun* (the name of the estate on which *Hamwic* was built) to Winchester.[120] Reconstitution elsewhere in Wessex is to be presumed as well for the northern borders of Wessex were not stabilized until the ninth century. Thus Wilton may have been the administrative centre for a dependent area (*Wiltunscir*) from the eighth century or earlier, but the exact bounds of its area must have varied depending on whether Mercia or Wessex was dominant and were probably not fixed until the ninth century.

It seems likely that Ine was responsible for replacing the West Saxon subkingships with ealdormanries. Although this no doubt strengthened the power of the West Saxon king, it seems to have done nothing to lessen the rivalries within the royal house or the rights of different lineages to claim the throne. It is possible that many of those who became ealdormen in the eighth century were themselves members of the royal house, as was certainly the case with the West Saxon ealdormanries in later centuries.[121] In this context it is interesting to note that when King Sigebert was deposed in 757 he was compensated with the control of *Hamtunscir* though unfortunately the *Chronicle* does not make clear what his exact status was after the deposition. On the other hand, none of those who became king in the eighth century can be found among the ealdormen who attested charters, so that the family connections of the ealdormen remain something of a mystery. But however much eighth-century kings wished to establish the supremacy of their own particular families, rival claimants had sufficient power to challenge them and all the West Saxon rulers of the eighth century are depicted in the *Chronicle* as fighting with æthelings. The detailed account of the rivalry between Cynewulf and the brothers Sigebert and Cyneheard shows that the ealdormen were closely involved in these disputes and supported different claimants.

So far we have scarcely mentioned any of the women of the royal house, but West Saxon queens seem to have been far from negligible. Seaxburh, the widow of Cenwalh, is the only Anglo-Saxon queen to appear as a ruler in a regnal list. Æthelburh, the wife of Ine, and Frithugyth, the wife of Æthelheard, are both mentioned in the *Chronicle*,[122] and one would dearly love to know what lay behind the enigmatic statement for 722 recording that 'Queen Æthelburh demolished Taunton, which Ine had built'. Æthelburh, Frithugyth and Eadburh, wife of Beorhtric, are all associated with grants of land made by their husbands,[123] and the last two seem also to have granted land in their own right.[124] Eadburh was the daughter of Offa of Mercia and her power within Wessex, on which Asser comments unfavourably, was no doubt connected with Offa's overlordship.[125] The family backgrounds of Æthelburh and Frithugyth are not known. A forged Glastonbury charter records that Æthelburh was the sister of King Æthelheard who succeeded Ine,[126] and although the identification may be no more than an educated guess based on the similarity of their names, it is not unlikely that alliances between rival kin-groups would have been sealed by marriage (as happened in Northumbria and Mercia) and that the queens as representatives of their kin-groups would be powerful individuals. Asser records that there was a reaction against the power of queens in ninth-century Wessex (which was perhaps connected with attempts to narrow access to the throne) and until the marriage of Æthelwulf and Judith there was a diminution in their status.[127]

It seems to have been difficult for much of the seventh and eighth centuries for any one branch of the royal house to win supremacy over the rest, though the descendants of Cutha, the brother of Ceawlin, are said to have done so from 592-672. At other times the successive kings in the regnal lists were generally only distantly related to each other, in so far as we can judge. One reason for the resilience of the different branches was probably the subkingships which can be glimpsed occasionally in the records. If control of certain areas was hereditary within different branches of the royal house it would provide them with a powerbase from which rival æthelings could launch their claims to the throne. The West Saxon regnal lists and the *Chronicle* provide a picture of successive dominant West Saxon kings, but in fact there seems to have been a tendency towards joint reigns and for the kingdom to split into disparate parts. The rights of the subgroups within the royal house seem to have been little affected by the substitution of shires under ealdormen for the subkingships, probably in the reign of Ine. Ine may have hoped to enhance the status of the dominant West Saxon king, but he could not suppress the claims of other male descendants of Cerdic to the throne or keep it within his own lineage. Those who climbed to the top of the heap in the eighth century may have been in a stronger position when they reached there than their predecessors of the seventh century, because of the suppression of the subkingdoms, but it would appear they found it equally difficult to pass their position on to their immediate heirs and competition for the throne remained as intense as ever it had been.

The West Saxon kingdom 802-99
A new phase of West Saxon history began in 802 when Egbert succeeded to the throne on the death of King Beorhtric. Egbert (802-39) was descended from Ingild, brother of King Ine, and the only one of his direct male ancestors to appear in the West Saxon regnal lists was King Ceawlin (see Table 16). The *Chronicle* records few events for Egbert's reign before the death of Cenwulf of Mercia in 821, though in 815 a campaign against the Cornish is mentioned. The troubles which unseated Ceolwulf of Mercia gave Egbert his opportunity. In 825 he won a decisive victory over King Beornwulf at *Ellandun* near Wroughton (Wilts) and followed it up by despatching part of the army to Kent to expel King Baldred. By the end of the year Egbert was in control of Kent, Surrey, the South Saxons and the East Saxons. In 829 Egbert invaded Mercia and ruled it for a year following the expulsion of King Wiglaf. The *Chronicle* triumphantly added Egbert's name to the list of seven great overlords from the *Ecclesiastical History* and declared him to be the eighth king who was 'bretwalda', the only early recorded use of the term.[128] Egbert's triumphant year ended with a submission from the Northumbrian king.

Wiglaf was back in control of Mercia in 830 and it is unlikely that Egbert had any significant authority in either Mercia or Northumbria after that time. But that does not detract from his substantial achievement in finally conquering Surrey, Sussex and Kent for Wessex. As Egbert also seems to have completed the West Saxon conquest of the Cornish, the West Saxons were in complete control of all the land south of the Thames, in addition to lands of the East Saxons north of the river. The new eastern areas were treated to begin with as a subkingdom of Wessex which was assigned to Egbert's son Æthelwulf to govern.[129] When Æthelwulf succeeded Egbert in 839, the subkingdom passed to Æthelwulf's son Athelstan.[130] By the time Æthelwulf left for Rome in 855, a second son, Æthelbert, was in charge of the area and when Æthelwulf drew up his will the eastern provinces seem to have been seen as an independent kingdom under Æthelbert's control.[131] However, eastern and western Wessex were united in 860 when Æthelbert succeeded to the western kingdom as well.

Not the least of Egbert's achievements was to secure the throne of Wessex for his own descendants; Egbert's son Æthelwulf (839-58) ruled after him, and Æthelwulf was followed successively by his sons Æthelbald (855-60), Æthelbert (860-66), Æthelred (866-71) and Alfred (871-99). Such dominance by one kin-group had been unknown in Wessex since the time of the sons and grandsons of Cutha. One of the differences between Egbert and the kings who immediately preceded him was that Egbert must have been much wealthier because of his new conquests, and such wealth could be used to purchase support. Two grants to Winchester and Canterbury seem to have been made on the condition that the bishops supported the claims of the heirs of Egbert and Æthelwulf.[132] The support of churchmen was particularly valuable as they performed the consecration ceremonies which helped create new kings and drew up documents such as wills which could help enforce royal decisions. The Carolingian Renaissance had raised consciousness of the importance both of the king having the support of God and of the king supporting the church. Both Egbert and Æthelwulf were generous to the church, but if we had more evidence of grants from them to laymen we would no doubt see them purchasing support from the secular world as well. Æthelwulf's 'Decimation' of his land in 855, shortly before his journey to Rome, seems to have benefited both churchmen and laymen and was perhaps designed to ensure security for his line on the eve of his departure.[133] The need to buy influential friends is a reminder that Egbert, Æthelwulf and their heirs were not necessarily the only possible claimants for the West Saxon throne. Presumably there were other male descendants of Cerdic still in existence in the ninth century even if we hear nothing about them directly.

The Egbertings were aware of the need for kings to consolidate their personal wealth. Egbert and Æthelwulf could be generous to the church, but were also careful to get acknowledgement that they were the lords of the Kentish monasteries in succession to the Kentish royal house.[134] Ultimately a number of estates that had belonged to monasteries in Kent and elsewhere came into their hands. According to Alfred's will, Egbert left land only to the males of the royal house so that estates should not be lost to the family. Alfred shows a similar awareness of the need to keep the family wealth together. According to his will, female relatives received estates for their lifetime only and after their deaths the estates were to return to the male line.[135] Alfred seems to have kept a careful balance between the open-handedness expected from a successful Anglo-Saxon king and the need to conserve his wealth. Asser, who was a recipient of Alfred's generosity and lovingly describes some of the gifts he received, also shows Alfred carefully assessing his revenues and planning his expenditure accordingly.[136]

Æthelwulf and his sons made arrangements amongst themselves about the pattern of succession they wished to achieve and the disposition of the family estates. Æthelwulf made his wishes clear in a will which we only know from descriptions of it in Asser's *Life of Alfred* and Alfred's will.[137] According to the latter Æthelwulf decreed that whichever of the three brothers, Æthelbald, Æthelred and Alfred, lived the longest should inherit the family possessions in western Wessex (Æthelbert was already provided for in the eastern kingdom). Æthelwulf recognized the importance of the king having considerable funds at his disposal and seems to have planned for his sons to succeed successively to the family assets (and perhaps to the kingdom as well). When Æthelbald died in 860, Æthelred and Alfred were too young to rule so Æthelbert took over the whole of the West Saxon kingdom, but made an agreement with his younger brothers that they would have the inheritance on his death. When Æthelbert died in 865 Æthelred and Alfred reached a similar agreement. Æthelred would have the family estates for his lifetime, but Alfred would succeed to the whole on Æthelred's death in preference to Æthelred's sons. When Æthelred died in 871 Alfred, the youngest of all Æthelwulf's sons, succeeded to the throne and the family inheritance. He was careful to get his agreement with Æthelred ratified by the West Saxon nobles to ensure the continuation of his line and to frustrate the ambitions of Æthelred's heirs.

In spite of such precautions it was impossible to eliminate competition within the kin-group. In 855 Æthelwulf went on pilgrimage to Rome and divided Wessex between his sons Æthelbald and Æthelbert who ruled west and east Wessex respectively. It might have been expected, following the precedents of Cædwalla and Ine, that Æthelwulf would not return from his journey, but the trip seems if anything to have rejuvenated him. When he came back in 856 Æthelwulf brought with him a twelve-year-old bride, Judith, a daughter of the western Frankish king Charles the Bald. Æthelbald, with the support of the bishop of Sherborne and the ealdorman of Somerset, rebelled and tried to prevent his father's return, but a compromise was reached by which Æthelwulf ruled the eastern half of the main West Saxon kingdom and Æthelbald the western.[138] It is not clear whether the coup was the result of real opposition to Æthelwulf's policies or of Æthelbald's fears for his position should Æthelwulf and Judith have a son.[139] As five of Æthelwulf's sons ruled (if we count Athelstan who ruled only in the eastern province), there were a number of rival æthelings in the next generation. Æthelred and Alfred both had sons, and so probably did at least one of the other brothers – an Oswald *filius regis* appears in a number of charters of the second half of the ninth century, but it is not known which king was his father.[140] Alfred used his position to ensure the succession of his eldest son Edward in accordance with his agreement with Æthelred. Alfred's wishes with regard to the succession were challenged, but ratified by a meeting of the West Saxon witan, though even this could not prevent one of his nephews attempting to take the throne after Alfred's death.[141]

In addition to such internal problems, the West Saxon rulers of the ninth century had a number of external threats to deal with. Mercia may have been weakened, but she was still a formidable force. Any West Saxon ambitions to conquer Mercia could only be achieved gradually. After the accession of Burgred the two royal houses began a period of peaceful cooperation. The kings issued compatible coinages[142] and marriage alliances were arranged. Burgred of Mercia married Æthelwulf's daughter Æthelswith in 854 and Æthelred of Mercia married Alfred's daughter Æthelflæd in the 880s.[143] The latter alliance eventually provided the pretext for a formal West Saxon takeover of Mercia in 918 when Alfred's son Edward ousted the daughter of Æthelred and Æthelflæd.[144] Edward could claim that he was following Alfred's injunction in his will that male kinsmen if they wished should lay claim to properties that were in the possession of their female relatives. Prior to Edward's acquisition of Mercia Alfred had begun to pave his way by patronizing Mercian churchmen, a number of whom received positions at the royal court or within the West Saxon church and were amongst Alfred's earliest helpers in the attempt to improve Christian standards in Wessex.[145] Alfred also extended his influence amongst the Welsh, the longtime enemies of Mercia, and induced a number of princes and religious houses to recognize his lordship.[146] Alfred's interest in Wales ultimately accounts for the presence of Asser at his court.

The main reason for the willingness of the Mercians and the Welsh to enter alliances with the West Saxons was the existence of even more formidable enemies, the Vikings. The first Viking raid on Wessex had been made in the reign of King Beorhtric, but serious attacks did not begin until 836. To begin with the West Saxons were reasonably successful against the Scandinavians, even when the invaders joined up with the Cornish, but after 851 they fared less well and were unable to prevent a Viking army from wintering in Thanet in that year. Alfred's four elder brothers died during the period of intensifying Viking attacks and, although we do not know the reasons for the deaths of any of them, it seems more than likely that some of them at least were attributable to injuries received during the campaigns against the Vikings. By the time the Great Heathen Army arrived in 865 the West Saxons had already been fighting major campaigns against Scandinavian forces for fourteen years, with substantial losses of personnel. The West Saxons were fortunate that the Vikings' priority seems to have been the conquest of northern England and of York in particular, but they nevertheless came close to being conquered. 871 was one crucial year in which nine battles were fought between Vikings and West Saxons; Æthelred died in the middle of the campaign. In 878 Alfred was nearly captured in a surprise midwinter raid; he was forced to retreat to the Somerset marshes (scene of the popular, but apocryphal, cake-burning episode), but rallied and won his decisive victory at Edington (Wilts) after which terms were reached with the Viking leader Guthrum.[147] In 886 Alfred recaptured London from the Vikings and although this did not lead to the recovery of all the lands the West Saxons had held in the former East Saxon territory, the victory seems to have been seen in Wessex and in other Anglo-Saxon areas as a sign that Alfred had mastered the Viking threat.[148] Alfred also succeeded in countering a major attack by a new Viking army between 892 and 896.

The *Chronicle* accounts concentrate on the set-piece battles between West Saxons and Vikings, but Asser's more detailed narrative allows us to see more of the logistical problems which the Viking wars introduced. It is clear from what Asser says that there was resentment within Wessex because of the long periods of military service and the other royal demands made upon the time and purses of the West Saxons.[149] Some refused to obey royal commands and we know of at least one ealdorman who defected to the Vikings;[150] a substantial portion of Wessex seems to have surrendered to the Vikings in 878 when Alfred's future seemed uncertain.[151] The bulk of the population might expect to reach reasonable terms with the Vikings which might ultimately leave them better off than they would be after a long period of resistance. But for the royal house there was no alternative but resistance, for the Vikings made a point of killing or expelling native kings when they conquered their kingdoms.

The West Saxon rulers had to develop new strategies and increase the demands they could make on their subjects in order to defeat the Vikings. They had precedents from Francia and Mercia (the latter too had drawn on Frankish advances) which they could follow.[152] One important innovation was the burh or fortress which could be used both as a local refuge and as a base for a militia to intercept Viking forces and hamper their manoeuvrability.[153] When Offa ruled Kent he had introduced the public services of fortress-work and bridge-work to help counter the first Viking attacks on the province so when the West Saxons conquered Kent they inherited the Mercian burhs there. The West Saxon burghal system has traditionally been associated with the reign of Alfred, but some of the West Saxon burhs, such as Wareham, were probably in existence before Alfred came to the throne, though he may deserve credit for extending the system and establishing a permanent militia in the fortresses.[154] Fortress-work only seems to have been regularly referred to in West Saxon charters from the reign of Æthelbald (855-60).[155] The fortifications themselves generally seem to have consisted of a timber-revetted bank with a ditch and even today some of the surviving ramparts such as those at Wareham are impressive structures.[156] The task of building the fortifications and manning them fell upon the population of the surrounding countryside. Asser reveals that fortress-work was one of the royal demands which was most resented and it would appear that Alfred had some difficulty in enforcing it.[157] However, if the West Saxons were to defeat the Vikings they had to persuade their subjects of the necessity of accepting greater royal control over their lives.

The Viking armies which attacked Wessex also operated in Francia and the *Chronicle* contains reports of the movements of the Viking forces across the Channel.[158] The Franks also built fortifications to try to contain the Scandinavian threat and there are some similarities between Frankish and West Saxon defences.[159] It was probably the common Viking threat which brought the Frankish and West Saxon royal houses closer together (though relations would have been established when Egbert spent three years in exile at the court of Charlemagne).[160] One result was the marriage of Charles the Bald's daughter Judith firstly to Æthelwulf of Wessex and then to Æthelwulf's son Æthelbald.[161] Such a marriage of stepmother and stepson was highly irregular by the ninth century and presumably reflects the importance placed on the Frankish–West Saxon alliance. By the reign of Alfred new powers were rising within the old western Frankish kingdom and towards the end of his reign Alfred married his daughter Ælfthryth to Count Baldwin II of Flanders.[162]

As a result of these links Francia continued to have a great influence on Wessex during the ninth century which can be most clearly seen in the cultural sphere. Æthelwulf had a Frankish secretary called Felix,[163] but the greatest period of Frankish influence came during the reign of Alfred. One thing which their Frankish contacts must have made abundantly clear to the West Saxons was the low standard of Christian culture in their kingdom compared to that of

Francia, and even to that of Mercia where the Carolingian Renaissance seems initially to have had more impact than in Wessex.[164] Alfred recruited the Frankish scholar Grimbald from Flanders and John the Old Saxon from eastern Francia to join Asser and the Mercian scholars at his court in the 880s.[165] This 'court school', which was perhaps a conscious imitation of the band of European scholars brought together by Charlemagne, belatedly brought the Carolingian Renaissance to Wessex. To begin with the Renaissance seems to have been a personal one for Alfred himself, but in the following decade Alfred sought to broaden its effect by making clear to his bishops and secular nobles that new standards of literacy and Christian knowledge were expected of them. Alfred also made available through his own translations and those of his scholarly advisers some of the books which he had found useful in his own personal odyssey and considered 'most necessary for all men to know'.[166]

Although several earlier Anglo-Saxon kings had been able to read and had interested themselves in learning, it was, as far as we know, unprecedented for a king to translate books from Latin to English for the benefit of his subjects.[167] The translations are particularly interesting as they contain a number of digressions and illustrative passages which seem to be based on the king's own experiences.[168] We seem to hear the authentic voice of the king speaking and when we put these passages alongside the intimate portrait of Alfred that Asser provides in his biography we have a much more rounded portrait of Alfred than we have for any earlier Anglo-Saxon ruler. Some caution must be exercised for Asser's Alfred is to a certain extent a literary construct and was influenced by Einhard's portrayal of Charlemagne.[169] Alfred in his translations was constrained by what his Latin texts said and was writing with didactic intent. Nevertheless the portrait which emerges is an interesting one. Alfred is not so much the gallant warrior king who saw off the Vikings as a sensitive, if not neurotic, scholar manqué who was much afflicted by ill health, but who eventually came to terms with his difficult life through his Christian studies.

Like Charlemagne, Alfred seems to have believed that many of his problems as king would be solved if his subjects developed a similar consciousness of doing their Christian duty. For according to the way these matters had been interpreted during the Carolingian Renaissance the subjects owed the same kind of obedience to their king that God demanded from the king himself.[170] Alfred's duty was to stand firm against the pagan Vikings; that of his subjects was to assist him by obeying his orders. A consciousness of doing one's duty in accordance with God's will was one of the messages which could be absorbed from Pope Gregory's *Pastoral Care* which was the most widely circulated of all Alfred's translations and a copy of which was sent to all the West Saxon dioceses.[171] The historical records produced during Alfred's reign can also be interpreted as part of his desire to galvanize his people against the Vikings.[172] The *Anglo-Saxon Chronicle*, for instance, celebrated past successes of the West Saxons under the leadership of the Cerdicings against other foreign enemies.

There is some truth in Wallace-Hadrill's maxim that 'we hold that Alfred was a great and glorious king in part because he rightly implies this',[173] but any manipulation of the written record by Alfred tends to enhance our admiration for the king. Alfred is a 'man for all seasons' and each age finds different things to admire in him. To the Victorians he was the ideal type of a muscular Christian and his biography was written by Thomas Hughes who was also the author of *Tom Brown's Schooldays*.[174] In the present day it could be said that it is his manipulation of the 'media' which has won admiration and enhanced his reputation.[175] But Alfred's victories over the Vikings and his battles for the hearts and minds of his people are impressive by any standards. However, although the Vikings were a formidable threat, in the long run they were extremely beneficial to the West Saxon rulers. In their brilliant campaigns of the 860s the leaders of the Great Heathen Army removed the rulers of all the surviving Anglo-Saxon kingdoms and their dynasties never recovered. Their actions left Alfred as the only Anglo-Saxon and the only Christian king in England, and he demonstrated his consciousness of the fact by adopting the title *rex Angul-Saxonum*. Asser went even further in the dedication of his *Life of Alfred* where he described the king as 'ruler of all the Christians of the island of Britain'.[176] The West Saxons could never have removed their rivals so easily, but the real heir to the Viking conquerors was Alfred's son Edward who, with the aid of Mercian forces under his sister Æthelflæd, defeated the scattered Viking settlers and thus added eastern Mercia and East Anglia to his kingdom.[177] To defeat the Vikings Alfred had to make his subjects accept greater public burdens than previously and once these greater powers of control had been won for the crown they were not given up and were another reason for the success of Alfred's descendants as kings of England.

Conclusion

When one looks back on West Saxon history, four reigns stand out in which the West Saxons seem to have made substantial advances – those of Ceawlin, Cædwalla, Ine and Alfred. There are grounds for suspicion about this selection for Alfred, Ine and Cædwalla were all descendants of Ceawlin, and it is possible that the Alfredian chronicler wanted readers to draw the conclusion that Wessex did best when it was ruled by descendants of Alfred's branch of the royal house. However, our assessment of the importance of Ceawlin, Cædwalla and Ine does not just depend on documents drawn up in the reign of Alfred and there seems no reason to doubt that they were rulers who enlarged the borders and powers of Wessex. It may be the case though that we do not hear as much as we should about other West Saxon kings who were not closely related to Alfred. Centwine is a case in point. The *Chronicle* makes very little of his reign, but charters and a brief reference from Aldhelm suggest that he was rather more significant than the two annal entries for his reign would otherwise lead one to imply. Centwine was a descendant of Cutha whose family dominated Wessex in the early seventh century when many of the foundations of later West Saxon greatness were laid. But the descendants of

Cutha were not closely related to the descendants of Ceawlin and the links may have been even more tenuous than the surviving genealogies admit for there are contradictions which cannot easily be explained other than by an editing of texts.

In the late sixth century the West Saxons were based in the Thames valley and seemed ideally situated to expand in all directions, though ultimately the success of Mercia concentrated their attention southwards and westwards. Cædwalla's success in conquering the Jutes and the South Saxons seems to have been regarded both within Wessex and outside as a turning-point in the growth of Wessex for it was during his reign that the title 'king of the Saxons' replaced 'king of the Geuissae'. The *Chronicle* contains the claim that the West Saxons were entitled to rule the Jutish territories because these areas had been conquered originally by Cerdic and Cynric who had appointed their kinsmen Stuf and Whitgar to rule in the Isle of Wight. It is unlikely that such claims are true, though it is not clear when they were formulated. The West Saxons seem to have been anxious to justify their advances in south-eastern England which were brought to their logical conclusion by Egbert's conquest of Kent and Sussex.

The westward expansion of Wessex was just as important as that to the east, but is very poorly recorded in spite of notices of some significant battles in the *Chronicle*. Although English place-names largely replaced their British predecessors in the western counties (with the exception of western Cornwall), there are few other signs of extensive Anglo-Saxon settlement in these areas. The West Saxons took over the estate and ecclesiastical organization that they found west of Selwood, but we can learn little of the details of interaction of Saxons and British within Wessex. The adoption of British name-elements by the West Saxon royal house may indicate that intermarriage and alliances with important British families helped West Saxon assimilation of British territory. British traditions may have enhanced the powers of West Saxon rulers, and British churchmen and other advisers may have helped shape the development of Wessex, but in the end we can only speculate on the significance of the West Saxons' British inheritance.

It is hard to say why Wessex was the only kingdom to survive intact to the end of the ninth century. It was not larger or richer than Northumbria or Mercia and its kings do not seem to have exercised any more considerable powers than those of other kingdoms; indeed, the evidence suggests that they claimed less in the way of public services than Mercia until the ninth century. Rivalries within the royal house were not dissimilar to those of other kingdoms during the eighth century, though the successes of Egbert resulted in succession being confined to one branch of the royal house in the ninth century which was not the case anywhere else in Anglo-Saxon England. However, Æthelbald's revolt against his father could have been the point at which everything collapsed into civil war if Æthelwulf had not been willing to compromise. One can point to times when the West Saxons were lucky not to be overwhelmed by the Vikings and give instances of outstanding skills of statesmanship by Alfred which ensured his eventual success. Above all, Alfred had the advantage that by his reign he could call upon at least three hundred years of Anglo-Saxon rule both within Wessex and elsewhere and the very substantial advances in royal government made in Carolingian Francia. In addition to military success, it was through drawing on the traditions of other kingdoms besides their own that the West Saxon rulers became the kings of England (see Fig. 14.7).

Chapter Eight

THE DEVELOPMENT OF KINGSHIP c. 600–900

In examining the histories of different Anglo-Saxon kingdoms one becomes aware of common problems and stimuli which the rulers of early Anglo-Saxon England faced. The concluding chapter examines four of the principal themes which have run through the earlier chapters and which helped shape the development of Anglo-Saxon kingship.

Kingship and overlordship

Anglo-Saxon kingship had its origins in warleadership. The breakdown of centralized authority during the subRoman period allowed power to pass into the hands of those who had military forces at their disposal, and various Anglo-Saxon leaders, some of whom may well have had forefathers who had been brought to Britain to provide military protection for the Romano-British, were able to seize the initiative and to establish kingdoms for themselves and their successors.[1] The superficial unity which the Roman empire had given to Britain south of the Hadrian and Antonine walls was lost and Roman Britain shattered into a number of small self-governing units. There seem to have been over thirty of such units, many of which were certainly controlled by kings, in the parts of Britain which the Anglo-Saxons had colonized by 600. By 800 only five Anglo-Saxon kingdoms are definitely known to have been still in existence, and a number of British kingdoms in the west of the country had disappeared as well. The major kingdoms had grown through absorbing smaller principalities and the means through which they did it and the character their kingdoms acquired as a result are one of the major themes of the period.

We know that from the time of Ælle of the South Saxons certain powerful individuals had been able to exercise a degree of authority over their peers. The first great military overlords, or 'bretwaldas' as they are sometimes known, came from southern England and in addition to Ælle, comprised Ceawlin of Wessex, Æthelbert of Kent and Rædwald of the East Angles. According to Bede they enjoyed an *imperium* over the other kingdoms south of the Humber.[2] After the death of Rædwald, the seat of power shifted from southern and eastern England to the Midlands and the north, and dominance was disputed between Northumbria and Mercia. The list Bede provides ends with the names of Edwin, Oswald and Oswiu of Northumbria, but additional information, including material from other chapters of the *Ecclesiastical History*, suggests a similar pre-eminence was achieved by Egfrith of Northumbria and by Penda, Wulfhere and

Æthelbald of Mercia, while at the end of the seventh century authority was disputed between Æthelred of Mercia and the West Saxon kings Cædwalla and Ine. These men oppressed not only other Anglo-Saxon principalities, but many of the Celtic kingdoms as well. At the height of their power the Northumbrian kings apparently claimed *imperium* over the whole of Britain.

Although Bede's use of the term *imperium* has been seen as significant in defining the status and powers of the bretwaldas,[3] in fact it is a word Bede used regularly as an alternative to *regnum*.[4] When we come to enquire what the exercise of a bretwalda's authority actually meant it seems to come down to little more than the collection of tribute. Oswiu's extension of overlordship over the Picts and Scots is expressed in terms of making them tributary.[5] Wulfhere of Mercia attacked Egfrith of Northumbria in c. 673 with the intention of placing the Northumbrians *sub tributo*, though as Wulfhere was defeated it was the Mercians who ended up paying tribute to the Northumbrians.[6] Earlier Oswiu had been obliged to offer Penda 'an incalculable and incredible store of royal treasures and gifts as the price of peace'.[7] Possibly the Sutton Hoo ship-burial, if it can be seen as representing some of the profits from Rædwald's period of overlordship, can give us some idea of the type of booty that might be acquired. No doubt the subject kings had to promise loyalty to their overlords and the handing over of great treasure without receiving commensurate gifts in return would symbolize their inferiority and subjection. Possibly military service could be demanded from the subject kings. Bede has an enigmatic reference to Rædwald retaining the *ducatus* of his own people while Æthelbert of Kent was bretwalda which presumably refers to some sort of military demand which a great overlord could usually make.[8] The appearance of thirty *duces regii* fighting on behalf of Penda when Oswiu challenged him for the overlordship at the battle of the *Winwæd* is suggestive, and Wulfhere is said to have led an army raised from all the southern peoples when he fought Northumbria in c. 673. But it cannot be demonstrated that these wide-ranging overlordships automatically allowed their holders to interfere in the domestic affairs of their subject kingdoms.[9]

The context in which the bretwaldas most frequently appear is a military one and everything which we can deduce about their warfare is consistent with the basis of their power being the use of military force to exact the payment of tribute. It is a form of power well evidenced in the Germanic world. Tacitus was aware of its operation among Germanic tribes in the first century AD and has various pertinent observations to make about the strengths and weaknesses of such a system.[10] In the eighth and ninth centuries tribute-taking by military force was as essential to Frankish kings as it was to their Viking contemporaries.[11] Warfare of tribute-takers was essentially offensive. Anglo-Saxon armies, like the Viking armies which later successfully campaigned in Britain, seem to have been able to move swiftly through the country and to campaign effectively away from their bases. When Cwichelm of Wessex attempted to have Edwin of Northumbria assassinated, Edwin retaliated with a raid on Wessex in which 'he either slew all whom he discovered to have plotted his death or forced them to surrender'.[12] Fear of such retribution would help keep tribute-payers loyal. The Northumbrian kings were able to attack from sea as well as on land; Edwin forced the submission of the Isle of Man, and Egfrith organized a raid on Ireland which ravaged churches and monasteries, presumably to take booty and encourage the payment of tribute.[13] Once again the parallels with the later Viking raiders are striking. It would presumably not have been necessary to fight every ruler to receive his submission. As Tacitus observed, in such societies reputation was sufficient to persuade kings of lesser armies to pay up rather than be needlessly slaughtered.[14] Only when a rival could command a comparable force would one of the major setpiece battles like those on the banks of the rivers *Winwæd* (655) and Trent (678) occur.[15]

Military overlordship could bring great short-term success and wealth, but the system had its disadvantages. Many of the overlords enjoyed their powers for a relatively short period. Oswiu of Northumbria (642-70) only won authority over the southern kingdoms after he ddefeated Penda at the battle of the *Winwæd* in 655 and must have lost it again soon after Wulfhere regained control in Mercia in 658. The situation did not remain static once overlordship had been achieved and rival kingdoms constantly intrigued and plotted alliances which would enable them to rise to pre-eminence. Oswiu himself colluded with other kingdoms before his defeat of Penda, and formed alliances with Sigebert of the East Saxons and with Penda's son Peada which were reinforced by the conversion of these rulers to Christianity.[16] An overlord had to be constantly on his guard against threats to his authority and to have an effective army always in readiness; Oswiu was the only one of the great Northumbrian bretwaldas not to be killed defending his position. There were no long-term gains with bretwaldaship, for the powers could not be passed from one generation to another and brought no permanent expansion of territory. Although three successive Northumbrian kings were overlords, each of them had to carve out the position for himself and none of them achieved any permanent gains south of the Humber. What enabled Northumbria to remain a secure and powerful kingdom once it had lost all pretensions to overlordship in southern England was the fact that it had permanently expanded its territory by absorbing the British kingdoms of Rheged and the Gododdin.[17]

There is a distinction between a superficial overlordship whose *raison d'être* was the collection of tribute (bretwaldaship) and the overlordship of one kingdom over another which was based on personal ties and obligations and which the superior party hoped would ultimately lead to the annexation of the lesser ruler's kingdom. As the more powerful kings tended to exercise both types of overlordship it has led to some confusion about what powers were inherent in bretwaldaship.[18] The distinction becomes clearer when we consider the powers of Æthelbert of Kent. Bede says that Æthelbert exercised an *imperium* over the other kingdoms of southern England, but when it came to enforcing Christianity, Æthelbert could only ensure the conversion of the East Saxons.[19] The ruler of the East Saxons, Sabert, was Æthelbert's nephew and possibly had other obligations towards Æthelbert as well.[20] Æthelbert had limited powers over many kingdoms, but there was only one kingdom into which he could walk and set up a bishopric.

Foundations had to be carefully laid to turn a tribute-paying underkingdom into a permanent acquisition. The detailed account that can be put together from the *Ecclesiastical History* of the Bernician absorption of Deira gives some idea of the likely different stages.[21] Bernicia's campaign began with marriage with a princess from the (temporarily) defeated Deiran dynasty. Æthelfrith of Bernicia married Edwin of Deira's sister and, according to Bede, their son Oswald was able to claim both kingdoms by inheritance.[22] Oswiu subsequently bolstered the claims of his descendants by also marrying a Deiran princess. Provision of a subking from the overlord's family for the underkingdom was also an important transitional stage. Oswiu ruled with first a nephew and then a son as subking in Deira, and although both subkings developed a desire for autonomy, Oswiu's son and successor Egfrith was able to unite Deira with Bernicia. By this time Deirans would have been the recipients of Bernician patronage and so many would have come to accept the Bernician rulers as their lords. The Bernicians were particularly assiduous in patronizing religious houses associated with Deiran princesses (Deiran princes having been eliminated) and these women, who from the intermarriages had become kinswomen of the Bernician kings, were able to exercise considerable political influence within the province.

Many parallel examples could be found from the other Anglo-Saxon kingdoms of the importance of personal links between rulers in the exercise of overlordship. As Bede was particularly interested in chronicling the progress of conversion to Christianity within England, much of what we can deduce about overlordship arrangements in the seventh century comes from this context. For one king to arrange for the conversion of another and to stand as his godfather seems to have created a strong bond between them, analogous, or even stronger, to that created by intermarriage of the two royal houses.[23] Anglo-Saxon kings were certainly fully aware that to accept conversion via another royal court was tantamount to acknowledging an inferiority that went beyond what was established by the mere payment of tribute. That is why Æthelbert preferred to be converted by missionaries from Rome, rather than by the Frankish bishop who had come with his bride.[24] It also explains why Rædwald was prepared to add an altar to the Christian God to his pagan temple, but was not prepared to go any further to accommodate Æthelbert's new religion.[25] Pagan overlords might influence their underkings in the opposite direction. Edwin of Northumbria probably delayed his conversion until after the death of Rædwald for he was under a particularly strong debt of personal obligation to Rædwald who had enabled him to take the Northumbrian throne.[26]

The history of Mercia provides a number of examples of how adjacent kingdoms were gradually brought into the Mercian fold.[27] Provinces, like those of the Middle Angles and the Magonsæte, which bordered Mercia, were naturally the first candidates for annexation and so the first to receive subkings from the Mercian royal house. More peripheral kingdoms might be bound to Mercia by ties of obligation. The Hwicce, for instance, seem to have had a royal house who were not of Mercian origin, but who came to power with Mercian military help or were ceded territory which had been conquered by the Mercians.[28] The Mercian kings retained various estates and rights over the territory in which they had a vested interest and eventually ousted the native dynasty in the course of the eighth century. As the screws tightened, the Hwiccian kings were obliged to acknowledge firstly that they were underkings of the Mercians and eventually that they were only ealdormen. By the end of the eighth century the former Hwiccian kingdom was a full Mercian ealdormanry administered by Mercian ealdormen.

A plethora of underkings can be found in sources for seventh-century England and the exact status of individuals is not always clear. It is hard, for instance, to be certain which subkings in the Mercian ambit were members of the Mercian royal house and which were members of provincial dynasties recognizing Mercian overlordship; Frithuwold, subking of Surrey during the reign of Wulfhere of Mercia, is a case in point.[29] Complex tiers of relationships might exist. When Wulfhere was trying to increase his influence over the South Saxons, he ceded control of the provinces of the Meonware and Wight to the South Saxon king. Wight at least had its own ruler who presumably recognized the authority of the South Saxon king who in turn recognized the overlordship of Wulfhere.[30] This example also demonstrates the point that alliances between the mighty and the not so mighty could be to the advantage in the short term of both parties. By the end of the seventh century, it must have become apparent that there was no future in being a very small kingdom and some leaders of smaller units may have surrendered to larger neighbours while there was still a chance of doing so on negotiated terms. When Tondbert of the Gyrwe married Æthelthryth, the daughter of King Anna of the East Angles, he virtually resigned his province to East Anglian control.[31] However through the marriage, Tondbert achieved kinship with a more powerful royal house, and as the only alternative was presumably absorption by Mercia, he may have made a conscious choice on the most advantageous terms he could achieve.

The smaller kingdoms did not disappear without trace once they were incorporated into larger polities; on the contrary their territorial integrity was preserved when they became ealdormanries or, depending on size, parts of ealdormanries within their new kingdoms. As the former subkingdoms were already functioning as assessed units there was presumably little incentive for internal reorganization. An obvious example of this tendency for later boundaries to preserve earlier arrangements is Sussex; the county boundary is essentially the same as that of the West Saxon shire and the Anglo-Saxon kingdom.[32] Although it has been recognized for some time that the shires of Wessex preserved earlier territorial arrangements, it had been thought that similar units had been lost in eastern Mercia because of dislocation caused by Viking settlement and the West Saxon reconquest. However, it now appears that the bounds of earlier provinces can be detected here as well and we may eventually be able to reach a clearer understanding of the nature of arrangements within the complicated Middle Anglian province.[33] Of course, not all the bounds of earlier provinces remained intact up to 900, let alone later. Provinces bordering the Thames seem to have been particularly affected by reorganization within the Middle Saxon period, for whereas the Thames may at one time have had united peoples who lived on its opposite banks by the end of the seventh century it had become a border zone between Wessex and Mercia. Although the number of political units had been severely reduced by the ninth century, earlier political groupings still influenced the organization of the larger kingdoms which may not have been as fully integrated as they superficially appear.

Royal resources

In one of King Alfred's digressions in his translation of Boethius' *Consolation of Philosophy*, he provided these observations about the resources which every king needed:

> In the case of the king, the resources and tools with which to rule are that he have his land fully manned: he must have praying men, fighting men and working men. You know also that without these tools no king may make his ability known. Another aspect of his resources is that he must have the means of support for his tools, the three classes of men. These, then, are their means of support: land to live on, gifts, weapons, food, ale, clothing and whatever else is necessary for each of the three classes of men.[34]

This is the first written appearance of the division of society into the 'three orders' which was to prove very popular in the Middle Ages.[35] Although it represents a great simplification of the complexities of medieval social organization, it is a good starting point for considering the practical organization of resources which was essential for the success of kingship in the early Anglo-Saxon world. Although raiding and the conquest of new territory may have provided rulers to begin with with much of the wealth that they needed, once a degree of stability had been reached and kings had to defend their enlarged borders, they had to make the most of the potential inherent in the land they ruled.

Basically the 'working men' provided the raw materials to support the other two classes. Kings exacted 'tribute' from the peasants who lived on their vast estates in the form of *feorm*, a render of food and other essential commodities which was collected at the royal vills to which various services might also appertain.[36] Food and drink might be consumed by king and court when they visited the vill or peasant labour could be utilized to transfer it wherever it was required; the Northumbrian thegn Imma, when he wished to conceal his identity from the Mercian thegn who had captured him, claimed that 'he was a poor peasant and married; and he declared that he had come to the army in company with other peasants to bring food to the soldiers'.[37] In such ways kings fulfilled their obligation to keep their attendant *comitatus* fed and watered, and to provide the great feasts which were so lovingly chronicled in Old English poetry and were essential for reinforcing the bonds between the king and his entourage.

The king could also provide for those in royal service by diverting part of the royal *feorm* to them, that is by the gift of land. Benedict Biscop, the founder of Wearmouth and Jarrow, and his cousin Eosterwine both entered the royal service as *ministri* when they were in their teens; presumably they became members of the king's *comitatus*. When they reached the ages of twenty-five and twenty-four respectively they received estates from the king 'suitable to their rank'.[38] On the basis of what Bede has to say in his *Letter to Egbert*,[39] such gifts of land were not permanent alienations, but temporary gifts which lasted for the lifetime of the recipient and after his death would return to the king, though no doubt the same estate could be granted out again to a kinsman or heir. The tenure seems to have been known to the Anglo-Saxons as *lænland* or *folcland*, though there are only a few instances where the vernacular terms were used, and such temporary grants seem to have been the regular way in which royal service was rewarded at the beginning of our period.[40] Those members of the nobility who went on to play major administrative roles as ealdormen or other royal officials would receive further gifts of estates on similar terms. However, it does appear that noble families also had land over which they had permanent control and that they were familiar with the concept of hereditary rights over land before the church reintroduced Roman concepts of land law.[41] However, the whole question of family holdings of the nobility is one of the most mysterious issues in early Anglo-Saxon England as practically all the evidence we have relates to royal land. How much land was permanently in the possession of noble families and what interest, if any, the king had in such estates are questions that cannot be answered, although they do need to be posed.

The advent of Christianity saw the introduction of new concepts of land tenure. The role of churchmen was analogous with that of the warriors of the *comitatus*; Bede was fond of the analogy that the soldiers of Christ waged heavenly warfare while the men of the *comitatus* engaged in earthly battles.[42] So as royal servants they would naturally be supported from the same stocks of land as the other royal retainers, and Bede makes it clear in the *Letter to Egbert* that this was indeed the case in Northumbria. But as we have seen grants to royal servants were essentially of a temporary nature whereas the church needed and expected permanent alienations in line with what was normal under the Roman Vulgar law known to the Continental churches.[43] Such gifts were recorded by the church in charters or 'books', as they were known in Old English (*boc*), hence the vernacular term 'bookland' (*bocland*) for the new type of tenure. It seems to have taken a while for the concept of permanent alienation of royal lands to have been accepted which is presumably why Anglo-Saxon charters utter dire threats to future kings who might try to revoke their predecessors' gifts.[44] Anglo-Saxon society also seems to have found it difficult to come to terms with the idea that estates granted to an individual in perpetuity in order to endow a church did not give automatic rights in the land to that individual's family. Benedict Biscop was extremely concerned that after his death his brother, who was a layman of dubious morality, would gain control of his monasteries and, in order to make doubly sure that his successor could come from outside his own family, obtained a letter of privilege from Pope Agatho.[45] The need to endow the church resulted in the permanent alienation of stocks of land which had previously only been granted out on a temporary basis and introduced the concept of a new type of hereditary land which could be freely alienated and was free of any family claims.

Kings were extremely generous in their gifts to the Church. Cædwalla granted Wilfrid a quarter of the Isle of Wight after he was convinced that the Christian God had helped him to victory,[46] and this gift represented a tiny proportion of the vast estates which Wilfrid accumulated during his lifetime.[47] Eorcenwald managed to acquire an endowment of three hundred hides for his foundation at Chertsey which, if the mode of assessment is the same, was the equivalent of half one of the smallest units found in the Tribal Hidage; the endowment of his sister's foundation at Barking seems to have been of comparable size.[48] Kings presumably believed that the support of the Christian God was worth the tremendous outlay, but one wonders whether the successors of those rulers who were swept away by the first flush of enthusiasm felt that the investment had paid sufficient dividends. Kings did not perhaps anticipate the effects of granting so much land to the church or perhaps did not appreciate that they would not be able to retain control over provinces over which they exercised a temporary overlordship; in other words, that there would not necessarily continue to be a renewal of the fisc, the stocks of land under royal control.

We know that there was something of a crisis because of the permanent alienation of royal estates in Northumbria from Bede's cogent analysis of the problems of his own day in his *Letter to Egbert*.[49] So much land had been granted away, says Bede, that there was a danger that there would no longer be enough to provide young warriors with the endowment they expected, let alone for any further provision for the church. The problem had been exacerbated in Northumbria because laymen had managed to acquire grants of land for themselves on the same terms as the church on the fictional pretext that they were founding monasteries. The minority of Osred had given those who ruled on his behalf the opportunity to reward themselves in this way, and, of course, the acquisition of permanent, rather than temporary, grants of royal land with rights of free alienation was a very attractive proposition. We do not have such a clear indication from any of the other kingdoms that comparable problems had arisen by the early years of the eighth century, but, given the size of gifts to the church, it seems likely, and the fiction that land was being granted to laymen for ostensibly religious purposes seems also to have been used in Mercia.[50]

As kingdoms and their borders grew in size, so the effort of maintaining and defending them became a greater burden. As kings were unable, and certainly ill-advised, to purchase more manpower through the indiscriminate granting of estates, their best way forward was to concentrate on the rights they could claim over estates which had already been alienated. There has been considerable debate about whether the new bookland tenure freed the land from all royal rights and claims.[51] Certainly monks would have been freed from personal service, but from analogy with Francia one would not expect that their lands would have been free from all royal demands and early charters do not claim general exemption from royal service.[52] What seems to have happened in Mercia in the eighth century was not so much that the Mercian kings were demanding hitherto unknown rights over churchland, but that they were making heavier demands than previously, including an insistance that monks should personally perform royal labour services. Such unheard of exactions brought protests from Boniface and other missionary bishops on behalf of Mercian churchmen.[53] In the end there was compromise. Mercian kings were prepared to remit certain rights they could claim, but insisted on the three common burdens of military service, the building of bridges and the construction of fortresses which 'the whole people perform by custom from their hereditary lands'.[54] The building of fortresses and bridges may have been new demands and may have represented considerable exactions. With the aid of these obligations, probably modelled on similar exactions in Francia, the Mercians produced new strategies for dealing with their Welsh enemies and subsequently adapted them for use against the Vikings. Offa imposed the common burdens on Kent when he conquered the kingdom. The formula was eventually copied by the West Saxons and ultimately refined by Alfred to enable him to overcome decisively the Viking threat to his kingdom through reorganizing fyrd-service and ringing his kingdom with a chain of fortified burhs.[55]

The principles behind the common burdens were important for the future development of kingship. They established that in order for a king to fulfil his responsibilities towards his people, particularly those concerned with defence, he had the right to make considerable exactions from the landowners of his kingdom. That was the point which Alfred was making in the passage quoted at the beginning: a king can only function properly if he is given the means to do so. Alfred's battles were not just with the Vikings; he also had to fight for the assent of his own people to substantial claims for military service and for contributions towards the cost of his campaigns. Some churches seem to have been forced to sell or mortgage lands to meet the king's demands,[56] and no doubt other landowners were similarly affected. Alfred met with some resistance,[57] but in the end gained important concessions on which his successors were able to build to make England one of the best ordered governments in tenth- and eleventh-century Europe.[58] The permanent alienation of land which had originally been granted on a temporary basis encouraged a shift away from the idea inherent in the organization of the *comitatus* that service to the king must be continually rewarded to one where obligations of royal service were inherited with land. It was still important that relations between nobles and the king were underpinned by personal service at the royal court and the giving of gifts, but the balance had undeniably shifted.

As well as establishing rights over land that had been granted away, kings had to administer their own estates effectively. Their lands had to provide them not only with the food and ale which Alfred mentions, but also with the wherewithal to acquire the weapons and gifts which kings also required. A king's estates could in many instances provide him with some essential raw materials such as the iron ore he needed for weapons; some charters suggest mineral deposits were being exploited by landowners,[59] and excavations at the royal estate of Ramsbury (Wilts) produced evidence for extensive iron-smelting and smithying.[60] But many of the raw materials that would have been needed for the expected gifts of jewellery and war-gear such as gold, silver, garnets and rock-crystal, could only be acquired by importing them from abroad, either through exchange mechanisms established by personal links with foreign kings or through trade.[61] What English kings could offer in exchange would presumably have been principally agricultural products or by-products like cloth, though hunting dogs, hawks and furs were additional possibilities.[62] Many of the items acquired from abroad seem to have reached England via Francia and in the sixth and early seventh century far more of such imports are known from Kent than from any other Anglo-Saxon king-dom. Early contacts between the Kentish and Merovingian royal houses are well-attested.[63] We cannot be certain that the Kentish kings had a monopoly on importing foreign goods into their kingdom, though the interest in trade in the early Kentish laws is suggestive. Gift-exchange between kings of Kent and other kingdoms may account for the presence of imported goods or items made from imported materials in rich burials like Taplow, Broomfield or, even, Sutton Hoo, though there is some evidence for separate trading links between eastern England and Austrasian Francia.[64]

In the seventh and eighth century, trade with the Continent seems to have become increasingly important to Anglo-Saxon kings, as can be seen from the development of the sceatta and penny coinages, the rise of the specialized trading base (*wic*) and the priority given to acquiring ports by kingdoms like Mercia and Wessex which to begin with were not ideally placed to participate in foreign trade. The *wics* had the potential to be more than just foreign trading bases, and Hamwic with its many specialist craftsmen may also have been a supply depot for surrounding royal estates and been involved in internal trade.[65] The great development of internal markets and trade was to come in the tenth century when the West Saxon kings developed the economic poten-tial of the burhs.

Beowulf, for all its heroic content, clearly makes the point that economic and military success were intimately linked.[66] A 'good' king was a generous king who through his wealth won the support which would ensure his supremacy over other kingdoms. But as Tacitus pointed out in the *Germania*, where military success was dependent on the ethos of the warband there was a need for continual warfare.[67] A large military following was necessary to prevent conquest from other kingdoms, but had to be held together by constant war and the giving of gifts, the former being necessary to acquire the means of providing the latter. The move from temporary grants of land for royal service to permanent alienation with hereditary tenure helped to get Anglo-Saxon kings off that particular treadmill and to establish that royal service was an obligation inherent in the ownership of land rather than something which had to be purchased continually. Nevertheless the rewards of royal service were still substantial. A gift like the Alfred Jewel with its exquisite workmanship in cloisonné enamelling and expensive materials of gold and rock-crystal was worth acquiring (see Fig. 5),[68] and the expansion of larger kingdoms at the expense of the smaller provided new opportunities for the nobility in royal administration. Although there were limits to the degree of loyalty which could be bought, as the murder of Æthelbald of Mercia by his household and the rebellion against Æthelwulf of Wessex demonstrated, the Anglo-Saxon kings on the whole seem to have been successful by the end of our period in using their resources to purchase the tools they needed in order to do their job effectively.

Royal and noble families

Although it has often been necessary to speak of the king and nobility as if they were two separate interest groups such a distinction should not be pushed too far. For the umbrella term 'nobility' included people who were members of the royal house and who would be linked to the king not only by ties of lordship, but also by the obligations and privileges of kinship. Membership of the royal family seems to have been broadly based and the genealogical information we possess suggests that any adult male who could claim descent in the male line from the founder king of the dynasty could be described as an 'ætheling', a prince eligible for the throne.[69] In some kingdoms, notably that of the East Saxons and the West Saxons until the middle of the seventh century, common descent and eligibility for the throne seem to have been expressed by use of names beginning with the same letter. This does not mean that we should think of the royal house as a monolithic agnatic clan as the genealogies might superficially suggest. Research on kinship structures suggests that the large clan was not characteristic of Anglo-Saxon England and that what was significant in most facets of life was a much narrower kinship group of close relatives which was essentially bilateral, that is composed of relatives of both the father and mother of any individual.[70] There is no reason to think that the royal house was any different. When we look at the activities of rulers for whom appropriate information survives we can see them actively promoting the interests of their own close relatives. When Cenwulf became king of Mercia he appointed one of his brothers as subking of Kent, made his son and another brother ealdormen and placed his daughter in charge of some choice religious houses. Two nephews were also prominent at his court, as were a number of other individuals whose names suggest that they too were closely related to Cenwulf.[71]

By the eighth century royal houses were composed of a number of separate royal lineages which appear in our sources as competing with each other to place a candidate on the throne and whose members, like Cenwulf's family, might adopt distinctive patterns of nomenclature. The evolution of distinct subgroupings within the royal house occurred naturally with the passage of time. Royal houses had started life as one close-knit family: Penda's power had been established, for instance, with the aid of his own immediate relatives. His brother had held a command on the Welsh border; one son ruled the Middle Angles, another the Magonsæte, while daughters provided valuable political alliances through marriages with princes of other kingdoms.[72] However, by the time that Cenwulf came to the throne of Mercia at the end of the eighth century the number of royal descendants had grown considerably. Men who had common ancestors who had been close relatives were themselves only distant cousins. Cenwulf's family was in competition with two other lineages, distinguished by names in 'B' and 'Wig' respectively, for control of the throne. It was not, of course, just a matter of concern to the individual claimant whether he became king or not, for it was of vital interest to the whole family group. If one of their number became king, they all stood to share from the patronage he would have available. Mutual self-interest might draw other important individuals into alliance with a particular kin-group and so the factions which seem to be characteristic of a number of kingdoms in the eighth and ninth centuries were born.

The pattern of succession in the different royal kingdoms varied with the fluctuating fortunes of the various royal lineages; a period of relatively stable succession in which successive kings were all closely related to one another might be followed by a much more unsettled phase in which a ruler was characteristically succeeded by a distant cousin. Northumbria, Mercia and Wessex all experienced these two periods of contrasting patterns of succession, but in Kent and East Anglia the succession remained with one descent-group (bar one or two interruptions connected with the ambitions of foreign rulers) for as long as we have appropriate genealogical information available (which in neither case covers the final period of the kingdom's independent history). In periods when the succession was exclusive generally those who ruled would themselves be the sons of kings; this was the pattern, for instance, in Kent where presumably more distant relatives were excluded, and in Wessex from the ninth century. In such periods a king might be succeeded by his son, but fraternal succession was just as common.

One might hazard that all kin-groups wished to obtain a monopoly of the throne, but that not all of them were able to do so. There was no recognized position of heir to the throne, but opportunities for designation could be created.[73] Abdication for religious purposes was apparently one possible way;[74] use of subkingships could give an heir opportunities to gain support and dispense patronage; and Offa tried to circumvent potential opposition by having his son crowned as king during his lifetime.[75] The kings who were most successful in ensuring the succession of their own descendants were those who were most successful in other spheres and, in particular, those who increased substantially the amount of territory under their control. Egbert and his son Æthelwulf were able to ensure that the succession remained in their branch of the West Saxon house by capitalizing on Egbert's great military successes which virtually doubled the size of the West Saxon kingdom. They could afford to buy support through gifts of land which political rivals could not hope to match, and the creation of the subkingdom of eastern Wessex not only eased those provinces into the West Saxon kingdom, but enabled first Æthelwulf and then his son Æthelbert to get valuable experiences of kingship before they succeeded to the main West Saxon throne.[76] Similar strategies had probably helped the families of Æthelbert of Kent, Æthelfrith of Bernicia and Penda of Mercia to establish themselves.

In Northumbria and Mercia branches of the royal house which dominated in the seventh century disappeared in the course of the eighth century. The initially dominant lineages may have begun to loosen their stranglehold on power when they began to be militarily and economically less successful; a natural corollary if their power had been based in the first instance on having more resources at their disposal than their rivals. In Northumbria the disastrous defeat of Egfrith at Nechtansmere led to a reduction in the territory under the control of his successors and so may have heralded the decline in power of the family of Æthelfrith.[77] But to remain buoyant a lineage had to be able to field an adult male candidate of the right calibre and the Æthelfrithings also failed in this department. To begin with family interests were protected by bringing Aldfrith, a half-brother of Egfrith, over from Ireland, but when Aldfrith died his sons were all under-age. The eldest Osred was kept going through a minority with the aid of influential kin and Northumbrian notables, but after his murder a distant collateral succeeded him.[78]

The natural tendency for some families to die out could give rival lineages the chance to take the throne. In addition to the hazards of infertility and high infant mortality, Anglo-Saxon princes were likely to meet an untimely end in battle or through the machinations of rivals. A variety of factors, for instance, caused the male line of the Deiran royal house to apparently die out within a few years of Edwin's death (see Table 9). One of Edwin's sons died with him at the battle of Hatfield; Edwin's cousin Osric who succeeded him was killed in battle against Penda and Cadwallon; Penda murdered a second son of Edwin and Oswiu murdered Osric's son Oswine; two infant sons and an infant grandson of Edwin died from natural causes.[79] The absorption of Christianity into Anglo-Saxon society increased the likelihood of lineages dying out by introducing new laws on marriage and legitimacy. By denying the throne to sons who were deemed illegitimate the church reduced the chances of lineages providing suitable claimants for the throne.[80] Aldfrith, for instance, was regarded in some quarters as illegitimate and if he had been born a century later would probably have been barred from acceding to the throne.[81]

But it still needs to be explained how distant collaterals were able to emerge to take the throne and why men who were as much as seven or eight generations away from an ancestor who had ruled were still regarded as eligible for the throne (something which would not be regarded as possible in later centuries).[82] A belief in the efficacy of royal blood and the need for an able ruler lie in the background, but a more immediate explanation can be found in the multiple rule which was a feature of Anglo-Saxon kingship in the seventh century. Although there are some instances of joint succession – most typically of several sons on the death of their father – in which power may have been held in common without any territorial division necessarily taking place,[83] in most instances multiple rule seems to have been linked initially with the need to provide a subsidiary ruler for a formerly independent area which was being taken over. Many such subkingships were shortlived and might disappear after one generation when the province was lost or was more firmly incorporated into the main kingdom. In other instances the subkingdom might remain under the control of the descendants of the first subking who would then begin to form a distinct subgroup within the royal house. We have examples of both types from Mercia; the Middle Angles were ruled as a subkingdom for only one generation under Penda's son Peada, but Merewalh of the Magonsæte (who was probably also a son of Penda) passed control of the province to his sons.[84]

It is likely that the multiple kingship systems we can see in operation among the East and West Saxons in the later seventh century originated from the granting of control of territories to individual members of the royal house who then passed rights on to their descendants, but we lack conclusive evidence. In the decade following the death of Cenwalh of Wessex in 673 it appears that it may not have been possible for any one ruler to assert authority over the rest, for, according to Bede, subkings divided the kingdom between them.[85] The resources of the subkingdom could be used to launch campaigns for the dominant position. Both Cædwalla and Ine, who were successful in establishing dominant West Saxon kingships, were the sons of West Saxon subkings. However, devolution of power was not the inevitable result of the creation of a subkingdom. In Kent the subkingdom of west Kent, which had probably been set up when the area was taken over in the sixth century, was utilized as part of the most carefully controlled succession system in early Anglo-Saxon England. In a number of instances the junior ruler in west Kent moved up to take the senior position on the death of his partner and it never became the preserve of a particular branch of the royal house.[86]

In the eighth century the subkingdoms were replaced by ealdormanries, but the tendency of rival branches of the royal house to challenge for the throne did not decline and in some kingdoms it increased. In a number of cases royal collateral lines which had provided subkings probably controlled the same areas as ealdormen. In Mercia and Northumbria we know that a number of the successful royal candidates were either ealdormen or the sons of ealdormen, and the powers inherent in the office of ealdorman may have helped the rival branches make their bids for power. Although removing the subkingships concentrated executive power in the hands of one king, which seems to have been of advantage in the kingdom's struggle for expansion and survival, the ealdormen inherited many of the regalian rights of the subkings and provincial kings whom they had succeeded.[87] Above all the armies of the provinces served under their ealdormen and would give their loyalty in the first instance to them.[88] The Northumbrian chronicle gives many instances of how combinations of ealdormen and their armed followings decided the success or failure of royal candidates.

There was probably a tendency, as in later Wessex, for ealdormanries to become hereditary which would increase the potential powers of the families who controlled them.[89] A number of ealdormen seem to have been the sons of ealdormen and the family of Berhtfrith of Northumbria exercised considerable power for three generations. Beornhæth, Berhtred and Berhtfrith seem to have been not just ealdormen, but to have enjoyed a rank second to that of the king, as Stephanus says of Berhtfrith.[90] In the eighth century the title of *patricius* was frequently applied to individuals in this position which seems to have been analogous to that of mayors of the palace in Francia (for whom Bede used the title *patricius*).[91] The position of *patricius* is known from Kent, Mercia and Northumbria in the eighth century. The *patricius* could deputize for the king as military leader and probably played a major role in the co-ordination of royal government. However, as in Francia the 'mayors of the palace' could be especially dangerous as well as potentially useful. Berhtfrith managed the kingdom during Osred's minority and must bear much of the responsibility for the abuses of power which occurred and at least two Northumbrian *patricii*, Æthelwold Moll and Osred II, went on to become kings.

Kings in the eighth and ninth centuries were in a difficult position. The primitive systems of government available to them required considerable reliance on ealdormen and delegation of some royal powers to them, but the surrender of such powers made the ealdormen a potential threat. Particularly dangerous were ealdormen who could claim royal descent for like the subkings of the seventh century they were potential candidates for the throne and had access to military and financial resources which would support their campaign. Some Mercian kings tried to pack the ealdormanries with their own relatives, but they would only have been able to fill a proportion of the offices in this way. Nor could they easily remove potential rivals from office, for they would face the opposition not only of the individual ealdorman concerned, but of that ealdorman's kinsmen and of other powerful nobles bound to the ealdorman by mutual ties of obligation. The Northumbrian chronicle shows how strong-arm tactics could lead to feud and counter-feud, and although Æthelbald and Offa of Mercia seem to have successfully dominated their ealdormen, their successors in the ninth century, like the eighth-century Northumbrian kings, only seem to have been able to command support from a section of the higher nobility.

Although we have so far talked exclusively of men, royal and noble women were also important in establishing and maintaining the power of their families. Anglo-Saxon women were not the equal of men in law, but though a daughter of a king might not enjoy equality with her brothers she was still a member of the kin-group and entitled to share in its success.[92] Only one queen, Seaxburh of Wessex, appears in a regnal list and unfortunately we do not know her ancestry. Normally women could not inherit the throne, but they do seem to have been able to pass royal blood on to their descendants. It was because Oswald's father, Æthelfrith of Bernicia, married a Deiran princess that Oswald was able to claim the thrones of both kingdoms by hereditary right.[93] It was probably for similar reasons that the rival Mercian princes Wigmund and Berhtfrith both wished to marry Ælfflæd, the daughter of King Ceolwulf, for her royal blood would greatly have enhanced the claims of their descendants to rule.[94] We cannot demonstrate that any individual succeeded to the throne purely through a claim passed by descent from a female, but neither can we categorically say that it did not occur; after all, Beowulf's claim to the throne of the Geats came through his mother.[95]

Women did not necessarily marry 'out' of their families; they could instead be seen as bringing new relatives into the family nexus, especially when the woman was of higher birth than her husband.[96] This was why marriages between princesses and rulers of kingdoms over which the princesses' kinsmen hoped to increase control were of great importance in a kingdom's strategy for growth; the in-laws were brought into the family structure of the dominant kingdom. The death of the Northumbrian prince Ælfwine at the battle of the Trent caused mourning in both the Northumbrian and Mercian courts for although Ælfwine had been the enemy of Æthelred of Mercia he was also his kinsman because he was his brother-in-law.[97] It should not be assumed that men describing themselves as kinsmen of a king could only be linked through a male of the royal house, for the descendants of female relatives were also likely to be important. In royal houses like that of the East Saxons where descendants in the male line adopted a distinctive nomenclature, members of the royal house, like Œthelred, who break the pattern could be the offspring of female members of the house.[98] It is a great pity that we know so little of marriages that took place within kingdoms. For instance, the marriage of King Alhred of Northumbria to Osgifu, daughter of King Oswulf and sister of King Ælfwold, provides a hint of an alliance between these two families against their rivals of the houses of Æthelwold Moll and Eadwulf.[99] If we had more information about such unions it is likely that the margin between royal and noble houses would become even less distinct than it appears at the moment.

King and Church

There can be little doubt that the conversion to Christianity had a profound effect upon the Anglo-Saxon kingdoms. Christianity brought with it not only a complex theology with quite different approaches to such ritual matters as the treatment of the dead,[100] but also a new morality and different expectations of legal and economic provision. It brought the Anglo-Saxons into closer contact with the late Roman world, but in doing so helped change facets of Anglo-Saxon life more radically than the first kings who embraced Christianity could have anticipated. The impact of Christianity is one of the best recorded aspects of early Anglo-Saxon England which is hardly surprising when our sources have been written by churchmen, but the interpretation of the records is not always straightforward. Churchmen like Bede wrote with a very clear idea of what the king's role within the Christian church should be and of the impact which they wished to have upon contemporary rulers.[101] When Bede wrote about the Northumbrian kings of the seventh century he projected upon them the ideals which he hoped contemporary rulers of the eighth century would espouse. So we get portraits like that of the saintly Oswald who was 'always wonderfully humble, kind, and generous to the poor and strangers' and prospered because he accepted the guidance of his spiritual advisor, Bishop Aidan, but who does not really live for us as the flesh and blood king who was so hated by the monks of the adjoining province of Lindsey that they were unwilling to house his body overnight.[102] It is much harder to interpret the motivation and understanding of rulers like Oswald than that of the churchmen who wrote about them.

Although royal families were initially cautious in their acceptance of Christianity, and in most kingdoms there was a temporary reaction in favour of paganism after the death of the first converted king,[103] once it was clear that Christianity was here to stay it was embraced with some enthusiasm at the royal courts. Kings not only made generous provision for churches in their kingdoms, but also showed in many cases a more personal commitment to the new religion. The number of kings abdicating to enter a monastery or to make the pilgrimage to Rome is remarkable.[104] It included not only kings like Ine who abdicated in old age after a reign of thirty-seven years in order to end his days in Rome, but younger men like King Sigebert of the East Angles who entered a monastery while apparently still in the prime of life.[105] Charismatic Irish or Irish-trained churchmen seem to have been particularly influential in causing kings to give up their worldly positions to concentrate on the journey to the better life in the world to come.[106] The Irish missionaries with their fearless determination to flout convention if it conflicted with Christian standards seem to have made a strong and positive impression; when an Irish-trained bishop cursed, an Anglo-Saxon king literally trembled and fell at his feet.[107] Once Irish influence was diluted after the synod of Whitby, Christianity came to fit much more comfortably with the even tenor of Anglo-Saxon life.

Right from the start when Æthelbert of Kent decided that it would be safer to be converted from Rome rather than via the ambitious Frankish court, there was a political dimension to Christianity within England which complicates our assessment of the relations between king and church. The conversion of one kingdom by another as recounted in the pages of the *Ecclesiastical History* was clearly connected with the pattern of overlordship. Overlords sought to increase their influence in subject kingdoms by arranging their conversion and by binding subject kings more closely to them by becoming their godfather.[108] That the Christian God was seen as a superior god of battle, replacing Woden from whom most Anglo-Saxon royal houses traced descent, also seems apparent from Bede's work, and many Anglo-Saxon kings were no doubt impressed by the type of arguments which

Bishop Daniel suggested Boniface should use on the pagan Continental Germans which stressed that the Christian nations were the most successful and prosperous in the known world.[109]

Charters articulate the belief of Anglo-Saxon kings that they were giving land to the church for the good of their souls, but there were other motives as well. The founding of monasteries in newly conquered territories was part of the consolidation process through which subjected areas were brought to identify themselves with the main kingdom and its royal house. The process would have been helped if, as was frequently the case, the founding member of the monastery came to be revered as a saint. The church saw the value of recognizing members of royal dynasties as saints for it not only encouraged more royal donations, but provided a model and a focus for the religious devotions of the local populations.[110] Kings too would have been alive to the political value of local saints' cults and to the kudos of possessing saintly relatives;[111] it was a role which female members of the royal house could fill, though royal males who died violent deaths, whether in battle like Oswald or through murder like Wigstan, were also eligible.[112] Retirement to a monastery provided elderly kings with a less taxing role and an opportunity to work off some of the sins which were an inescapable part of being a medieval ruler. It also seems to have carried the added bonus of being able to nominate one's heir, as there are a number of well-attested instances where kings like Sigebert of East Anglia, Ine of Wessex, Æthelred of Mercia, and Ceolwulf of Northumbria resigned their thrones for religious purposes and appointed their successors.[113] However, abdication to enter a monastery or to journey to Rome could have a more sinister connotation. In eighth-century Northumbria several kings like Osred II were forcibly tonsured and incarcerated in a monastery as a way of getting rid of them – once accepted into holy orders they were not eligible for secular offices.[114] One wonders whether all those kings whose abdications for religious purposes are recorded in the *Ecclesiastical History* went quite as joyfully as Bede implies; one thinks in particular about Cenred of Mercia and Offa of the East Saxons whose departure was politically very convenient for relatives they left behind.[115]

Although the church had a great potential to bring about change in Anglo-Saxon society some of its impact was muted to begin with because of the need of the church to adapt itself to Anglo-Saxon society to win acceptance.[116] Churchmen had to accept that kings expected to be heads of the churches in their respective kingdoms which meant that they appointed the bishops and made many of the key decisions. Although kings could be advised and might accept quite severe rebukes from charismatic church leaders, there were limits to the degree of interference they would allow, as Bishop Wilfrid of Northumbria discovered. Wilfrid earned the wrath of Egfrith of Northumbria by meddling in his marriage, by amassing exceptionally large endowments for his religious houses and by accepting the patronage of enemy kings.[117] All Wilfrid's wealth was of no avail when Egfrith decided to exile him and neither he nor his successor Aldfrith were prepared to accept papal judgements which said Wilfrid should be reinstated. Other churchmen, including Bishop Cuthbert and Bede,[118] seem to have taken a more pragmatic attitude, perhaps taking their lead from Pope Gregory who had advised his missionaries to ease the Anglo-Saxons into Christianity by associating the new religion with aspects of the old.[119] Particularly notable was the fusion of the ideals of the church and the warband.[120] However, there were limits to the degree of rapprochement which could be achieved between Christianity and the traditional forms of Anglo-Saxon life without damaging the tenets of the former, and some of the aristocratic churchmen of the eighth century who were rebuked by Bede and Alcuin for preferring feasting and hunting to church services, seem to have had a poor grasp of the expected differences between ecclesiastical and secular life.[121]

Nevertheless some changes did begin to have an effect soon after the establishment of Christianity. The introduction of bookland and some of its consequences have already been mentioned. Although kings diverted large resources in land to the church, royal houses, like other important lay families, also took advantage of the new tenure to establish their own proprietary monasteries. Many of these were double monasteries controlled by females of the royal house, but, if Boniface's correspondents in Kent can be relied upon, subject to supervision and demands from the king.[122] The concentration of land and wealth in church hands gave the church a potential political power and in eighth-century Northumbria churchmen were not infrequently allied with different factions leading to attacks on churchmen and their property as part of the internal feuding.[123] In 750 King Eadbert had the bishop of Lindisfarne imprisoned and his church besieged so that he could capture a rival ætheling who had taken refuge there, and at the beginning of the ninth century Archbishop Eanbald II of York toured the country with a large following of thegns and their armed men who included enemies of the current king.[124]

The church was also very concerned from the start with controlling marriage practices within England and a number of the questions which Augustine put to Pope Gregory were concerned with the permitted degrees of consanguinity.[125] The Gregorian mission was nearly expelled from Kent because it forbad King Eadbald's marriage with his stepmother; only a timely epileptic fit persuaded Eadbald to accept the church's ruling.[126] Marriage was still a source of contention in the eighth century when King Æthelbald of Mercia was rebuked for not taking a legitimate wife, but having instead many concubines, some of whom had once been nuns (no doubt from the proprietary nunneries of the Mercian royal house).[127] The papal legates reiterated the importance of adhering to the church's laws on marriage on their visit in 786.[128] But there was more involved here than just questions of morality. The laws on marriage also defined offspring as legitimate or illegitimate and, as the papal legates specifically stressed, only the legitimate offspring of a king could be recognized by the church as eligible for the throne. The laws of the church interfered with traditional strategies of heirship and gave churchmen considerable political influence through being able to rule which unions were legitimate or which mariages might be dissolved.[129] However, although kings showed increasing respect for church laws as our period progressed and from the second half of the eighth century made increasing use of the coronation ceremony to legitimize succession to the throne,[130] they were not always prepared to accept their rulings if there was sufficient motivation to resist them. The question of marriage with a stepmother surfaced again in the ninth century when King Æthelbald of Wessex married his father's second wife, Judith, the daughter of the Frankish king Charles the Bald.[131] Presumably such a prestigious bride and such an important alliance with Francia was too tempting to relinquish.

The Carolingian Renaissance heightened appreciation within England of the role of king and church in a Christian state. Anglo-Saxon kings like Offa and Alfred were quick to perceive the advantages which Charlemagne had seen in a revived church which stressed how the king was set apart from his subjects as Christ's representative on earth and owed unquestioning loyalty and obedience by his people.[132] The church helped pave the way to political unity in southern England by emphasizing its spiritual unity under the archbishop of Canterbury.[133] In exchange for the advantages the church could bring, these ambitious kings were prepared to use their earthly powers to protect the church and promote Christian principles in their kingdoms. Offa was praised by Alcuin for establishing 'good, modest and chaste customs' among the Mercians;[134] he received the papal legates and presided over other synods of the southern English church – the presidency helped emphasize his dominant political position south of the Humber.[135] Alcuin, who as advisor to Charlemagne played a major part in formulating the Carolingian views of kingship, considered Offa a model Renaissance prince (in spite of having arranged the deaths of a number of relatives), in contrast to the contemporary Northumbrian kings who failed miserably on a number of counts as role models for their people.

Alcuin's tendency to berate contemporary Anglo-Saxon rulers as if he were some latter-day Old Testament prophet reveals another facet of the Carolingian Renaissance which stressed the need of the king to receive guidance from his churchmen. In fact, in the ideal Christian state the king was in second place to the church which should guide all royal policy.[136] The Carolingian Renaissance spoke to Anglo-Saxon churchmen as well as to their kings, and encouraged them to carry out their own reforms without waiting for royal initiative, as well as to stand up to rulers if it was necessary. One of the issues over which church and state fell out was the control of proprietary monasteries, and, more particularly, over whether the Mercian kings could take over the proprietary houses of the kings of the Hwicce and Kent whom they had replaced. Opposition from archbishops of Canterbury and bishops of Worcester forced the Mercian kings to compromise and they did not acquire as much land as they had hoped.[137]

The West Saxon kings were also interested in annexing the lands of defunct monasteries, and seem ultimately to have been more successful than the Mercians in acquiring former church lands in Kent.[138] Alfred himself is said to have taken over the former monastery of Abingdon and its lands,[139] and early in Alfred's reign Pope John VIII felt obliged to send him a letter of admonishment and to urge him to show obedience to the archbishop of Canterbury.[140] Alfred's exactions seem to have been considerable and forced churchmen to sell estates, but he could plead necessity, and churchmen were only too aware that if the Vikings had taken over southern England the church would have been likely to lose even more land. Like Charlemagne, Alfred found that as a result of surrounding himself with eager churchmen, whom he had recruited from outside his own kingdom and who were working with him for a common goal, much would be forgiven him and that in the long run his virtues would be seen to counteract any vices. In his own works Alfred seems to accept the principles and precepts with which Bede had clothed the kings he wrote about in the *Ecclesiastical History* in the hope that by so doing others might be led to truly espouse them.

Conclusion

In the period between 600 and 900 major changes took place in the kingdoms of Anglo-Saxon England. Whereas in 600 there was a profusion of kingdoms of different sizes, in 900 the West Saxon royal house was the only one still in power and was poised to take over the former kingdoms of the Mercians and East Angles. The changes we have traced took place for varied reasons. Some, like the appearance of kingship itself and the use of subkings, reflect a common response to common problems. Anglo-Saxon kingdoms also learnt from each other so that an advance in one kingdom, such as the production of coinage, was likely to be copied in the others. But the main political model which the Anglo-Saxon kings had to follow was the Frankish kingdom and many of the innovations of the Anglo-Saxon kings – written lawcodes, the penny coinage, the use of fortresses – can be traced back to Frankish precedents. The church also, of course, stimulated change and introduced Anglo-Saxon England to the legacy of learning from the Roman world. However, some of its introductions like bookland had an impact that was probably not anticipated by either king or church.

It is more difficult to say why Wessex survived while the other Anglo-Saxon kingdoms did not. The kingdoms which were initially most successful in the sixth and early seventh centuries were those in coastal locations in eastern and southern England which had the advantage of trade and other contacts with Francia to boost them. However, ultimately the advantage was to lie with the middle kingdoms which could expand in all directions and particularly at the expense of British communities to the west and north. Sometimes we can identify policies which seem to have been mistaken and may have contributed to a kingdom's decline. The kings of Northumbria in the later seventh century, for instance, seem to have relied too much on temporary overlordships and overestimated the size of the territory they could control, while at the same time granting out too much land from the royal fisc to churches and to members of the nobility, including potential rivals of the royal house. But it is not always possible to be categoric about whether developments were advantageous or not. For instance, the kingship system of Kent initially seems to have much to recommend it and may have been a factor in the early success of the kingdom. One king was dominant, but a subsidiary kingship was used to help manipulate the succession so that eligibility to the throne was confined to a narrow group of those who were themselves sons of kings. Although it did not completely reduce friction within the royal house Kent suffered far less than many king- doms from succession disputes. But the system had its disadvantages as well for if the group eligible for the throne was too narrow there was less choice of candidates with the result that the man chosen to be king might not be of the highest calibre and there was a danger, as happened with the English crown in the eleventh century, of the royal house dying out altogether leading to foreign conquest. We do not know whether any of these factors helped the Mercian conquest of Kent, but some of the problems of Northumbria in the eighth century were the result of the Æthelfrithings and their supporters being deter- mined to hang on to power although they did not have a suitable candidate for the throne on the death of Aldfrith.

Probably no one living in the eighth century would have predicted that the great Mercian empire would be destroyed and that the West Saxons with their poor track record for feuds and infighting within the royal house would emer- ge as the dominant kingdom in the ninth century. However, Mercia may not have been quite as impressive as a state as it superficially appears. The power- ful Mercian rulers Æthelbald, Offa and Cenwulf failed to solve all the prob- lems inherent in the government of Mercia. In addition – and this was also a crucial matter in a kingdom's survival – all failed to produce sons who survived them. Egbert of Wessex made the most of the opportunities offered by family feuding in Mercia in the ninth century, but in the end the Viking armies were the deciding factor. If the Great Heathen Army had begun with the conquest of Wessex, rather than leaving it to last, subsequent history might have been rather different. The Anglo-Saxons believed in 'luck' as a random element in the affairs of man and so would probably have agreed that there is a limit to the extent one can understand why one kingdom failed while another succeeded.

NOTES

Chapter One
INTRODUCTION: THE ORIGINS OF
THE ANGLO-SAXON KINGDOMS

1. *HE* I, 23; Mayr-Harting 1972, 51–77; Brooks 1984, 3–14.
2. Winterbottom (ed. and trans.) 1978. See O'Sullivan 1978, Sims-Williams 1983a, Lapidge and Dumville (eds.) 1984 for date and general discussion.
3. Gildas ch. 23–6.
4. Gildas ch. 27–36.
5. Davies 1982.
6. Alcock 1988a; Charles-Edwards 1989.
7. Jackson 1969; Charles-Edwards 1978.
8. *HE* I, 15; Miller 1975; Sims-Williams 1983b, 5–26.
9. The context of Gildas' words could be taken to imply that the first settlement was in the north-east not the south-east: Thompson 1979, 217–19; Sims-Williams 1983a, 20–1.
10. *HE* Preface.
11. See Brooks 1989a, 58–64 and below ch. 2, 26.
12. Sims-Williams 1983b, 26–41.
13. Sims-Williams 1983a, 22–4; Brooks 1989a, 58–64.
14. Turville-Petre 1957; Moisl 1981.
15. Sims-Williams 1983b, 29.
16. Sims-Williams 1983b, 5–21; Wallace-Hadrill 1988, 212–15.
17. Dumville 1985.
18. Dumville 1985, 50–6.
19. *HE* II, 15; see also below ch. 4, 61.
20. See below ch. 3, 46.
21. Dumville 1977a, 90–3.
22. Hills 1979a; Arnold 1988, 1–16.
23. Myres 1969 and 1986; Hills 1979.
24. Hawkes and Dunning 1961; Clarke 1979, 389–403; Crummy 1981, 1–23; Jones, M.U. 1980.
25. Welch 1971; Johnson 1980, 124–49; Myres 1986.
26. Hills 1979, 297–308; Sims-Williams 1983a, 20–1.
27. See maps in Arnold 1988a, 42–3.
28. Hawkes 1982, 65.
29. *HE* I, 15.
30. Myres 1970; Hills 1979, 313–17.
31. Hills 1979, 313–17; Myres 1986, 104–13.
32. *HE* V, 9.
33. Hines 1984.
34. Evison 1965.
35. Grierson 1959; Hodges 1982, 1–28.
36. Hawkes 1966 and 1982, 72–4; Wood, I. 1983.
37. Reece 1980; Arnold 1984 – but these views are controversial; for a more conventional view see Salway 1984, 348–414.
38. Barker 1980; Bidwell 1979 and 1980.
39. Tatton-Brown 1984, 5–12; Biddle 1983, 111–15.
40. Reece 1980; Arnold 1984, 48–83.
41. Gracie and Price 1979 (see also Heighway 1987, 3–4); Rodwell and Rodwell 1985, especially 68–75.
42. Jones 1966.
43. Alcock 1987, 153–71, but see also Burrow 1981.
44. Alcock 1987, 172–214.

45. These remarks are not intended to apply to the Celtic kingdoms of northern Britain which were never fully incorporated into the Roman empire and so retained more distinctive 'Celtic' features – Alcock 1987, 285–311.
46. Hayes 1972 and 1980.
47. Arnold 1984, 121–41.
48. Hills 1980.
49. Jones 1979.
50. Gelling 1978, 87–105.
51. Bonney 1976; Davies 1979; Drury and Rodwell 1980; Everitt 1986, 69–92 and see n. 25 above.
52. Hall 1988.
53. For example, Finberg 1955; Jones 1976; Davies 1979; Hooke 1985; Rodwell and Rodwell 1986.
54. Foard 1985, 201–3.
55. Jones 1976; Campbell 1978, 48–50. The territories described here should not be regarded as identical with the fully developed economic model of the later Celtic multiple estates. The multiple estates may have developed from similar territorial arrangements in Celtic Britain.
56. Sawyer 1983; Charles-Edwards 1989.
57. Bassett 1989a, 17–23.
58. Hope-Taylor 1977.
59. Millett and James 1983.
60. James, Marshall and Millett 1984.
61. Shephard 1979; Arnold 1988b.
62. Clark, Cowie and Foxon 1985.
63. Hines 1984, 285.
64. Bruce-Mitford 1974, 222–52.
65. Stephens 1884; Smith 1903, 320–6.
66. The text is based on Loyn 1984, 35–6 and Dumville 1989c.
67. Davies and Vierck 1974, 224–36; Dumville 1989a, 129–30; but the case for a Northumbrian origin is put in Brooks 1989b, 167–8.
68. Davies and Vierck 1974, 224–36; the case for a later date is put in Hart 1971, 157.
69. Charles-Edwards 1972; Loyn 1984, 34–6.
70. Davies and Vierck 1974, 228–9; Loyn 1984, 36. For instance, *HE* IV, 16 assesses the Isle of Wight at the time of Cædwalla's conquest at 1,200 hides, exactly twice its Tribal Hidage total. Bede stresses Cædwalla's punitive treatment of the island and this is presumably reflected in the higher hidage assessment.
71. Sawyer 1978, 110–11.
72. The name is generally emended to 'Wreocensæte' 'dwellers of the Wrekin', the form given in the Latin manuscripts – Davies and Vierck 1974, 230–1.
73. *HE* IV, 23 (Elmet) (to be read in conjunction with *HB* ch. 63); IV, 16 (Wight).
74. *HE* IV, 19.
75. Maps consulted for the preparation of map 1 include Hart 1971, 137 and 1977, 50–1; Davies and Vierck 1974, fig. 8; Hill 1981, 76; together with information from regional studies, especially Courtney 1981.
76. Campbell 1979, 5–8.
77. *HE* III, 24.
78. See n. 71 and Faull 1977.
79. Davis 1982.
80. Dumville 1989a, 129–34.
81. Bassett 1989a, 17–23.
82. Yorke 1983; Brooks 1989a, 67–74; and see below ch. 2, 27.
83. Bailey 1989; Blair 1989; Dumville 1989a.
84. Jackson 1953, 419–20, 600–3 and 701–5; Brooks 1989a, 57–8; Eagles 1989, 210–11.
85. Wallace-Hadrill 1971, 1–20; James 1989.
86. Chadwick 1907, 49–50.
87. *Ibid.*, 114–36; Sisam 1953a, 306–7.
88. Sisam 1953a, 322–31.
89. Bruce-Mitford 1974, 35–55; 1978, 91–99, 205–25, but see also below ch. 4, 61.
90. Dumville 1977a, 78–9; Moisl 1981 (for how Bede may have interpreted Woden see Harrison 1976b).

91. Yorke 1985, 13–14.
92. Brooks 1989a, 59.
93. Wallace-Hadrill 1971, 1–20; Dumville 1979, 15–18.
94. James 1989.
95. Reuter 1985; Charles-Edwards 1989, 29–31.
96. John 1966, 1–63; Yorke 1981; Wormald 1983; an alternative reading of the title – *brytenwalda/*'wide ruler' – appears in all the *Chronicle* texts except 'A'.
97. *HE* II, 5.
98. Chadwick 1961; John 1966, 11–12; Wood, I. 1983, 13–14.
99. Tacitus ch. 13–14.
100. Owen 1981, 8–22.
101. Bruce-Mitford 1978.
102. *Ibid.*, 311–93; Enright 1983.
103. Nelson 1980, 44–6.
104. Bruce-Mitford 1974, 223–52, but see also the Coppergate helmet found on its own in a pit in York – Hall 1984, 34–42.
105. Tacitus ch. 13–14.
106. Green 1965 *passim*; Campbell 1979, 8–9.
107. Hume 1974.
108. Cramp 1957; Millett and James 1983, 227–46.
109. Bruce-Mitford 1983.
110. *Beowulf* lines 230–51, 1900–4.
111. Liebermann (ed.) 1903, I, 3–8; *EHD* I, 391–4; Wallace-Hadrill 1971, 32–44; Brooks 1989a. For general problems in interpretation of lawcodes see Wormald 1977a.
112. Wallace-Hadrill 1975, 19–38.
113. Sawyer 1977.
114. Wood, I. 1983.
115. Hawkes 1982; Owen-Crocker 1986, 57–63.
116. Hodges 1982, 104–29; Huggett 1988.
117. Hicks 1986.
118. Charles-Edwards 1983; Wallace-Hadrill 1988, 30.
119. Enright 1983; C. Hicks in Bruce-Mitford 1978, 378–82.
120. Hunter 1974.
121. *HE* II, 16.
122. Bruce-Mitford 1974, 7–17; 1978, 350–7.
123. Hope-Taylor 1977, 241–4; Brooks 1984, 24–5.
124. Kirby 1978, 160–73; Welch 1983 and 1989.
125. Levison 1946, 249–59.
126. Whitelock 1972, and see also ch. 4, 58–9.
127. Stenton 1927; Eagles 1989.
128. Stenton 1955; Brooks 1974.
129. Chaplais 1965 and 1969.
130. Wormald 1984, 14.
131. John 1966, 64–127; Wormald 1984; and see below ch. 8, 163–5.
132. *HE* III, 1; Wallace-Hadrill 1988, 87–8.
133. Sisam 1953a; Dumville 1977a.
134. Dumville 1976.
135. Whitelock 1951; Girvan 1971.
136. Chase (ed.) 1981.
137. Cramp 1957; Bruce-Mitford 1974, 253–61; Wallace-Hadrill 1971, 120–3; Wormald 1978, 120–3.
138. Green 1965 *passim*; Wormald 1978.
139. Out of numerous studies see in particular, Thompson (ed.) 1935; Campbell 1966; Bonner (ed.) 1976; Wallace-Hadrill 1971, 77–97 and 1988.
140. McClure 1983.
141. Kirby 1966.
142. Harrison 1976a, 76–98.
143. Kirby 1980.
144. *HE* V, 23; Wallace-Hadrill 1988, 199.
145. Stenton 1958; Blunt, Lyon and Stewart 1963.

Chapter Two

KENT

1. Meyvaert 1964; Wallace-Hadrill 1988, 31.
2. Dumville 1976, 31, 33 and 37.
3. James 1912, I, 399. The manuscript is Corpus Christi College Cambridge 173 (55v).
4. For example, the reign of Hlothere

- see Harrison 1976a, 80–4, 142–6. See also the reigns of Æthelbert II and Eadric, below, 30–1.
5. Liebermann (ed.) 1903, I, 3–14; Attenborough (trans.) 1922, 4–31; *EHD* I, 391–415.
6. Rollason 1982.
7. See above ch. I, 3–4.
8. Sims-Williams 1983b; Brooks 1989a, 58–64.
9. *HE* II, 5; Brooks 1989a, 58–64.
10. *HE* I, 15; Chadwick 1907, 49–50.
11. Hawkes 1982, 70–2.
12. *Ibid.*, 72–8. For arguments in favour of substantial Frankish settlement see Joliffe 1933 and Evison 1965.
13. Wood, I. 1983.
14. Arnold 1980, 81–142.
15. Tatton-Brown 1984; Brooks 1984, 16–30.
16. Everitt 1986; see also Brooks 1989a, 67–74. These discussions supersede Joliffe 1933.
17. Brooks 1989a, 57–8.
18. Hawkes 1982, 64–78.
19. Yorke 1983 and below, 32–4.
20. See map in Hill 1981, 14.
21. Sims-Williams 1983b, 24–5.
22. Arnold 1982, 26–8, 50–72 and 106–7.
23. Gregory of Tours IV, 26 and IX, 26.
24. Wood, I. 1983, 15–16; Brooks 1989a, 65–7.
25. Brooks 1984, 5–6; 1989a, 65–7.
26. *HE* II, 5.
27. *HE* II, 3 and below ch. 3, 46–8.
28. *HE* II, 15; Colgrave 1968, 98–101; Plummer 1896, II, 93–4.
29. *HE* I, 25.
30. Wallace-Hadrill 1971, 27–32; Angenendt 1986, 778–81.
31. *EHD* I, 790–1; Brooks 1984, 6.
32. *HE* II, 5.
33. Rollason 1982, 75, 77, 80–6, 92 and 114; Werner 1985, 42.
34. See table 3; Witney 1984.
35. *HE* II, 5 and 9.
36. Liebermann (ed.) 1903, I, 9–11; Attenborough 1922, 22–3.
37. S 1165; Blair 1989, 100–2.
38. *HE* IV, 26; Welch 1989, 78–9.
39. *HE* II, 20.
40. *HE* III, 29; Brooks 1984, 69–70.
41. *HE* IV, 12.
42. See Rollason 1982, 39 for Æthelred as the possible avenger of the murdered princes Æthelbert and Æthelred.
43. *Chronicle* sa 686 and 687; Thomas of Elmham 232–8.
44. S 233; Stenton 1933, 189–90.
45. *Chronicle* sa 694.
46. Pertz (ed.) 1841, 2.
47. Harrison 1976a, 142–6; Yorke 1985, 21.
48. *HE* IV, 26; Yorke 1983, 8.
49. S 10 and 12, but see also Scharer 1982, 80–3.
50. For Wihtred's dates see *HE* IV, 26 and V, 8; Plummer (ed.) 1896 II, 284; Dumville 1986b, 13.
51. S 17.
52. *HE* V, 23.
53. Thomas of Elmham 324; Witney 1982, 182; Dumville 1986b, 13.
54. See S 25, 28 and 29.
55. S 30 and 31; Yorke 1983, 9–11.
56. S 91, see also S 86–8.
57. Brooks 1984, 80–1.
58. S 32.
59. S 33.
60. S 33 and 105; Brooks 1984, 111–14.
61. S 34 and 37.
62. Stenton 1971, 207–8.
63. S 35 and 36.
64. S 38.
65. Brooks 1984, 113–17, 321–2.
66. Brooks 1984, 114.
67. *Chronicle* sa 796; Blunt, Lyon and Stewart 1963, 4.
68. *HS* III, 523–5; *EHD* I, 861–2; *Historia Regum* sa 798.
69. Brooks 1984, 129–35.
70. Blunt, Lyon and Stewart 1963, 5; Brooks 1984, 136.
71. Yorke 1983.
72. Levison 1946, 174–233; Yorke 1983, 5–6.
73. *HE* II, 8; Blair 1971, 7–8.
74. Rollason 1982.
75. *HE* II, 5, 6 and 8.
76. S 27.
77. Yorke 1983, 13–17.
78. S 27.
79. S 10–14.

80. S 33.
81. Chadwick 1905, 192–3, 271.
82. See table 2.
83. Yorke 1983, 16–19.
84. *HE* IV, 26.
85. Rollason 1982; see table 2.
86. Ward 1938.
87. *HE* IV, 26.
88. S 32; see also Brooks 1984, 349, n. 16.
89. James 1984.
90. Tangl (ed.) 1916, no. 14; for speculation about Eangyth and Heahburh's relationship to the main royal line see Witney 1984.
91. See table 3.
92. *HE* II, 9.
93. *HE* III, 15, and see below ch. 4, 78–80.
94. *V. Wilfredi* ch. 2 and 3; *HE* III, 25.
95. S 20; *HS* III, 238–40; Bateson 1889.
96. Rollason 1982, 43–7; Witney 1984.
97. Brooks 1984, 203–6.
98. Some versions of the Mildrith Legend wrongly equate Domne Eafe with her sister Eormenburh, the mother of Mildrith; both Eormenburh and Æbbe/Eafe attest S 20.
99. Rollason 1982, 43–7.
100. S 29 and 143.
101. Tangl (ed.) 1916, no. 30; *EHD* I, 747.
102. Tangl (ed.) 1916, no. 105.
103. Tangl (ed.) 1916, no 14.
104. Godfrey 1976; Rollason 1982, 47–9; Everitt 1986, 181–258.
105. *HE* I, 30.
106. *HS* III, 195 (ch. VI, 8); McNeill and Gamer (trans.) 1979, 204.
107. Brooks 1984, 180–97.
108. *HE* II, 20.
109. *HE* III, 8; Bateson 1889; Rigold 1968.
110. Wood, I. 1983.
111. Hodges 1982, 29–46; Huggett 1988.
112. Sawyer 1977.
113. For example, S 29.
114. Hawkes 1982.
115. Hawkes 1982, 76; see also Astill 1985 and Evison 1987, 168–75.
116. For the available evidence see Hodges 1982, 104–29.
117. Huggett 1988.
118. *HE* II, 3.
119. Liebermann (ed.) 1903, I, 9–11; Attenborough (trans.) 1922, 22–3.
120. Stewart 1978.
121. *HE* III, 8.
122. Grierson and Blackburn 1986, 158–9.
123. Hill and Metcalf (eds.) 1984, 5–70 and 165–74.
124. Blunt 1961.
125. *HE* II, 5; Wallace-Hadrill 1971, 32–44; Wormald 1977a *passim*.
126. Wallace-Hadrill 1971, 37–8; Wood, I. 1983, 12–13.
127. Joliffe 1933, 98–120; Evison 1965.
128. Sawyer 1977.
129. S 7–14.
130. S 1182 and 29 respectively.
131. S 33.
132. Tangl (ed.) 1916, no. 14.
133. S 29.
134. Everitt 1986, 69–92; Brooks 1989a, 67–74.
135. Brooks 1984, 184–6; Crick 1988.
136. Brooks 1984, 114–15.
137. Brooks 1984, 140–2.

Chapter Three
THE EAST SAXONS

1. *HE* Preface and III, 22.
2. *HE* IV, 11 and Yorke 1985, 2.
3. *HE* III, 30.
4. Yorke 1985, 3–4, 8–11; see table 5.
5. Gibbs (ed.) 1939, 1–8; S 1783–7, 1791.
6. See below, 55.
7. Bascombe 1987; Huggins 1978.
8. Rodwell and Rodwell 1986; Bassett 1989a, 24–6.
9. Drury and Rodwell 1980.
10. Jones, W.T. 1980.
11. Smith 1903, 320–6.
12. Priddy 1987, 104.
13. Huggins 1988 *passim*.
14. Crummy, Hillam and Crossan 1982.
15. Jones, M.U. and Jones, W.T. 1980.
16. Yorke 1985, 13–16.
17. *HE* II, 3.
18. See above ch. 2, 27.

19. Brooke and Keir 1975, 16–17.
20. Whitelock 1975, 4–11.
21. Yorke 1985, 27–36; Hart 1987, 57–60.
22. S 65 (704); Bailey 1989, 111–12.
23. Dumville 1989a, 134–6.
24. *HE* IV, 6; Gover *et al.* 1934, xii–xv.
25. S 1165; Blair 1989.
26. Blair 1989, 105–7.
27. Bailey 1989, 114–22; Blair 1989, 98–103.
28. For example, 'the province called *Sunninges'* (Sonning) referred to in S 1165; see map in Bailey 1989, 116.
29. *HE* II, 3.
30. *HE* II, 5 and 6.
31. *HE* II, 5; Plummer (ed.) 1896, II, 88.
32. *HE* III, 22.
33. S 1246; Yorke 1985, 19.
34. *HE* III, 22.
35. *HE* III, 30.
36. *HE* III, 30 and 7.
37. S 1165; Hart 1966, 117–18; Blair 1989, 104–5.
38. *Ibid.*
39. See above ch. 2, 40.
40. Blair forthcoming.
41. S 1171 and 1246; Hart 1966, 121; Whitelock 1975, 7–8.
42. S 10, 12, 65, 1246 and 1783.
43. Whitelock 1975, 10–11; Chaplais 1978.
44. See table 5.
45. *HE* III, 30.
46. S 233; Stenton 1933, 189–90.
47. See above ch. 2, 30.
48. S 10, 13, 14 and 233; Yorke 1983, 8.
49. *HE* V, 8; Plummer (ed.) 1896, II, 284.
50. *HE* IV, 11 and V, 19.
51. S 65 and see n. 42 for his other East Saxon grants.
52. See, for instance, Bascombe 1987.
53. S 65, 1785 and 1787.
54. *HE* V, 19; Stancliffe 1983, 157, 166–71.
55. See, for instance, *V. Wilfredi*, ch. 57.
56. *Historia Regum* II, 32.
57. Yorke 1985, 4 and 23; see table 5.
58. S 100, 106 and 119 (Mddx); S 136, 151 and 1791 (Herts). S 151 is of dubious authenticity.
59. S 86–8, 91, 98 and 1788.
60. Metcalf 1977 and Stewart 1986.
61. Grimes 1968, 204–9; Haslam 1987, 83.
62. Metcalf 1976, 9–13.
63. S 151; *Chronicle* F, sa 798.
64. S 165, 168, 170 and 187; Yorke 1985, 24.
65. Hart 1987, 57–60.
66. S 1791.
67. Yorke 1985, 25–7; Dumville 1989a, 136–40.
68. *HE* III, 30.
69. But see Dumville 1989a, 138.
70. S 64 and 1784.
71. S 64; *HE* V, 19.
72. S 1171; the term used, *parens*, cannot mean 'father' as Seaxred was Sæbbi's father, so possibly 'kinsman' was intended (see Latham 1965, 332 for cognate words).
73. S 1171 and 1246; Hart 1966, 144–5; Chaplais 1968, 327–32.
74. Scharer 1982, 133.
75. Bascombe 1987, 86.
76. S 1784 and 1787.
77. Reaney 1935, xxxi and 174.
78. S 10.
79. S 1171 and 1246; Chaplais 1968, 332.
80. Hohler 1966; Bethell 1970.
81. Bascombe 1987.
82. *HE* IV, 6; S 1246; Hart 1966, 141–2.
83. Huggins 1978.
84. S 1171, 1246 and 1248; Hart 1966, 141–2.
85. S 10 and 11.
86. Hart 1966, 145.
87. *HE* IV, 7–11.
88. Priddy 1987, 104.
89. Whitelock 1975, 5.
90. *Ibid.*, 5–10.
91. S 1165; Blair 1989, 103–5.
92. *V. Wilfredi* ch. 43.
93. Liebermann (ed.) 1903, I, 88; *EHD* I, 398–9.
94. Lapidge and Herren 1979.
95. Scharer 1982, 129–41; Wormald 1984, 9–11.
96. *HE* IV, 6.
97. Whitelock, 1975, 6.
98. *HE* IV, 11.
99. *HE* II, 3; Biddle 1984; Vince 1984; Tatton-Brown 1986.
100. Metcalf 1984, 56.

Chapter Four
THE EAST ANGLES

1. Davis 1955; Whitelock 1972, 1–2.
2. *HE* Preface.
3. Wallace-Hadrill 1988, 112–13.
4. Stenton 1959.
5. Ridyard 1988, 176–96.
6. *V. Guthlaci*, prologue and 15–19.
7. Thacker 1985, 5–7.
8. Whitelock 1972, 6.
9. James 1917; Thacker 1985, 16–18.
10. Winterbottom (ed.) 1972, 67–87; Whitelock 1969.
11. Bruce-Mitford 1975, 1978 and 1983.
12. Bruce-Mitford 1975, 488–573; see also Evison 1980; Vierck 1980; Carver 1986, 94–6.
13. J. Kent in Bruce-Mitford 1975, 578–61.
14. Brown 1981.
15. Bruce-Mitford 1975, 683–717.
16. Bruce-Mitford 1975, 693–8; see also Kirby 1963, 522.
17. *HE* II, 12.
18. *HE* II, 15; and see discussion in Plummer (ed.) 1896, II, 106 for date of Eorpwald's reign.
19. Carver and Evans 1989.
20. *HE* II, 15.
21. *HB* ch. 59.
22. Böhme 1986; Carver 1989, 147–8.
23. Hines 1984, 35–109, 270–85.
24. Bruce-Mitford 1975, 693 and 1986, 195–210.
25. Bruce-Mitford 1974, 55–60.
26. O'Loughlin 1964.
27. Evans 1986, 114–16.
28. Hines 1984, 286–91.
29. Hicks 1986.
30. Warner 1988.
31. See further below, 69–70.
32. *HE* II, 15.
33. *HE* II, 5; Vollrath-Reichelt 1971, 80–8; Wallace-Hadrill 1988, 59, 220–2.
34. *HE* II, 12.
35. *HE* II, 15.
36. *HE* III, 18.

37. *HE* III, 7. 637/8 is given for the death of Sigebert in *FW* and *LE* respectively, but Bede's words suggest a longer reign. *LE* I, 18, states that Anna was killed in the nineteenth year of his reign.
38. Whitelock 1972, 6–12; West and Scarfe 1984, 295; Thacker 1985, 17–18.
39. *HE* III, 18.
40. *HE* III, 21.
41. *HE* III, 24; see Prestwich 1968 for a textual amendment concerning the role of Æthelhere at *Winwæd*.
42. *HE* II, 15.
43. *HE* IV, 17; Plummer (ed.) 1896, II, 15.
44. *HE* III, 22.
45. *HE* IV, 19.
46. *Chronicle* I, 34–5.
47. *V. Guthlaci* ch. 49 and 52.
48. *Ibid.* ch. 1–2.
49. The names Hun and Beonna have been run together as one name in *HS*, but are usually assumed to represent two people; *EHD* I, 240 and n. 9.
50. D. Sherlock in Fenwick 1984, 44–50; Grierson and Blackburn 1986, 277–8.
51. James 1917, 222 and 236.
52. Blunt 19961, 49–50.
53. *Ibid.* and *Chronicle* I, 54–5.
54. Grierson and Blackburn 1986, 281 and 293.
55. Pagan 1982 and Archibald 1982.
56. *Chronicle* I, 60–1; Pagan 1982.
57. Loomis 1932; Whitelock 1969; Smyth 1977, 201–13.
58. Grierson and Blackburn 1986, 294.
59. Davies 1973; Campbell 1979, 4–6; and see above ch. 1, 20.
60. Courtney 1981.
61. Darby 1934.
62. Müller-Wille 1974.
63. Evans 1986; Carver 1986, 102–8.
64. Bruce-Mitford 1975, 578–681; see also Grierson 1970.
65. *HE* II, 15 and III, 18.
66. Wallace-Hadrill 1988, 77–8, 223.
67. *HE* III, 19; Whitelock 1972, 5–6; Wallace-Hadrill 1988, 114–15.

68. *HE* III, 8 and IV, 23.
69. Dunmore *et al.* 1975; Hodges 1982, 70–3.
70. Hurst 1976, 299–303.
71. Hodges 1982, 87–94.
72. Metcalf 1984, 58–9; Stewart 1984, 9–10, 15–16.
73. Grierson and Blackburn 1986, 277–8.
74. *HE* II, 15; Whitelock 1972, 3–8.
75. *HE* III, 18.
76. *HE* IV, 22.
77. See n. 38. A niece (Eormenburh) of Queen Seaxburh (daughter of King Anna) married King Merewalh of the Magonsæte.
78. *HE* II, 12.
79. *HE* IV, 23.
80. *Historia Abbatum* (Anon); Plummer (ed.) 1896, I, 389; *EHD* I, 759; Whitelock 1972, 10–11.
81. *HE* Preface.
82. *HE* IV, 19.
83. Dumville 1976, 31, 33–4 and 37; see table 7.
84. Stenton 1959.
85. Glass 1962.
86. James 1917, 222 and 236.
87. Warner 1988.
88. Whitelock 1972, 4.
89. *HE* IV, 5; Whitelock 1972, 8.
90. Hart 1971, 153–4.
91. *HE* III, 18.
92. *HE* III, 22 and 24.
93. Bruce-Mitford 1952.
94. Fenwick 1984; Carr, Tester and Murphy 1988.
95. Whitelock 1972, 16–17; and see below, 71.
96. See below, 70.
97. Johnson 1983.
98. *HE* III, 19; Whitelock 1972, 5–6.
99. *HE* III, 19.
100. *HE* IV, 3.
101. *HE* IV, 22.
102. *HE* IV, 19.
103. Miller 1951, 8–15; Courtney 1981.
104. *HE* IV, 19; Rollason 1982, 34, 38, 84 and 87. For the possible association of Eormenhild's daughter Werburh with Ely see *LE* I, 15; Thacker 1985, 4; Ridyard 1988, 179–81.
105. *V. Guthlaci* 146–9.
106. *LE* II, 53; Ridyard 1988, 59, 180–1.
107. Rollason 1982, 84, 85 and 87.
108. *Chronicle* F sa 798.
109. Ridyard 1988, 176–96.
110. *LE* I, 1; Ridyard 1988, 219–20.
111. *LE* I, 7.
112. *Chronicle* I, 28–9; West and Scarfe 1984.
113. Tangl (ed.) 1916, no. 81.
114. Fenwick 1984; Carr, Tester and Murphy 1988.
115. Whitelock 1972, 17–22.

Chapter Five
NORTHUMBRIA

1. Kirby 1966, 342–57; see below ch. 1, n. 139 for general works on the *Ecclesiastical History*.
2. Poole 1934; Kirby 1963.
3. Levison 1946, 265–79; Harrison 1976a, 81–5; Miller 1979; Wood, S. 1983.
4. The author of the *V. Wilfredi* is often referred to as Eddius Stephanus, but see Kirby 1983.
5. *V. Wilfredi* ch. 59.
6. Jackson 1963; Dumville 1977c.
7. Blair 1949, 105–12; Duncan 1981, 15–16.
8. Blair 1948; see *HE*, 572–7.
9. Blair 1963; *EHD* I, 263–80.
10. Hart 1982; Lapidge 1982.
11. Lyon 1957 and 1987; Pagan 1969; Grierson and Blackburn 1986, 298–301.
12. Craster 1954; Hart 1975, 131–8.
13. Myres 1935; Blair 1948, 98–104, but see also Wallace-Hadrill 1988, 87, 226–8.
14. Jackson 1953, 701–5; Smyth 1984, 19–21; for the boundary between Bernicia and Deira see Cramp 1988, 72–4.
15. *HB* ch. 38; Blair 1947; Dumville 1977b.
16. *HB* ch. 57; Dumville 1989b, 218.
17. Dumville 1973; *HB* ch. 56.
18. For a list of these kings see table 8, and for a discussion of them see Blair 1950; Kirby 1963, 523–7.

19. Blair 1950; Miller 1979, 49.
20. *HB* ch. 61 which seems to imply that Bamburgh was being added to areas already controlled by the Bernicians. For various views of the campaign see Stenton 1971, 74–6; Hope-Taylor 1977, 284–308; Higham 1986, 256–8.
21. Cramp 1983.
22. Miller 1979.
23. Bede *Chronica Majora*; see Miller 1979, 41. However, the *Chronicle* has dates of 560–88 for Ælle.
24. This depends on a combination of evidence from *HE* I, 34; III, 6 and *HB* ch. 61.
25. *HE* II, 12.
26. *HE* III, 1; Moisl 1983, 116–24.
27. *HE* II, 5, 9, 12 and 15; Kirby 1963, 552–3; Mayr-Harting 1972, 66–7.
28. *HE* II, 20.
29. *HE* III, 1.
30. *HE* III, 6.
31. *HE* III, 3.
32. *HE* III, 9–13; Wallace-Hadrill 1971, 83–5; Folz 1980; Clemoes 1983.
33. *HE* II, 20 and III, 11.
34. *HE* III, 14.
35. *HE* III, 24.
36. *HE* III, 25; *V. Wilfredi* ch. 7–10; John 1970; Mayr-Harting 1972, 103–13; Abels 1988.
37. *HE* III, 24.
38. *HE* IV, 21–2.
39. Blair 1949.
40. *HE* III, 14 and 24.
41. *HE* IV, 23; Fell 1981; Blair 1985.
42. Colgrave (ed.) 1968, 42–4, 47–8.
43. Miller 1979, though she prefers Gilling as the place where the names were preserved.
44. *HE* III, 24.
45. Colgrave (ed.) 1968, 31–45; Kirby 1974a, 19–20.
46. *HE* II, 14.
47. *HE* II, 5; *V.Wilfredi* ch. 20.
48. *HE* II, 9 and 20; III, 15.
49. *HE* IV, 23; Stenton 1959.
50. *HE* IV, 19.
51. *HE* II, 9.
52. Dumville 1979, 79–81.
53. Stenton 1927; Eagles 1989.
54. *HE* II, 20.
55. *HE* III, 24.
56. *HE* III, 21.
57. *HE* III, 11; see table 9.
58. *HE* IV, 21.
59. *HE* V, 24; Finberg 1972, 176–7.
60. Kemp 1987.
61. Booth 1984.
62. Faull, 1981, 171.
63. Sawyer 1978, 22–7; Higham 1986, 250–74.
64. Moisl 1983, 103–16.
65. Jackson 1959, but see also Dumville 1989b, 215–16.
66. Dumville 1977b.
67. *HE* II, 2; Stenton 1971, 78–9.
68. *V. Wilfredi* ch. 17.
69. *Ibid.*; Faull 1981.
70. *HE* I, 34.
71. Jackson 1969; Charles-Edwards 1978.
72. Blair 1959, 156–8; Chadwick 1963a; Duncan 1981, 16–19; Moisl 1983, 112–15.
73. *HE* II, 5, III, 1.
74. Blair 1959, 161–5.
75. *HE* III, 6.
76. Jackson 1959.
77. Blair 1959, 160–2; Smyth 1984, 31–4.
78. Kirby 1976; Miller 1978.
79. *HE* IV, 12 and 26.
80. *V. Wilfredi* ch. 17; Roper 1974.
81. *HE* IV, 26.
82. Moisl 1983, 120–4.
83. *HE* III, 27 and IV, 4; Hughes 1971.
84. *HE* IV, 26. Moisl 1983, 120–4 suggests a Pictish-Irish alliance to end Northumbrian overlordship and establish the half-Irish Aldfrith as king of Northumbria.
85. Miller 1978.
86. *HB* ch. 57; Jackson 1963, 41–2.
87. Blair 1959, 160; Miller 1978.
88. *HE* III, 3.
89. Anon. *V. Cuthberti* II, 4; Bede *V. Cuthberti* ch. 11; Blair 1959, 165–8.
90. Jackson 1956; Higham 1986, 263–74.
91. Faull 1981, 179–80.
92. Faull 1977.
93. Jones 1975 and 1976; Kapelle 1979, 50–85.
94. Hope-Taylor 1977.

95. *HE* II, 14; Alcock 1988b, 17–20.
96. Bede *Letter to Egbert* (*EHD* I, 799–810); Tangl (ed.) 1916, no. 73 (*EHD* I, 816–22).
97. *V. Wilfredi* ch. 59.
98. *V. Wilfredi* ch. 60; Kirby 1974a.
99. *Chronicle* sa 731; Dumville 1976, 30–7; see table 11.
100. *HE* V, 23–4.
101. Kirby 1974a; details of events come from the Northumbrian Chronicle, as preserved in the *Historia Regum* (see n. 9), unless otherwise stated.
102. Booth 1984, 72–80.
103. Stenton 1971, 187–9; Mayr-Harting 1972, 240–61 *passim*; McNeill and Gamer (trans.) 1979, 237–48.
104. Dumville 1976, 30–7; *HB* ch. 57.
105. Dümmler (ed.) 1895, no. 109; *EHD* I, 785–6.
106. Kirby 1974a.
107. It is proposed here that the first cousins Ceolwulf and Eadbert should be seen as coming from the same kin-group of collaterals (see table 11). Ceolwulf appointed Eadbert's brother Egbert as bishop of York in 734 and apparently voluntarily resigned his throne to Eadbert in 737.
108. Kirby 1974a.
109. *HE* IV, 26.
110. Bede *Letter to Egbert*; John 1966, 78–83.
111. *HE* III, 24.
112. Roper 1974; Hart 1975, 131–9.
113. *HS* III, 394–6; *EHD* I, 830–1.
114. *HE* II, 9 and 13.
115. *HE* V, 4 and 5.
116. Wormald 1984, 19–23.
117. Bede *Historia Abbatum* ch. 11; Wormald 1976, 152–4.
118. *V. Wilfredi* ch. 17.
119. *Ibid.* ch. 38.
120. *Ibid.* ch. 19.
121. *Historia Regum* sa 867; Thacker 1981, 107.
122. Blair 1959, 170–1; Duncan 1981, 14–15.
123. *V. Wilfredi* ch. 60.
124. Thacker 1981, 213–17.
125. Bede *Letter to Egbert*.
126. Campbell (ed.) 1967, ch. 2–4.
127. See above, 89.
128. For Æthelwold see *EHD* I, 830–1 and Osbald *Historia Regum* sa 799.
129. See n. 113.
130. *Historia Regum* sa 788, 793 and 796; see also Kirby 1974a, 24–9.
131. Dümmler (ed.) 1895 nos. 232 and 233; *EHD* I, 795–7.
132. *HE* III, 5.
133. Dümmler (ed.) 1895 no. 16; *EHD* I, 842–4 and see n. 131.
134. For a survey see Blair 1970.
135. The marriage can be deduced from *Historia Regum* sa 768 and 788.
136. Bede *Letter to Egbert*.
137. *HE* V, 23.
138. Smyth 1984, 28–9.
139. *Ibid.*, 71–6.
140. *HE* 'continuations', 572–7.
141. *Historia Regum* sa 801; Sawyer 1978, 107–8.
142. Thacker 1985, 15–16.
143. Radford 1976.
144. Wallace-Hadrill 1975, 171–2.
145. Levison 1946; Wallace-Hadrill 1983, 143–62.
146. Levison 1946, 113–14.
147. *HS* III, 447–62; *EHD* I, 836–40.
148. For example, *EHD* I, 849–56, 862–6; Allott (trans.) 1974, 14–35.
149. Levison 1946, 114.
150. *EHD* I, 277–8; 281–4; Pagan 1969.
151. *EHD* I, 341–2; Levison 1946, 114; Booth 1987; Kirby 1987, 17.
152. Kirby 1987 for more detailed discussion of chronology.
153. Pagan 1969; Metcalf (ed.) 1987 *passim*.
154. For the disputed chronology of these reigns see Pagan 1969; Grierson and Blackburn 1986, 299–303.
155. See, for instance Dümmler (ed.) 1895, no. 17; *EHD* I, 844–6 and n. 133.
156. Booth 1987.
157. Smyth 1977, 169–88.
158. *Chronicle* sa 867; Kirby 1987.
159. Kapelle 1979, 3–49; Higham 1986, 307–13.
160. Lyon 1957; Pirie 1986; Metcalf (ed.) 1987 *passim*.
161. *EHD* I, 875–8; Cramp 1978; Kirby 1987, 15–16.
162. Craster 1954; Bonner 1989; Cambridge 1989.

Chapter Six
MERCIA

1. Kirby 1966, 368–70.
2. Page 1965–66; Bailey 1980.
3. Stenton 1933.
4. Hearne (ed.) 1723 I, 242 and II, 369; Ker 1948.
5. See above ch. 1, 10–13.
6. Thacker 1985.
7. *Ibid.* 6–7.
8. Hartland 1916; Rollason 1983, 9–10; Thacker 1985, 8–12.
9. Rollason 1981; Thacker 1985, 12–14.
10. Williams, Shaw and Denham 1985.
11. Stafford 1985, 97–108.
12. Sisam 1953a, 329.
13. *V. Guthlaci* ch. 2.
14. Dumville 1976, 30–7; see Table 13 .
15. *HE* II, 14.
16. Davies 1977.
17. *Chronicle* sa 593.
18. *HE* III, 24.
19. Hart 1977, 53–4; Brooks 1989b, 160–2.
20. Brooks 1989b, 160–2.
21. Blair 1948.
22. Brooks 1989b, 160–2.
23. *HE* III, 24.
24. Davies 1977, 20–2; Brooks 1989b, 164–7.
25. Brooks 1989b, 165–6.
26. *HE* II, 20.
27. *HB* ch. 65.
28. *HE* II, 20; for this translation see Wallace-Hadrill 1988, 84.
29. Stenton 1971, 31–49.
30. Kirby 1977; Davies 1982, 90–102; Brooks 1989b, 168–70.
31. *HE* III, 24.
32. *HB* ch. 64; Jackson 1963, 35.
33. Stenton 1918, 49–50; Vollrath-Reichelt 1971, 122–51.
34. *V. Wilfredi* ch. 20.
35. *HE* IV, 21; *V. Wilfredi* ch. 24.
36. Stenton 1918, 50–2.
37. See above ch. 2, 30.
38. Vollrath-Reichelt 1971, 88–94.
39. *HE* III, 16.
40. *HE* IV, 12.
41. See above ch. 1, 10–13.
42. Brooks 1989b, 161–2.
43. Hart 1977, 44–54.
44. Hart 1971; Davies and Vierck 1974.
45. *HE* III, 24.
46. Davies 1973.
47. Hart 1977, 43–54; Foard 1985, 193–201.
48. See *HE* I, 15; III, 21; IV, 3; Campbell 1979, 3–5; Bailey 1980; Dumville 1989a, 123–35.
49. *V. Guthlaci* ch. 1–2.
50. Stenton 1933; Dornier 1977a, 155–68; Wormald 1983, 112.
51. Blair 1989.
52. Stenton 1934, 193–6; Pretty 1989.
53. Finberg 1972, 197–224; Thacker 1985, 4–5.
54. Rollason 1982.
55. *V. Wilfredi* ch. 40; S 1169.
56. S 1166, see also S 71 and 73.
57. *HB* ch. 65; Jackson 1963, 39. For reservations about the identification of the battle site see Gelling 1989, 188–9.
58. For a radically different interpretation of Eowa's reign see Brooks 1989b, 167–9.
59. S 1165; Blair 1989, 105–7.
60. Stenton 1927; Dumville 1976, 30–7, 45–7; *HE* II, 16.
61. *HE* IV, 19; see above ch. 4, 64–5.
62. Ozanne 1962.
63. Finberg 1972, 167–80.
64. *Ibid.* and Stubbs 1862, 237–8; Bassett 1989a, 6 prefers to see the royal house as native Hwiccians.
65. Bassett 1985, 82–4 and 1989a, 6–17.
66. Heighway 1987, 22–31.
67. Stenton 1971, 44–6; Brooks 1989b, 163–4.
68. Yorke 1985, 27–33; Dumville 1989a, 134–7; and see above ch. 3, 50.
69. S 65.
70. *HE* IV, 13; Yorke 1989, 90–3.
71. Finberg 1972, 181–3.
72. Stenton 1933; Dornier 1977a.
73. Finberg 1972, 167–80, 197–216.
74. S 1165 (Chertsey); Hart 1966, 117–45 (Barking); Stenton 1913, 20–1 (Abingdon); S 71 and 73 (Malmesbury).

75. *HE* IV, 19 and V, 19; *Chronicle* sa 716.
76. Thacker 1985, 1–4.
77. *Ibid.*, 4–8.
78. Blair 1989, 105–7.
79. *HE* V, 19.
80. *Ibid.* and see above ch. 3, 50.
81. *HE* V, 24; Tangl (ed.) 1916, no. 73; *EHD* I, 816–22.
82. Hearne (ed.) 1723, II, 369; see also *Chronicle* B and C sa 716.
83. Tangl (ed.) 1916, no. 73; *EHD* I, 816–22.
84. S 54 and 1177 (Hwicce); Finberg 1972, 197–216 (Magonsæte); S 65 (East Saxons) and for fens see above ch. 4, 63.
85. *V. Guthlaci* ch. 34; *Chronicle* sa 715.
86. *V. Guthlaci* ch. 49 and 52.
87. Tangl (ed.) 1916, no. 10.
88. Dumville 1976 (Mercia II and III); see Table 13, 104.
89. See S 116, 117 and 146.
90. Thacker 1981, 217–18.
91. S 1257.
92. *Chronicle* sa 757; Bede 'continuations' sa 757; Hearne (ed.) 1723, II, 369.
93. *HE* V, 23; Stenton 1918, 53–64.
94. Finberg 1972, 221–4.
95. Stenton 1971, 45–6; S 113.
96. Stenton 1927; S. Keynes in Roper forthcoming.
97. Yorke 1985, 31–6; and see above ch. 3, 51.
98. S 1258; Stenton 1913, 22–4; Brooks 1984, 103–4.
99. *HS* III, 447–62; *EHD* I, 770–4.
100. Asser ch. 14–15; Stafford 1981a, 3–4.
101. Brooks 1984, 111–14.
102. Stenton 1971, 206–9.
103. See ch. 4, 64.
104. Stenton 1927.
105. See ch. 5, 95.
106. Stenton 1918; Yorke 1981; Wormald 1983, 109–11.
107. For reservations see Wormald 1983, 110–11.
108. S 86–8 and 91.
109. Dümmler (ed.) 1895, no. 100; *EHD* I, 848–8; Wallace-Hadrill 1965.
110. Metcalf 1977.
111. Blunt 1961; Stewart 1986.
112. Metcalf 1977.
113. Blunt 1961, 46–7; Grierson and Blackburn 1986, 270–82.
114. John 1966, 27–35; Nelson 1980.
115. Dümmler (ed.) 1895, no. 104, and see also no. 101; Wallace-Hadrill 1971, 98–123.
116. Levison 1946, 111–13.
117. Wallace-Hadrill 1965.
118. Tangl (ed.) 1916, no. 73; *EHD* I, 816–22.
119. Brooks 1971.
120. Dümmler (ed.) 1895, no. 101; *EHD* I, 849–51.
121. Levison 1946, 29–32, 257–8.
122. *HS* III, 447–62; *EHD* I, 836–40.
123. Cramp 1977; Parsons 1977; Taylor 1987.
124. Biddle and Kjølbye-Biddle 1985.
125. Levison 1946, 30–2.
126. S 120 and 1257 (Bath); Levison 1946, 31 (Winchcombe).
127. S 1257.
128. S 1258; *EHD* I, 508–10.
129. Levison 1946, 30–1; Wormald 1982, 110.
130. Brooks 1984, 111–20.
131. Fox 1955; Hill 1977; Wormald 1982, 120–1; Noble 1983; Abels 1988, 54–5.
132. For forts see Musson and Spurgeon 1988.
133. Shoesmith 1982.
134. Haslam 1987.
135. Dümmler (ed.) 1895, no. 27; *EHD* I, 854–6.
136. Nelson 1980.
137. Dumville 1976 (Mercia IV); see tables 13 and 14.
138. S 135, 1412 (described as *princeps*); Thacker 1985, 10.
139. For full references see Thacker 1985, 10–11.
140. Brooks 1984, 180–6.
141. Levison 1946, 32.
142. Levison 1946, 249–59; Bassett 1985.
143. Hartland 1916; Rollason 1983, 9–10; Thacker 1985, 8–12.
144. Thacker 1985, 13.

145. Rollason 1981; Thacker 1985, 12–14.
146. Biddle 1986, 16–22; Taylor 1987.
147. See nn. 55, 56 and 59.
148. See S 135, 187, 1433 and 204 respectively.
149. See above ch. 4, 64.
150. *Historia Regum* 798; Dümmler (ed.) 1895, no. 127; *EHD* I, 861–2.
151. For Cuthred see S 39–41.
152. Yorke 1985, 24 and 36.
153. See above ch. 5, 95.
154. Stenton 1971, 230–1; Davies 1982, 113.
155. Brooks 1984, 120–32; see *EHD* I, 858–61 and 867–9.
156. Brooks 1984, 133–5, 175–86.
157. Stenton 1971, 230–1.
158. Brooks 1984, 136–7.
159. *Ibid.*.
160. *Chronicle* sa 823 and see below ch. 7, 148.
161. Although the *Chronicle* seems to date his invasion of East Anglia and death to 825, Brooks 1984, 136 shows that Beornwulf was still alive in 826.
162. *Chronicle* sa 827; Hearne (ed.) 1723, II, 369; S 188.
163. Stenton 1913, 25–9.
164. Brooks 1979.
165. Stenton 1913, 25–9; Gelling 1976, 838–47.
166. S 1201 and see also S 214.
167. *Chronicle* sa 853; Blunt and Dolley 1961.
168. Smyth 1977, 195–200.
169. *Chronicle* sa 874; Smyth 1977, 240–5.
170. Hearne (ed.) 1723, I, 212; S 215–16; Blunt and Dolley 1961.
171. Asser ch. 75, 80 and 83; *Chronicle* sa 893.
172. S 217–23; see also Æthelweard sa 893.
173. Wainwright 1959.
174. *Chronicle* B and C sa 919.
175. Williams 1982, 161–4.
176. S 1791; Yorke 1985, 24 and 36; Hart 1987, 57.
177. Dyer 1980, 13–15.
178. Asser ch. 77.
179. Sisam 1953b, 1–28; Morrish 1986.
180. Taylor 1957; Foard 1985.
181. Hart 1977, 53–4; Hooke 1985, 85–6.
182. Stenton 1913; Blair 1989.
183. Hooke 1985, 12–20.
184. S 197; Hart 1975, 68–9.
185. S 190, 192, 193 and 207.
186. Brooks 1971.
187. Thacker 1981, 220–1.
188. *Ibid.*, 217–20.
189. S 197; see also S 1624.

Chapter Seven
THE WEST SAXONS

1. Bately 1978, 96.
2. Stenton 1926, 119; see also Harrison 1976a, 132–41.
3. Sisam 1953a; Dumville 1976, 30–7; see table 16.
4. Dumville 1985 and 1986a.
5. *Chronicle* II, cii–civ; *EHD* I, 30, n. 5.
6. The series is published by D.S. Brewer Ltd. To date editions of MSS A, B and the *Annals of St Neots* have appeared.
7. Stenton 1925; Bately 1978, 116–29; Keynes 1986, 196–8.
8. Davis 1971.
9. Davis 1971; Keynes and Lapidge 1983, 40–1; but see also Whitelock 1978.
10. Asser ch. 12 and 13.
11. Stevenson 1904; Schütt 1957; Kirby 1971; Keynes and Lapidge 1983, 48–58 (translation of Asser, 65–110).
12. Kirby 1966, 364–6; Wallace-Hadrill 1988, 97–8.
13. Yorke 1989.
14. *V. Wilfredi*, ch. 41–2.
15. Keynes and Lapidge 1983, 171–8; 193–4; Davis 1982; Hill 1969.
16. Liebermann (ed.) 1903, I, 15–123; *EHD* I, 398–415; Richards 1986, 172–6.
17. Finberg 1964a, 214–48.
18. Wormald 1984; Edwards 1988.
19. Lapidge and Herren 1979; Lapidge and Rosier 1985.
20. Levison 1946, 70–93; Reuter (ed.) 1980.

21. Tangl (ed.) 1916 *passim*, and for translations of many of the letters Talbot 1954, 65–149.
22. Waitz (ed.) 1887; Talbot 1954, 205–26.
23. Chadwick 1907, 19–32; Stenton 1926; Copley 1954; Myres 1985, 144–72.
24. Harrison 1971; Sims-Williams 1983b; Dumville 1985; Yorke 1989.
25. Sisam 1953a, 337–8; Dumville 1985, 59–60.
26. Harrison 1971.
27. Dumville 1985.
28. Yorke 1989, 89–92.
29. Leeds 1913; Myres 1969 and 1985; Biddle 1976.
30. Myres 1985, 149–62.
31. *HE* IV, 16; Yorke 1985, 89–91.
32. Dumville 1985, 46, 58–9.
33. Bately 1978, 102–3.
34. Hawkes 1986.
35. *HE* III, 7.
36. Walker 1956; Yorke 1989, 93–4.
37. *HE* II, 5.
38. Sawyer 1983, 274–9.
39. Sims-Williams 1983b, 32–3 for a sceptical view.
40. Dumville 1985, 46. For correction of the dates of Æthelbert I of Kent which have a bearing on those of Ceawlin see above ch. 2, 28.
41. See below, 42.
42. *Chronicle* sa 597.
43. Hoskins 1970; Todd 1987, 270–3.
44. Lapidge and Rosier 1985, 40–1, 47–9.
45. Heighway 1987, 22–31.
46. *HE* III, 7.
47. *Ibid.*; *Chronicle* sa 661.
48. Finberg 1964a, 215; Yorke 1982.
49. *V. Wilfredi* ch. 40.
50. Edwards 1988, 85–127.
51. *HE* IV, 16.
52. Finberg 1964b, 98–9; Edwards 1988, 15–17, 65–6 and 243–53.
53. Levison 1946, 70–1.
54. Stenton 1971, 295–7; Hart 1971, 156–7.
55. *Chronicle* sa 685; *HE* IV, 15; *V. Wilfredi* ch. 42.
56. Lapidge and Rosier 1985, 40–1, 47–9.
57. *HE* IV, 16; Stenton 1971, 69–71.
58. *Chronicle* sa 687; see also S 10.
59. *HE* V, 7; Stancliffe 1983, 170–1.
60. Stenton 1971, 71; Wallace-Hadrill 1988, 178–9.
61. Yorke 1989, 92–3.
62. *HE* IV, 13.
63. Walker 1956; Yorke 1989, 93–4. The title 'King of the West Saxons' was regularly used from 760 – Edwards 1988, 309.
64. *Chronicle* sa 688.
65. *Chronicle* sa 692.
66. S 45; Edwards 1988, 292–7.
67. Stenton 1971, 72–3; Whitelock 1975, 10–11.
68. Liebermann (ed.) 1903, 88–123; *EHD* I, 398–407.
69. Wormald 1977a *passim*.
70. Pearce 1982b and c, 1985; Todd 1987, 273–5.
71. Chadwick 1907, 28–9; Stenton 1971, 69–70.
72. Hare 1975; Hase 1988; Blair forthcoming.
73. Stenton 1971, 71–3; Edwards 1988, especially 23–40 and 105–114.
74. Pearce 1982b and c, 1985; Todd 1987, 240–52.
75. Finberg 1964b; Barker 1982; Edwards 1988, 64–5 and 243–53.
76. Lapidge and Herren 1979, 9–10.
77. S 252; Edwards 1988, 168–77.
78. *Chronicle* sa 718; Lapidge and Rosier 1985, 40–9.
79. Holdsworth 1984; Andrews forthcoming; Morton forthcoming.
80. Metcalf 1988, 17–36.
81. Hodges 1982, 185–98; Arnold 1988a, 51–93.
82. Wrenn 1941; Bately 1978, 106–7.
83. See, for instance, S 96 and 1410.
84. See, for instance, S 256–7.
85. S 149 and 265; Stenton 1913, 22–4; Edwards 1988, 121–3 and 223–7.
86. *HS* III, 447–62; *EHD* I, 770–4.
87. Andrews and Metcalf 1984.
88. *Chronicle* sa 787; Asser ch. 14 and 15.
89. *Chronicle* sa 839.
90. Brooks 1971, 80–7; Grierson and Blackburn 1986, 282.
91. S 149; Edwards 1988, 52–5.
92. S 262; *Chronicle* sa 757.

93. For example, S 257, 1678, 1680–8 (Glastonbury); S 256 and 260 (Malmesbury); Edwards 1988, 243–53 (Sherborne).
94. See Talbot 1956 *passim*; Reuter (ed.) 1980 *passim*.
95. Todd 1987, 273–4.
96. Yorke 1982.
98. Dumville 1979, 14–19.
99. Kirby 1965; Dumville 1985, 60–1.
100. Sisam 1953a.
101. S 236, see also S 238, 1170 and 1665; Lapidge and Herren 1979, 170.
102. *HE* II, 9.
103. S 241 and 45 respectively; Edwards 1988, 297–99.
104. *HE* III, 7.
105. S 1164; Edwards 1988, 229–34.
106. S 241.
107. Kirby 1965.
108. S 1164; *Chronicle* sa 718.
109. *Chronicle* sa 860 and 871.
110. Asser ch. 98.
111. *Chronicle* sa 900; Ross 1985, 31–2.
112. *HE* IV, 12.
113. *FW* I, 272; Kirby 1965, 18–20.
114. Lapidge and Rosier 1985, 40–1, 47–9.
115. Ch. 8, 36 and 39; Chadwick 1905, 282–90. See above, n.16.
116. Thacker 1981, *passim*.
117. For instance, S 260–2; Chadwick 1905, 282; Edwards 1988, 60.
118. Chadwick 1905, 288.
119. Hinton 1981, 63–4; Yorke 1989, 96.
120. Yorke 1982.
121. Hart 1973; Williams 1982.
122. *Chronicle* sa 722 and 737.
123. S 251, 253 and 268 respectively.
124. S 1677 and 270a respectively; Edwards 1988, 56–9.
125. Asser ch. 14.
126. S 250, see also *Gesta* I, 35–6.
127. Asser ch. 13; Stafford 1981a.
128. John 1966, 7–8, 35–7; Yorke 1981, 171–4; Wormald 1983.
129. S 280 and 286.
130. *Chronicle* sa 839.
131. Asser ch. 16; *Chronicle* sa 855.
132. S 281 and 1438; Brooks 1984, 146–7.
133. Finberg 1964a, 187–213; Abels 1988, 60–1.
134. Brooks 1984, 197–206.
135. Keynes and Lapidge 1983, 174–8, 324–5.
136. Asser ch. 81, 99–102.
137. Asser ch. 16; Keynes and Lapidge 1983, 174–8; Williams 1978, 145–8; Dumville 1979, 21–4.
138. Asser ch. 11–13; Stafford 1981a, 143.
139. Enright 1979; Stafford 1981a.
140. S 340, 1201 and 1203.
141. See Alfred's will and *Chronicle* sa 900.
142. Dolley and Skaare 1961.
143. *Chronicle* sa 853; Asser ch. 75.
144. *Chronicle* sa 918; Wainwright 1959.
145. Asser ch. 77; Morrish 1986.
146. Asser ch. 79–80; Kirby 1971, 16–20.
147. Smyth 1977, 240–54; Whitelock 1978; Davis 1982.
148. Asser ch. 83.
149. Asser ch. 91; see also *Chronicle* sa 892.
150. S 362.
151. Asser ch. 52–3; Whitelock 1978, 4–6.
152. Brooks 1971 *passim*.
153. Hill 1969; Keynes and Lapidge 1983, 193–4, 339–41.
154. Brooks 1979, 17–20.
155. Brooks 1971, 78–54.
156. RCHM 1959.
157. See n. 149.
158. Wallace-Hadrill 1975, 201–36.
159. Hill and Hassall 1970; Brooks 1971, 81–3.
160. *Chronicle* sa 839.
161. See n. 139.
162. Æthelweard, 2.
163. Stevenson 1904, 225–6.
164. Morrish 1986.
165. Asser ch. 78; Grierson 1940; Bately 1966.
166. Prose preface to Alfred's translation of Pope Gregory's *Pastoral Care* – Keynes and Lapidge 1983, 124–7 (see also 26–41).
167. Wormald 1977b, 102–14.
168. Keynes and Lapidge 1983, 131–52; Waterhouse 1986.
169. Schütt 1957; Wallace-Hadrill 1975, 211–12.
170. Green 1965 *passim*; Wallace-Hadrill 1971, 124–51.
171. Keynes and Lapidge 1983, 124–30, 293–8; Shippey 1979.

172. Wallace-Hadrill 1975, 209–15.
173. Wallace-Hadrill 1975, 213.
174. Hughes 1906; Keynes and Lapidge 1983, 44–8.
175. Davis 1971.
176. Stevenson 1904, 147–52; Keynes and Lapidge 1983, 227–8.
177. Wainwright 1959; Stenton 1971, 319–39.

Chapter Eight
THE DEVELOPMENT OF KINGSHIP
c. 600–900

1. See ch. 1, 2–6.
2. *HE* II, 5.
3. John 1966, 1–63; Vollrath-Reichelt 1971, *passim*.
4. Yorke 1981; Wormald 1983, 107–9.
5. *HE* II, 5.
6. *V. Wilfredi* ch. 20.
7. *HE* III, 24.
8. Vollrath-Reichelt 1971, 80–8; Wallace-Hadrill 1988, 59, 220–2.
9. Wormald 1983.
10. Tacitus ch. 13–14.
11. Reuter 1985.
12. *HE* II, 9.
13. *HE* II, 5; IV, 26.
14. Tacitus ch. 13.
15. *HE* III, 24; IV, 21.
16. *HE* III, 21–22.
17. See ch. 5, 83–6.
18. Wormald 1983.
19. *HE* II, 5; II, 3.
20. See ch. 3, 46–8.
21. See ch, 5, 74–81.
22. *HE* III, 6.
23. Campbell 1973, 8; Goody 1983, 194–204; Angenendt 1986, 755–66.
24. *HE* I, 25; Angenendt 1986, 779–81.
25. *HE* II, 15.
26. Kirby 1963, 552–3; Mayr-Harting 1972, 66–7.
27. See ch. 6, 105–11.
28. Finberg 1972, 167–80; see ch. 6, 108–9.
29. S 1165; Blair 1989; ch. 3, 47.
30. *HE* IV, 13; Campbell 1979, 7–8.
31. *HE* IV, 19; see ch. 4, 70.

32. Welch 1989; however, the Hæstingas may originally have been independent from the main province.
33. Foard 1985.
34. Keynes and Lapidge 1983, 132,
35. Duby 1980, especially 99–109.
36. Campbell 1978, 43–51; Sawyer 1983.
37. *HE* IV, 22.
38. *Historia Abbatum* ch. 1 and 8 (Plummer (ed.) 1896, I, 364 and 371); Charles-Edwards 1976, 181–4.
39. Plummer (ed.) 1896, I, 405–23; *EHD* I, 799–810.
40. John 1966, 64–127.
41. Wormald 1984, 19–23.
42. For example, *HE* III, 24.
43. Levy 1951.
44. Wormald 1984, 21.
45. *Historia Abbatum* ch. 11; Wormald 1976, 152–4.
46. *HE* IV, 16.
47. John 1970; Roper 1974.
48. Hart 1966, 117–45.
49. See n. 39.
50. Wormald 1984, 23.
51. Brooks 1971 and Wormald 1984 *contra* Stenton 1955, John 1966, 64–127 and Abels 1988, 43–57.
52. Brooks 1971, 73; Wormald 1984, 20–1.
53. Tangl (ed.) 1916, no. 73; *EHD* I, 816–22; Brooks 1971.
54. S 177; Brooks 1971.
55. Abels 1988, 58–78.
56. S 354 and 1278; Yorke 1984, 64–5; Brooks 1984, 149–52.
57. Asser ch. 91.
58. Campbell 1975.
59. For example, S 12 and 1624.
60. Haslam 1980.
61. Grierson 1959; Huggett 1988.
62. Hodges 1982, 104–29.
63. Hawkes 1982; see ch. 2, 39–41.
64. Huggett 1988, 90–4.
65. Hodges 1982, 66–86; 130–50.
66. Campbell 1979, 8–9.
67. Tacitus ch. 14.
68. Hinton 1974, 29–48; Keynes and Lapidge 1983, 203–6.

69. Dumville 1979.
70. Lancaster 1958; Loyn 1974; Goody 1983, 222–39.
71. See ch. 6, 118–19.
72. See ch. 6, 107–11.
73. Dumville 1979.
74. See below, 174.
75. *Chronicle* sa 787; Wallace-Hadrill 1971, 114–20.
76. See ch. 7, 148.
77. *HE* IV, 26.
78. Kirby 1974a; see ch. 5, 86–8 and table 11.
79. Miller 1979; see table 9.
80. Goody 1983, especially 133–56.
81. *HE* IV, 26; Kirby 1974a, 19–20; Moisl 1983, 122–3; Wallace-Hadrill 1988, 232–3.
82. Kirby's suggestion (1974a, 20–1) that only male kindred up to seven generations in descent from the founder king were eligible for the throne has not received general support; see Dumville 1979, 16–17.
83. For instance, among the East Saxons on the death of Sabert and among the Hwicce; see Dumville 1989a, 138–9.
84. See ch. 6, 107–8.
85. *HE* IV, 12; see ch. 7, 145–6.
86. Yorke 1983; see ch. 2, 32–5 and table 1.
87. See ch. 6, 124–6.
88. Abels 1988, 58–60.
89. Chadwick 1905, 292–307.
90. *V. Wilfredi* ch. 60; see ch. 5, 92.
91. Thacker 1981, 213–21.
92. Klinck 1982, 111–14.
93. *HE* III, 6.
94. Thacker 1985, 8–12; see ch. 6, 119–20 and table 14.
95. *Beowulf* lines 371–5.
96. Leyser 1968, especially 33.
97. *HE* IV, 21.
98. See ch. 3, 53–6.
99. *Historia Regum* sa 768 and 788.
100. Bullough 1983.
101. Campbell 1966, 70–5.
102. *HE* III, 6 and 11.
103. Angenendt 1986, 749–54.
104. Stancliffe 1983.
105. *HE* V, 7 and III, 18 respectively.
106. Stancliffe 1983.
107. *HE* III, 22; Mayr-Harting 1972, 99–102.
108. Campbell 1973, 18; Angenendt 1986, 755–66.
109. Tangl (ed.) 1916, no. 23; *EHD* I, 795–7.
110. Brown, P. 1981.
111. Thacker 1985.
112. Rollason 1983.
113. Dumville 1979, 18–19.
114. James 1984.
115. *HE* V, 19; see ch. 3, 49–50.
116. Wormald 1978.
117. John 1970; Farmer 1974.
118. Thacker 1983, 146–9.
119. *HE* I, 30.
120. Green 1965; Wormald 1978.
121. Bede, *Letter to Egbert*; Dümmler (ed.) 1895, no. 20 (*EHD* I, 845–6).
122. Tangl (ed.) 1916, no. 14; see ch. 2, 38.
123. Kirby 1974a, 17–34.
124. Dümmler (ed.) 1895, no. 174; *EHD* I, 865–6; Abels 1988, 27.
125. *HE* I, 27; Goody 1983, 35–47.
126. *HE* II, 5.
127. Tangl (ed.) 1916, no. 73; *EHD* I, 816–27; Ross 1985, 131–3.
128. *HS* III, 447–62; *EHD* I, 836–40.
129. Goody 1983.
130. Dumville 1979, 19–21; Nelson 1980.
131. Asser ch. 17.
132. Wallace-Hadrill 1971, 98–151.
133. Wormald 1983, 120–9.
134. Dümmler (ed.) 1895, no. 122; *EHD* I, 854–6; see also Dümmler no. 101; *EHD* I, 849–51.
135. See ch. 6, 116.
136. Ullmann 1969.
137. Brooks 1984, 129–54.
138. *Ibid.*; Fleming 1985.
139. Stenton 1913, 31–2; Fleming 1985, 250–1.
140. *EHD* I, 881–3.

BIBLIOGRAPHY AND ABBREVIATIONS

Abels, R 1988: *Lordship and Military Obligation in Anglo-Saxon England.* California

Æthelweard: *The Chronicle of Æthelweard.* ed A Campbell, London, 1962

Alcock, L 1987: *Economy, Society and Warfare Among the Britons and Saxons.* Cardiff

Alcock, L 1988a: 'The activities of potentates in Celtic Britain, AD 500–800: a positivist approach.' Driscoll and Nieke (eds) 1988, 22–46

Alcock, L 1988b: *Bede, Eddius, and the Forts of the North Britons.* Jarrow lecture

Allott, S (trans) 1974: *Alcuin of York.* York

Andrews, P forthcoming: *Excavations in Hamwic: volume 2, excavations at Six Dials 1977–86*

Andrews, P and Metcalf, D 1984: 'A coinage for King Cynewulf?' Hill and Metcalf (eds) 1984, 175–9

Angenendt, A 1986: 'The conversion of the Anglo-Saxons considered against the background of the early medieval mission.' *Angli e Sassoni al di qua e al di la del Mare*, Spoleto Settimane di Studio **32**, II, 747–81

Archibald, M 1982: 'A ship type of Æthelstan I of East Anglia.' *British Numismatic Journal* **52**, 34–40

Arnold, C 1980: 'Wealth and social structure: a matter of life and death.' Rahtz, Dickinson and Watts (eds) 1980, 81–142

Arnold, C 1982: *The Anglo-Saxon Cemeteries of the Isle of Wight.* London

Arnold, C 1984: *Roman Britain to Saxon England.* London

Arnold, C 1988a: *An Archaeology of the Early Anglo-Saxon Kingdoms.* London

Arnold, C 1988b: 'Territories and leadership: frameworks for the study of emergent polities in early Anglo-Saxon southern England.' Driscoll and Nieke (eds) 1988, 111–27

Asser: *Asser's Life of King Alfred.* ed W H Stevenson, Oxford, 1904

Astill, G 1985: 'Archaeology, economics and early medieval Europe.' *Oxford Journal of Archaeology* **4**, 215–32

Attenborough, F L (trans) 1922: *The Laws of the Earliest English Kings.* Cambridge

Bailey, J 1980: *The Early Christian Church in Leicester and its Region.* Vaughan Paper No 25, Leicester

Bailey, K 1989: 'The Middle Saxons.' Bassett (ed) 1989b, 108–22

BAR: British Archaeological Reports, Oxford. British series unless otherwise stated

Barker, K 1982: 'The early history of Sherborne.' Pearce (ed) 1982a, 77–116

Barker, P 1980: *Wroxeter Roman City: Excavations 1966–80.* London

Bascombe, K 1987: 'Two charters of King Suebred of Essex.' Neale (ed) 1987, 85–96

Bassett, S 1985: 'A probable Mercian royal mausoleum at Winchcombe, Gloucestershire.' *Antiquaries' Journal* **65**, part I, 82–100

Bassett, S 1989a: 'In search of the origins of Anglo-Saxon kingdoms.' Bassett (ed) 1989b, 3–27

Bassett, S (ed) 1989b: *The Origins of Anglo-Saxon Kingdoms.* Leicester

Bately, J 1966: 'Grimbald of St Bertin's.' *Medium Ævum* **35**, 1–10

Bately, J 1978: 'The compilation of the Anglo-Saxon Chronicle 60 B.C. to A.D. 890: vocabulary as evidence.' *Proceedings of the British Academy* **64**, 93–129

Bateman, T 1861: *Ten Years Digging*. London

Bateson, M 1889: 'Origin and early history of double monasteries.' *Transactions of the Royal Historical Society* **13**, 137–98

Beowulf: ed C L Wrenn, 3rd ed, London, 1973

Bethell, D 1970: 'The lives of St Osyth of Essex and St Osyth of Aylesbury.' *Analecta Bollandiana* **88**, 75–127

Biddle, M 1976: 'Hampshire and the origins of Wessex.' *Problems in Economic and Social Archaeology*, ed G de G Sieveking, I H Longworth and K E Wilson, London

Biddle, M 1983: 'The study of Winchester: archaeology and history in a British town, 1961–1983.' *Proceedings of the British Academy* **69**, 93–135

Biddle, M 1984: 'London on the Strand,' *Popular Archaeology*, July, 23–7

Biddle, M 1986: 'Archaeology, architecture and the cult of saints in Anglo-Saxon England.' *The Anglo-Saxon Church*. ed L Butler and R Morris, CBA report 60, 1–31

Biddle, M and Kjølbye-Biddle, B 1985: 'The Repton stone.' *Anglo-Saxon England* **14**, 233–92

Bidwell, P T 1979: *The Legionary Bath-House and Basilica and Forum at Exeter. Exeter Archaeological Reports 1*

Bidwell, P T 1980: *Roman Exeter: Fortress and Town*, Exeter

Blackburn, M (ed) 1986: *Anglo-Saxon Monetary History. Essays in Memory of Michael Dolley*. Leicester

Blair, J 1989: 'Frithuwold's kingdom and the origins of Surrey.' Bassett (ed) 1989b, 97–107

Blair, J forthcoming: *Landholding, Church and Settlement in Early Medieval Surrey*. Surrey Archaeological Society

Blair, P Hunter 1947: 'The origins of Northumbria.' *Archaeologia Aeliana* 4th series, **25**, 1–51

Blair, P Hunter 1948: 'The Northumbrians and their southern frontier.' *Archaeologia Aeliana* 4th series, **26**, 98–126

Blair, P Hunter 1949: 'The boundary between Bernicia and Deira.' *Archaeolgia Aeliana* 4th series, **27**, 46–59

Blair, P Hunter 1950: 'The *Moore Memoranda* on Northumbrian history.' *The Early Cultures of North-West Europe*. ed C Fox and B Dickins, Cambridge

Blair, P Hunter 1959: 'The Bernicians and their northern frontier.' *Studies in Early British History*. ed N K Chadwick, Cambridge, 137–72

Blair, P Hunter 1963: 'Some observations on the *Historia Regum* attributed to Symeon of Durham.' Chadwick (ed) 1963b, 63–118

Blair, P Hunter 1970: *The World of Bede*. London

Blair, P Hunter 1971: 'The letters of Pope Boniface V and the mission of Paulinus to Northumbria.' Clemoes and Hughes (eds) 1971, 5–15

Blair, P Hunter 1985: 'Whitby as a centre of learning in the seventh century.' *Learning and Literature in Anglo-Saxon England*. ed M Lapidge and H Gneuss, Cambridge, 3–32

Blunt, C E 1961: 'The coinage of Offa.' Dolley (ed), 1961, 39–62

Blunt, C E and Dolley, R H M 1961: 'The chronology of the coins of Alfred the Great 871–99.' Dolley (ed) 1961, 77–95

Blunt, C E, Lyon, C S S and Stewart, B H 1963: 'The coinage of southern England, 796–840.' *British Numismatic Journal* **32**, 1–74

Böhme, H W 1986: 'Das Ende der Romerherrschaft in Britannien und die angelsächsische Besiedlung Englands im 5. Jahrhundert.' *Jahrbuch des Romisch-Germanischen Zentral Museum* **33**, 466–574

Bonner, G (ed) 1976: *Famulus Christi: Essays in Commemoration of the Thirteenth Centenary of the Birth of the Venerable Bede*. London

Bonner, G 1989: 'St Cuthbert at Chester-le-Street.' Bonner, Rollason and Stancliffe (eds) 1989, 387–96

Bonner, G, Rollason, D and Stancliffe, C (eds) 1989: *St Cuthbert, His Cult and His Community*. Woodbridge

Bonney, D J 1976: 'Early boundaries and estates in southern England.' Sawyer (ed) 1976, 72–82

Booth, J 1984: 'Sceattas in Northumbria.' Hill and Metcalf (eds) 1984, 71–112

Booth, J 1987: 'Coinage and Northumbrian history: c790–c810.' Metcalf (ed) 1987, 57–89

Brooke, C N L and Keir, G 1975: *London, 800–1216: The Shaping of a City*. London

Brooks, N 1971: 'The development of military obligations in eighth- and ninth-century England.' Clemoes and Hughes (eds) 1971, 69–84

Brooks, N 1974: 'Anglo-Saxon charters: the work of the last twenty years.' *Anglo-Saxon England* 3, 211–32

Brooks, N 1979: 'England in the ninth century: the crucible of defeat.' *Transactions of the Royal Historical Society* 5th series, 29, 1–20

Brooks, N 1984: *The Early History of the Church of Canterbury*. Leicester

Brooks, N 1989a: 'The creation and early structure of the kingdom of Kent.' Bassett (ed) 1989b, 55–74

Brooks, N 1989b: 'The formation of the Mercian kingdom.' Bassett (ed) 1989b, 159–70

Brown, D 1981: 'The dating of the Sutton Hoo coins.' *Anglo-Saxon Studies in Archaeology and History* 2, BAR 92, 71–90

Brown, P 1981: *The Cult of the Saints: its Rise and Function in Latin Christianity*. Chicago

Bruce-Mitford, R 1952: 'The Snape Boat-Grave.' *Proceedings of the Suffolk Institute of Archaeology* 26, 1–26

Bruce-Mitford, R 1974: *Aspects of Anglo-Saxon Archaeology*. London

Bruce-Mitford, R 1975, 1978 and 1983: *The Sutton Hoo Ship-Burial*, vols. I, II and III, London

Bruce-Mitford, R 1986: 'The Sutton Hoo ship-burial: some foreign connections.' *Angli e Sassoni al di qua e al di la del Mare*, Spoleto Settimane di Studio 32, I, 143–218

Buckley, D G (ed) 1980: *Archaeology in Essex to AD 1500*. CBA report 34, London

Bullough, D 1983: 'Burial, community and belief in the early medieval west.' Wormald *et al* (eds) 1983, 177–201

Burrow, I C G 1981: *Hillforts and Hill-top Settlement in Somerset in the first to eighth centuries AD*. BAR 91

Cambridge, E 1989: 'Why did the community of St Cuthbert settle at Chester-le-Street?' Bonner, Rollason and Stancliffe (eds) 1989, 367–86

Campbell, A (ed) 1967: *Æthelwulf, De Abbatibus*. Oxford

Campbell, J 1966: 'Bede', *Latin Historians*, ed T A Dorey, London, 159–90

Campbell, J 1973: 'Observations on the conversion of England.' *Ampleforth Journal* 78, ii, 12–26

Campbell, J 1975: 'Observations on English government from the tenth to the twelfth century.' *Transactions of the Royal Historical Society* 5th series, 25, 39–54

Campbell, J 1978: 'Bede's words for places.' *Names, Words, and Graves: Early Medieval Settlement*. ed P Sawyer, Leeds, 34–54

Campbell, J 1979: *Bede's Reges and Principes*. Jarrow Lecture (Campbell 1986, 85–98)

Campbell, J (ed) 1982: *The Anglo-Saxons*. Oxford

Campbell, J 1986: *Essays in Anglo-Saxon History*. London

Campbell, J 1989: 'Elements in the background to the life of St Cuthbert and his early cult.' Bonner, Rollason and Stancliffe (eds), 3–19

Carr, R D, Tester, A and **Murphy, P** 1988: 'The Middle-Saxon settlement at Staunch Meadow, Brandon.' *Antiquity* **62**, 371–7

Carver, M 1986: 'Sutton Hoo in context.' *Angli e Sassoni al di qua e al di la del Mare.* Spoleto Settimane di Studio **32**, I, 77–117

Carver, M 1989: 'Kingship and material culture in early Anglo-Saxon East Anglia.' Bassett (ed) 1989b, 141–58

Carver, M and **Evans, A C** 1989: 'Anglo-Saxon discoveries at Sutton Hoo, 1987–8.' *Bulletin of the Sutton Hoo Research Committee*, 6, 4–13

Casey, P J (ed) 1979: *The End of Roman Britain.* BAR 71

CBA: Council for British Archaeology (London)

Chadwick, H M 1905: *Studies on Anglo-Saxon Institutions.* Cambridge

Chadwick, H M 1907: *The Origin of the English Nation.* Cambridge

Chadwick, N K 1961: 'Bretwalda. Gweldig. Vortigern.' *Bulletin of the Board of Celtic Studies* V.**19**, 225–30

Chadwick, N K 1963a: 'The battle of Chester: a study of sources.' Chadwick (ed) 1963b, 167–85

Chadwick, N K (ed) 1963b: *Celt and Saxon: Studies in the Early British Border.* Cambridge

Chaplais, P 1965: 'The origin and authenticity of the royal Anglo-Saxon diploma.' *Journal of the Society of Archivists* **3**, 48–61

Chaplais, P 1968: 'Some early Anglo-Saxon diplomas on single sheets: originals or copies?' *Journal of the Society of Archivists* **3**, 315–36

Chaplais, P 1969: 'Who introduced charters into England? The case for Augustine.' *Journal of the Society of Archivists* **3**, 526–42

Chaplais, P 1978: 'The letter from Bishop Wealdhere of London to Archbishop Brihtwald of Canterbury.' *Medieval Scribes, Manuscripts and Libraries: Essays Presented to N.R. Ker,* ed M B Parkes and A G Watson, London, 3–23

Charles-Edwards, T M 1972: 'Kinship, status and the origins of the hide.' *Past and Present* **56**, 3–33

Charles-Edwards, T M 1976: 'The distinction between land and moveable wealth in Anglo-Saxon England.' Sawyer (ed) 1976, 180–7

Charles-Edwards, T M 1978: 'The authenticity of the Gododdin: an historian's view.' *Astudiaethau ar yr Hengerdd (Studies in Old Welsh Poetry),* ed R Bromwich and R B Jones, Cardiff, 44–71

Charles-Edwards, T M 1983: 'Bede, the Irish and the Britons.' *Celtica* 15, 42–52

Charles-Edwards, T M 1989: 'Early medieval kingships in the British Isles.' Bassett (ed) 1989b, 28–39

Chase, C (ed) 1981: *The Dating of Beowulf,* Toronto

Chronicle: Two of the Saxon Chronicles Parallel, ed C Plummer and J Earle, 2 vols, Oxford, 1892

Clarke, D V, Cowie, T G and **Foxon, A** 1985: *Symbols of Power at the Time of Stonehenge.* Edinburgh

Clarke, G N 1979: *The Roman Cemetery at Lankhills.* Winchester Studies 3, part 2, Oxford

Clemoes, P (ed) 1959: *The Anglo-Saxons: Studies in Some Aspects of their History and Culture Presented to Bruce Dickins.* London

Clemoes, P 1983: *The Cult of St Oswald on the Continent.* Jarrow lecture

Clemoes, P and **Hughes, K** (eds) 1971: *England Before the Conquest. Studies in Primary Sources Presented to Dorothy Whitelock.* Cambridge

Colgrave, B (ed) 1927: *The Life of Bishop Wilfred by Eddius Stephanus.* Cambridge

Colgrave, B (ed) 1940: *Two Lives of Saint Cuthbert.* Cambridge

Colgrave, B (ed) 1956: *Felix's Life of Saint Guthlac*. Cambridge
Colgrave, B (ed) 1968: *The Earliest Life of Gregory the Great*. Cambridge
Copley, G J 1954: *The Conquest of Wessex in the Sixth Century*. London
Courtney, P 1981: 'The early Saxon fenland: a reconsideration.' *Anglo-Saxon in Archaeology and History* 2, 91–9
Cramp, R 1957: '*Beowulf* and archaeology.' *Medieval Archaeology* 1, 57–77
Cramp, R 1977: 'Schools of Mercian sculpture.' Dornier (ed) 1977b, 191–234
Cramp, R 1978: 'The Anglian tradition in the ninth century.' *Anglo-Saxon and Viking Age Sculpture and its Context.* ed J Laing, BAR 49, 1–32
Cramp, R 1983: 'Anglo-Saxon settlement.' *Settlement in Northern Britain, 1000 BC-AD 1000.* ed J C Chapman and H C Mytum, BAR 118, 263–97
Cramp, R 1988: 'Northumbria: the archaeological evidence.' Driscoll and Nieke (eds) 1988, 69–78
Craster, H E 1954: 'The patrimony of St Cuthbert.' *English Historical Review* 69, 177–99
Crick, J 1988: 'Church, land and local nobility in early ninth-century Kent: the case of Ealdorman Oswulf.' *Bulletin of the Institute of Historical Research* 61, 251–69
Crummy, P 1981: *Aspects of Anglo-Saxon and Norman Colchester*. CBA report 39
Crummy, P, Hillam, J and Crossan, C 1982: 'Mersea island: the Anglo-Saxon causeway.' *Essex Archaeology and History* 14, 77–86
Darby, H C 1934: 'The Fenland frontier in Anglo-Saxon England.' *Antiquity* 8, 185–201
Davies, W 1973: 'Middle Anglia and the Middle Angles.' *Midland History* 2, 18–20
Davies, W 1977: 'Annals and the origin of Mercia.' Dornier (ed) 1977b, 17–29
Davies, W 1979: 'Roman settlements and post-Roman estates in south-east Wales.' Casey (ed) 1979, 153–73
Davies, W 1982: *Wales in the Early Middle Ages*. Leicester
Davies, W and Vierck, H 1974: 'The contexts of Tribal Hidage: social aggregates and settlement patterns.' *Frühmittelalterliche Studien* 8, 223–93
Davis, K Rutherford 1982: *Britons and Saxons. The Chiltern Region 400–700*. Chichester
Davis, R H C 1955: 'East Anglia and the Danelaw.' *Transactions of the Royal Historical Society* 5th series, 5, 23–39
Davis, R H C 1971: 'Alfred the Great: propaganda and truth.' *History* 56, 169–82
Davis, R H C 1982: 'Alfred and Guthrum's frontier.' *English Historical Review* 97, 803–10
Dolley, R H M (ed) 1961: *Anglo-Saxon Coins: Studies Presented to F.M.Stenton*. London
Dolley, R H M and Skaare, K 1961: 'The coinage of Æthelwulf, king of the West Saxons, 839–58.' Dolley (ed) 1961, 63–75
Dornier, A 1977a: 'The Anglo-Saxon monastery at Breedon-on-the-Hill, Leicestershire.' Dornier (ed) 1977b, 155–68
Dornier, A (ed) 1977b: *Mercian Studies*. Leicester
Driscoll, S T and Nieke, M R (eds) 1988: *Power and Politics in Early Medieval Britain and Ireland*. Edinburgh
Drury, P J and Rodwell, W 1980: 'Settlement in the later Iron age and Roman periods.' Buckley (ed) 1980, 59–75
Duby, G 1980: *The Three Orders: Feudal Society Imagined*. London
Dümmler, E (ed) 1895: *Alcuini Epistolae*, MGH Epist. Karol. Aevi II, Berlin
Dumville, D N 1973: 'A new chronicle-fragment of early British history.' *English Historical Review* 88, 312–14
Dumville, D N 1976: 'The Anglian collection of royal genealogies and regnal lists.' *Anglo-Saxon England* 5, 23–50
Dumville, D N 1977a: 'Kingship, genealogies and regnal lists.' Sawyer and Wood (eds) 1977, 72–104
Dumville, D N 1977b: 'Sub-Roman Britain: history and legend.' *History* 62, 173–92

Dumville, D N 1977c: 'On the Northern British section of the *Historia Brittonum*.' *Welsh History Review* **8**, 345–54

Dumville, D N 1979: 'The ætheling: a study in Anglo-Saxon constitutional history.' *Anglo-Saxon England* **8**, 1–33

Dumville, D N 1985: 'The West Saxon Genealogical Regnal List and the chronology of Wessex.' *Peritia* **4**, 21–66

Dumville, D N 1986a: 'The West Saxon Genealogical Regnal List: manuscripts and texts.' *Anglia* **104**, 1–32

Dumville, D N 1986b: 'The local rulers of England to AD 927.' *Handbook of British Chronology*, ed E B Fryde, D E Greenway, S Porter and I Roy, 3rd ed, London, 1–25

Dumville, D N 1989a: 'Essex, Middle Anglia and the expansion of Mercia in the South-East.' Bassett (ed) 1989b, 123–40

Dumville, D N. 1989b: 'The origins of Northumbria: some aspects of the British background.' Bassett (ed) 1989b, 213–22

Dumville, D N 1989c: 'The Tribal Hidage: an introduction to its texts and their history.' Bassett (ed) 1989b, 225–30

Duncan, A 1981: 'Bede, Iona, and the Picts.' *The Writing of History in the Middle Ages*. ed R H C Davis and J M Wallace-Hadrill, Oxford, 1–42

Dunmore, S, Gray, V, Loader, T and Wade, K 1975: 'The origin and development of Ipswich: an interim report.' *East Anglian Archaeology* **1**, 57–67

Dyer, C 1980: *Lords and Peasants in a Changing Society. The Estates of the Bishopric of Worcester, 650–1540*. Cambridge

Eagles, B 1989: 'Lindsey.' Bassett (ed) 1989b, 202–12

Edwards, H 1988: *The Charters of the Early West Saxon Kingdom*. BAR 198

EHD I: *English Historical Documents volume I, c. 500–1042*. ed D Whitelock, 2nd ed, London, 1979

Evans, A C 1986: *The Sutton Hoo Ship Burial*. London

Enright, M J 1979: 'Charles the Bald and Æthelwulf of Wessex: the alliance of 856 and the strategies of royal succession.' *Journal of Medieval History* **5**, 291–302

Enright, M J 1983: 'The Sutton Hoo whetstone sceptre: a study in iconography and cultural milieu.' *Anglo-Saxon England* **11**, 119–34

Everitt, A 1986: *Continuity and Colonization. The Evolution of Kentish Settlement*. Leicester

Evison, V 1965: *The Fifth-Century Invasions South of the Thames*. London

Evison, V 1979: *Wheel-thrown Pottery in Anglo-Saxon Graves*. London

Evison, V 1980: 'The Sutton Hoo coffin.' Rahtz, Dickinson and Watts (eds) 1980, 357–62

Evison, V 1987: *Dover: The Buckland Anglo-Saxon Cemetery*. London

Farmer, D H 1974: 'Saint Wilfrid.' Kirby (ed) 1974b, 35–59

Faull, M 1977: 'British survival in Anglo-Saxon Northumbria.' *Studies in Celtic Survival*. ed L Laing, BAR 37, 1–55

Faull, M 1981: 'West Yorkshire: the post-Roman period.' *West Yorkshire: an Archaeological Survey to AD 1500*. vol I, ed M Faull and S Moorhouse, Wakefield, 171–224

Fell, C 1981: 'Hild, Abbess of Streonæshalch.' *Hagiography and Medieval Literature: a Symposium*. ed H Bekker-Nielsen *et al.*, Odense, 76–99

Fenwick, V 1984: 'Insula de Burgh: excavations at Burrow Hill, Butley, Suffolk 1978–1981.' *Anglo-Saxon Studies in Archaeology and History*, **3**, 34–54

Finberg, H P R 1955: *Roman and Saxon Withington, a Study in Continuity*. Leicester

Finberg, H P R 1964a: *The Early Charters of Wessex*. Leicester

Finberg, H P R 1964b: 'Sherborne, Glastonbury, and the expansion of Wessex.' *Lucerna. Studies of Some Problems in the Early History of England*. London, 95–115

Finberg, H P R 1972: *The Early Charters of the West Midlands*. 2nd ed, Leicester

Fleming, R 1985: 'Monastic land and England's defence in the Viking age.' *English Historical Review* **100**, 247–65

Flores: *Rogeri de Wendover Chronica sive Flores Historiarum*. ed H O Coxe, 4 vols and appendix, London, 1881–84

Foard, G 1985: 'The administrative organization of Northamptonshire in the Saxon period.' *Anglo-Saxon Studies in Archaeology and History* **4**, 185–222

Folz, R 1980: 'Saint Oswald roi de Northumbrie, étude d'hagiographie royale.' *Analecta Bollandiana* **98**, 49–74

Fox, C 1955: *Offa's Dyke*. London

FW: *Florentii Wigorniensis Monachi Chronicon ex Chronicis*. ed B Thorpe, 2 vols, London, 1848–49

Gelling, M 1976: *The Place-Names of Berkshire, Part 3*. English Place-Name Society vol 51

Gelling, M 1978: *Signposts to the Past*. London

Gelling, M 1989: 'The early history of western Mercia.' Bassett (ed) 1989b, 184–201

Gesta: *Willelmi Malmesbiriensis Monachi De Gestis Regum Anglorum*. ed W Stubbs, 2 vols, London, 1887–88

Gibbs, M (ed) 1939: *Early Charters of the Cathedral Church of St Paul, London*. Camden Society, 3rd series 58, London

Gildas: Winterbottom (ed) 1978

Girvan, R 1971: *Beowulf and the Seventh Century*. 2nd ed, London

Glass, S 1962: 'The Sutton Hoo Ship-Burial.' *Antiquity* **36**, 179–93

Godfrey, J 1976: 'The place of the double monastery in the Anglo-Saxon minster system.' Bonner (ed) 1976, 344–50

Goody, J 1983: *The Development of the Family and Marriage in Europe*. Cambridge

Gover, J E B, Mawer, A, Stenton, F M and **Bonner, A** 1934: *The Place-Names of Surrey*. English Place-Name Society vol 11

Gracie, H S and **Price, E G** 1979: 'Frocester Court Roman villa: second report.' *Transactions of the Bristol and Gloucestershire Archaeological Society* **97**, 9–64

Green, D H 1965: *The Carolingian Lord*. Cambridge

Gregory of Tours: *Decem Libri Historiarum*. ed B Krusch and W Levison, MGH, Scriptores Rerum Merovingicarum, Hanover, 1951

Grierson, P 1940: 'Grimbald of St Bertin's.' *English Historical Review* **55**, 529–61

Grierson, P 1959: 'Commerce in the Dark Ages: a critique of the evidence'. *Transactions of the Royal Historical Society* 5th series, **9**, 123–40

Grierson, P 1970: 'The purpose of the Sutton Hoo coins.' *Antiquity* **44**, 14–18

Grierson, P and **Blackburn M** 1986: *Medieval European Coinage with a Catalogue of the Coins in the Fitzwilliam Museum*. Cambridge

Grimes, W F 1968: *The Excavation of Roman and Medieval London*. London

Hall, D 1988: 'The late Saxon countryside: villages and their fields.' Hooke (ed) 1988, 99–122

Hall, R 1984: *The Viking Dig: The Excavations at York*. London

Hare, M 1975: 'The Anglo-Saxon church of St Peter, Titchfield.' *Proceedings of Hampshire Field Club and Archaeological Society* **32**, 5–48

Harrison, K 1971: 'Early Wessex annals in the Anglo-Saxon Chronicle.' *English Historical Review* **86**, 527–33

Harrison, K 1976a: *The Framework of Anglo-Saxon History to A.D. 900*. Cambridge

Harrison, K 1976b: 'Woden.' Bonner (ed) 1976, 351–6

Hart, C 1966: *The Early Charters of Eastern England*. Leicester

Hart, C 1971: 'The Tribal Hidage.' *Transactions of the Royal Historical Society* 5th series, **21**, 133–57

Hart, C 1973: 'Athelstan "Half King" and his family.' *Anglo-Saxon England* **2**, 115–44

Hart, C 1975: *The Early Charters of Northern England and the North Midlands.* Leicester

Hart, C 1977: 'The kingdom of Mercia.' Dornier (ed) 1977b, 43–62

Hart, C 1982: 'Byrhtferth's Northumbrian Chronicle.' *English Historical Review* 97, 558–82

Hart, C 1987: 'The ealdordom of Essex.' Neale (ed) 1987, 57–81

Hartland, E S 1916: 'The legend of St. Kenelm.' *Transactions of the Bristol and Gloucestershire Archaeological Society* 39, 17–24

Hase, P H 1988: 'The mother churches of Hampshire.' *Minsters and Parish Churches. The Local Church in Transition 950–1200.* ed J Blair, Oxford, 45–66

Haslam, J 1980: 'A Middle Saxon smelting site at Ramsbury, Wiltshire.' *Medieval Archaeology* 24, 1–68

Haslam, J 1987: 'Market and fortress in England in the reign of Offa.' *World Archaeology* 19, part 1, 76–93

Hawkes, S Chadwick 1966: 'Review of V.I. Evison, *The Fifth Century Invasions South of the Thames.*' *Antiquity* 40, 322–3

Hawkes, S Chadwick 1982: 'Anglo-Saxon Kent c 425–725.' *Archaeology in Kent to AD 1500.* ed P E Leach, London

Hawkes, S Chadwick 1986: 'The early Saxon period.' *The Archaeology of the Oxford Region.* ed T Rowley *et al,* Oxford

Hawkes, S Chadwick and Dunning, G C 1961: 'Soldiers and settlers in Britain, fourth to fifth century.' *Medieval Archaeology* 5, 1–70

Hayes, J W 1972: *Late Roman Pottery.* London

Hayes, J W 1980: *Supplement to Late Roman Pottery.* London

HB: *Nennius: British History and the Welsh Annals.* ed and trans J Morris, Chichester, 1980

HE: *Bede's Ecclesiastical History of the English People.* ed B Colgrave and R A B Mynors, Oxford, 1969

Hearne, T (ed) 1723: *Hemingi Chartularium Ecclesiae Wigorniensis.* 2 vols, Oxford

Heighway, C 1987: *Anglo-Saxon Gloucestershire.* Gloucester

Hicks, C 1986: 'The birds on the Sutton Hoo purse.' *Anglo-Saxon England* 15, 153–66

Higham, N 1986: *The Northern Counties to AD 1000.* Harlow

Hill, D 1969: 'The Burghal Hidage: the establishment of a text.' *Medieval Archaeology* 13, 84–92

Hill, D 1977: 'Offa's and Wat's Dykes: some aspects of recent work.' *Transactions of the Lancashire and Cheshire Antiquarian Society* 79, 21–33

Hill, D 1981: *Atlas of Anglo-Saxon England.* Oxford

Hill, D and Hassall, J M 1970: 'Pont de l'Arche: Frankish influence on the West Saxon burh?' *Archaeological Journal* 127, 188–95

Hill, D and Metcalf, D M (eds) 1984: *Sceattas in England and on the Continent.* BAR 128

Hills, C 1979: 'The archaeology of Anglo-Saxon England in the pagan period: a review.' *Anglo-Saxon England* 8, 297–329

Hills, C 1980: 'Anglo-Saxon cremation cemeteries with particular reference to Spong Hill, Norfolk.' Rahtz, Dickinson and Watts (eds) 1980, 197–207

Hines, J 1984: *The Scandinavian Character of Anglian England in the pre-Viking Period.* BAR 124

Hinton, D 1974: *A Catalogue of the Anglo-Saxon Ornamental Metalwork 700–1100 in the Department of Antiquities Ashmolean Museum.* Oxford

Hinton, D 1981: 'Hampshire's Anglo-Saxon origins.' *The Archaeology of Hampshire* ed S J Shennan and R T Schadla Hall, Hampshire Field Club and Archaeological Society, 56–65

Historia Abbatum (Anon): Plummer (ed) 1896, 388–404

Historia Abbatum (Bede): Plummer (ed) 1896, 364–87

Historia Regum: *Symeonis Monachi Opera Omnia.* ed T Arnold, vol II, London, 1885

Hodges, R 1982: *Dark Age Economics: The Origins of Towns and Trade A.D. 600–1000.* London

Hodgkin, R H 1952: *A History of the Anglo-Saxons.* 3rd ed, Oxford

Hohler, C 1966: 'St Osyth and Aylesbury.' *Records of Buckinghamshire* 18.1, 61–72

Holdsworth, P 1984: 'Saxon Southampton', *Anglo-Saxon Towns in Southern England*, ed J Haslam, Chichester, 331–44

Hooke, D 1985: *The Anglo-Saxon Landscape. The Kingdom of the Hwicce.* Manchester

Hooke, D (ed) 1988: *Anglo-Saxon Settlements.* Oxford

Hope-Taylor, B 1977: *Yeavering: An Anglo-British Centre of Early Northumbria.* London

Hoskins, W G 1970: *The Westward Expansion of Wessex.* Leicester

HS: *Councils and Ecclesiastical Documents Relating to Great Britain and Ireland.* ed A W Haddan and W Stubbs, 3 vols, Oxford, 1869–71

Huggett, J W 1988: 'Imported grave goods and the early Anglo-Saxon economy.' *Medieval Archaeology* **32**, 63–96

Huggins, P J 1978: 'Excavations of a Belgic and Romano-British farm with Middle Saxon cemetery and churches at Nazeingbury, Essex, 1975–6.' *Essex Archaeology and History.* 3rd series, **10**, 29–117

Huggins, P J 1988: 'Excavations on the north side of Sun Street, Waltham Abbey, Essex 1974–5.' *Essex Archaeology and History.* 3rd series, **19**, 117–53

Hughes, K 1971: 'Evidence for contacts between the churches of the Irish and English from the Synod of Whitby to the Viking Age.' Clemoes and Hughes (eds) 1971, 49–68

Hughes, T 1906: *Alfred the Great.* London

Hume, K 1974: 'The concept of the hall in Old English poetry.' *Anglo-Saxon England* **3**, 63–74

Hunter, M 1974: 'Germanic and Roman antiquity and the sense of the past in Anglo-Saxon England.' *Anglo-Saxon England* **3**, 29–50

Hurst, J 1976: 'The pottery.' *The Archaeology of Anglo-Saxon England.* ed D M Wilson, London, 283–348

Jackson, K 1953: *Language and History in Early Britain.* Edinburgh

Jackson, K 1959: 'Edinburgh and the Anglian occupation of Lothian.' Clemoes (ed) 1959, 35–42

Jackson, K 1963: 'On the Northern British section in Nennius.' Chadwick 1963b, 20–62

Jackson, K 1969: *The Gododdin: The Oldest Scottish Poem.* Edinburgh

James, E 1984: 'Bede and the tonsure question.' *Peritia* **3**, 85–98

James, E 1988: *The Franks.* Oxford

James, E 1989: 'The origins of barbarian kingdoms: the continental evidence,' Bassett (ed) 1989b, 40–52

James, M R 1912: *A Descriptive Catalogue of the Manuscripts in the Library of Corpus Christi College, Cambridge.* 2 vols, Cambridge

James, M R 1917: 'Two Lives of St Æthelbert, King and Martyr.' *English Historical Review* **32**, 14–44

James, S, Marshall, A and **Millett, M** 1984: 'An early medieval building tradition.' *Archaeological Journal* **141**, 182–215

John, E 1966: *Orbis Britanniae and other studies.* Leicester

John, E 1970: 'The social and political problems of the early English church.' *Land, Church, and People.* ed J Thirsk, British Agricultural History Society Supplement, 39–63

Johnson, S 1980: *Later Roman Britain.* London

Johnson, S 1983: 'Burgh Castle, excavations by Charles Green 1958–61.' *East Anglian Archaeology* **20**

Joliffe, J E A 1933: *Pre-Feudal England. The Jutes.* Oxford

Jones, A H M 1966: *The Decline of the Ancient World.* London

Jones, G R 1975: 'Early territorial organisation in Gwynedd and Elmet.' *Northern History* 10, 3–27

Jones, G R 1976: 'Multiple estates and early settlement'. Sawyer (ed) 1976, 15–40

Jones, M E 1979: 'Climate, nutrition and disease: an hypothesis of Romano-British population.' Casey (ed) 1979, 231–51

Jones, M U 1980: 'Mucking and Early Saxon rural settlement in Essex.' Buckley (ed) 1980, 82–6

Jones, W T 1980: 'Early Saxon cemeteries in Essex.' Buckley (ed) 1980, 87–95

Kapelle, W E 1979: *The Norman Conquest of the North*. London

Kemp, R 1987: 'Anglian York – the missing link.' *Current Archaeology* **104**, 259–63

Ker, N 1948: 'Hemming's Chartulary.' *Studies in Medieval History Presented to Frederick Maurice Powicke*. ed R Hunt, W Pantin and R Southern, Oxford, 49–75

Keynes, S 1986: 'A tale of two kings: Alfred the Great and Æthelred the Unready.' *Transactions of the Royal Historical Society*, 5th series, **36**, 195–217

Keynes, S and **Blackburn, M** 1985: *Anglo-Saxon Coins. An Exhibition*. Cambridge

Keynes, S and **Lapidge, M** 1983: *Alfred the Great*. Harmondsworth

Kirby, D 1963: 'Bede and Northumbrian chronology.' *English Historical Review* **78**, 514–27

Kirby, D 1965: 'Problems of early West Saxon history.' *English Historical Review* **80**, 10–29

Kirby, D 1966: 'Bede's Native Sources for the *Historia Ecclesiastica*.' *Bulletin of the John Rylands Library* **48**, 341–71

Kirby, D 1971: 'Asser and his *Life of King Alfred*.' *Studia Celtica* **6**, 12–35

Kirby, D 1974a: 'Northumbria in the time of Wilfrid.' Kirby (ed) 1974b, 1–34

Kirby, D (ed) 1974b: *Saint Wilfrid at Hexham*. Newcastle upon Tyne

Kirby, D 1976: '. . . per universas Pictorum provincias.' Bonner (ed) 1976, 286–324

Kirby, D 1977: 'Welsh bards and the border.' Dornier (ed) 1977b, 31–42

Kirby, D 1978: 'The church in Saxon Sussex.' *The South Saxons*. ed P Brandon, Chichester, 160–73

Kirby, D 1980: 'King Ceolwulf of Northumbria and the *Historia Ecclesiastica*.' *Studia Celtica* **14–15**, 168–73

Kirby, D 1983: 'Bede, Eddius and the *Life of Wilfrid*.' *English Historical Review* **98**, 101–14

Kirby, D 1987: 'Northumbria in the ninth century.' Metcalf (ed) 1987, 11–25

Klinck, A 1982: 'Anglo-Saxon women and the law.' *Journal of Medieval History* **8**, 107–22

Lancaster, L 1958: 'Kinship in Anglo-Saxon society.' *Journal of British Sociology* **9**, 230–50, 359–77

Lapidge, M 1982: 'Byrhtferth of Ramsey and the early sections of the *Historia Regum* attributed to Symeon of Durham.' *Anglo-Saxon England* **10**, 97–122

Lapidge, M and **Dumville, D N** (eds) 1984: *Gildas: New Approaches*. Woodbridge

Lapidge, M and **Herren, M** 1979: *Aldhelm: The Prose Works*. Woodbridge

Lapidge, M and **Rosier, J** 1985: *Aldhelm: The Poetic Works*. Woodbridge

Latham, R E 1965: *Revised Medieval Latin Word-List*. London

LE: *Liber Eliensis*. ed E O Blake, Camden Society, 3rd series, **92**, London, 1962

Leeds, E T 1913: *The Archaeology of the Anglo-Saxon Settlements*. Oxford

Levison, W 1946: *England and the Continent in the Eighth Century*. Oxford

Levy, E 1951: *West Roman Vulgar Law*. Memoirs of the American Philosophical Society 29, Philadelphia

Leyser, K 1968: 'The German aristocracy from the ninth to the early twelfth century.' *Past and Present* **41**, 25–53

Liebermann, F (ed) 1903–16: *Die Gesetze der Angelsachsen*. 3 vols, Halle

Loomis, G 1932: 'The growth of the Saint Edmund legend.' *Harvard Studies and Notes in Philology and Literature* **14**, 83–113

Loyn, H R 1962: *Anglo-Saxon England and the Norman Conquest*. London

Loyn, H R 1974: 'Kinship in Anglo-Saxon England.' *Anglo-Saxon England* 3, 197–209
Loyn, H R 1984: *The Governance of Anglo-Saxon England 500–1087*. London
Lyon, C S S 1957: 'A reappraisal of the sceatta and styca coinage of Northumbria.' *British Numismatic Journal* 28, 227–43
Lyon, C S S 1987: 'Ninth-century Northumbrian chronology.' Metcalf (ed) 1987, 27–41
McLure, J 1983: 'Bede's Old Testament kings.' Wormald *et al.* (eds) 1983, 76–98
McNeill, J T and Gamer, H M (trans) 1979: *Medieval Handbooks of Penance*. New York
Mayr-Harting, H 1972: *The Coming of Christianity to Anglo-Saxon England*. London
Metcalf, D M 1976: 'Twelve notes on sceatta finds.' *British Numismatic Journal* 46, 1–18
Metcalf, D M 1977: 'Monetary affairs in Mercia in the time of Æthelbald (716–757)' Dornier (ed) 1977b, 87–106
Metcalf, D M 1984: 'Monetary circulation in southern England in the first half of the eighth century.' Hill and Metcalf (eds) 1984, 27–70
Metcalf, D M 1987 (ed): *Coinage in Ninth-Century Northumbria*. BAR 180, Oxford
Metcalf, D M 1988: 'The coins.' *Southampton Finds, Volume 1; The Coins and Pottery from Hamwic*. ed P Andrews, Southampton, 17–36
Meyvaert, P 1964: *Bede and Gregory the Great*. Jarrow lecture
Miller, E 1951: *The Abbey and Bishopric of Ely*. Cambridge
Miller, M 1975: 'Bede's use of Gildas.' *English Historical Review* 90, 241–61
Miller, M 1978: 'Eanfrith's Pictish son.' *Northern History* 14, 47–66
Miller, M 1979: 'The dates of Deira.' *Anglo-Saxon England* 8, 35–61
Millett, M and James, S 1983: 'Excavations at Cowdery's Down, Basingstoke, Hampshire, 1978–81.' *Archaeological Journal* 140, 151–279
Moisl, H 1981: 'Anglo-Saxon genealogies and Germanic oral tradition.' *Journal of Medieval History* 7, 215–48
Moisl, H 1983: 'The Bernician royal dynasty and the Irish in the seventh century.' *Peritia* 2, 103–26
Morrish, J 1986: 'King Alfred's letter as a source on learning in England.' Szarmach (ed) 1986, 87–107
Morton, A forthcoming: *Excavations in Hamwic: volume 1, excavations 1946–83, excluding Six Dials.*
Müller-Wille, M 1974: 'Boat graves in northern Europe.' *International Journal of Nautical Archaeology* 3, 187–204
Musson, C R and Spurgeon, C J 1988: 'Cwrt Llechrhyd, Llanelwedd: an unusual moated site in Central Powys.' *Medieval Archaeology* 32, 97–109
Myres, J N L 1935: 'The Teutonic settlement of northern England.' *History* 20, 250–62
Myres, J N L 1969: *Anglo-Saxon Pottery and the Settlement of England*. Oxford
Myres, J N L 1970: 'The Angles, the Saxons and the Jutes.' *Proceedings of the British Academy* 56, 145–74
Myres, J N L 1986: *The Anglo-Saxon Settlements*. Oxford
Neale, K (ed) 1987: *An Essex Tribute. Essays Presented to F.G. Emmison*. London
Nelson, J 1980: 'The earliest English coronation Ordo.' *Authority and Power: Studies Presented to Walter Ullmann*. ed B Tierney and P Linehan, Cambridge, 29–48
Noble, F 1983: *Offa's Dyke Reviewed*. BAR 114
O'Loughlin, J L N 1964: 'Sutton Hoo – the evidence of the documents.' *Medieval Archaeology* 8, 1–19
O'Sullivan, T D 1978: *The De Excidio of Gildas, Its Authenticity and Date*. Leiden
Owen, G 1981: *Rites and Religions of the Anglo-Saxons*. Newton Abbot
Owen-Crocker, G 1986: *Dress in Anglo-Saxon England*. Manchester
Ozanne, A 1962: 'The Peak-Dwellers.' *Medieval Archaeology* 6, 15–52

Pagan, H E 1969: 'Northumbrian numismatic chronology in the ninth century.' *British Numismatic Journal* 38, 1–15

Pagan, H E 1982: 'The coinage of the East Anglian kingdom from 825 to 870.' *British Numismatic Journal* 52, 41–83

Page, R I, 1965–66: 'Anglo-Saxon episcopal lists.' *Nottingham Medieval Studies* 9–10, 71–95, 2–24

Parsons, D 1977: 'Brixworth and its monastery church.' Dornier (ed) 1977b, 173–90

Pearce, S 1978: *The Kingdom of Dumnonia*. Padstow

Pearce, S (ed) 1982a: *The Early Church in Western Britain and Ireland*. BAR 102

Pearce, S 1982b: 'Church and society in South Devon AD 350–700.' *Devon Archaeological Society Proceedings* 40, 1–18

Pearce, S 1982c: 'Estates and church sites in Dorset and Gloucestershire: the emergence of a Christian society.' Pearce (ed) 1982a, 117–38

Pearce, S 1985: 'The early church in the landscape: the evidence from North Devon.' *Archaeological Journal* 142, 255–75

Pertz, G H (ed) 1841: *Annales Sancti Germani Minores, Monumenta Germaniae Historica*, Scriptores IV, Berlin

Pirie, E 1986: 'Finds of "sceattas" and "stycas" of Northumbria.' Blackburn (ed) 1986, 67–90

Plummer, C (ed) 1896: *Venerabilis Bædae Opera Historica*. 2 vols, Oxford

Poole, R L 1934: *Studies in Chronology and History*. Oxford

Prestwich, J O 1968: 'King Æthelhere and the battle of the Winwæd.' *English Historical Review* 83, 89–95

Pretty, K 1989: 'Defining the Magonsæte.' Bassett (ed) 1989b, 171–83

Priddy, D 1987: 'Excavations at Barking.' *Essex Archaeology and History* 18, 104

Radford, C R 1976: 'The church of St Alkmund, Derby', *Derbyshire Archaeological Journal* 96, 26–61

Rahtz, P, Dickinson, T and **Watts, L** (eds) 1980: *Anglo-Saxon Cemeteries 1979*. BAR 82

RCHM 1959: 'Wareham West Walls. Excavations by the Royal Commission on Historical Monuments (England).' *Medieval Archaeology* 3, 120–38

Reaney, P H 1935: *The Place-Names of Essex*. English Place-Name Society vol 12, Cambridge

Reece, R 1980: 'Town and country: the end of Roman Britain.' *World Archaeology* 12, 77–92

Reuter, T (ed) 1980: *The Greatest Englishman*. Exeter

Reuter, T 1985: 'Plunder and tribute in the Carolingian empire.' *Transactions of the Royal Historical Society* 5th series, 35, 75–94

Richards, M P 1986: 'The manuscript contexts of the Old English laws: tradition and innovation.' Szarmach 1986 (ed), 171–92

Ridyard, S J 1988: *The Royal Saints of Anglo-Saxon England*. Cambridge

Rigold, S 1968: 'The double monasteries of Kent and their analogies.' *Journal of the British Archaeological Association* 3rd series, 13, 27–37

Rodwell, W J and **Rodwell, K A** 1985: *Rivenhall: Investigations of a Villa, Church and Village, 1950–1977*. CBA 55

Rollason, D W 1981: *The Search for Saint Wigstan*. Vaughan Papers No 27, Leicester

Rollason, D W 1982: *The Mildrith Legend: A Study in Early Medieval Hagiography in England*. Leicester

Rollason, D W 1983: 'The cults of murdered royal saints in Anglo-Saxon England.' *Anglo-Saxon England* 11, 1–22

Roper, M 1974: 'Wilfrid's landholdings in Northumbria.' Kirby (ed) 1974, 61–79

Roper, M forthcoming: *Charters of Selsey*.

Ross, M Clunies 1985: 'Concubinage in Anglo-Saxon England.' *Past and Present* 108, 3–34

S: P Sawyer, *Anglo-Saxon Charters: An Annotated List and Bibliography*. London, 1968

Salway, P 1984: *Roman Britain*. Oxford

Sawyer, P (ed) 1976: *Medieval Settlement: Continuity and Change*. London

Sawyer, P 1977: 'Kings and Merchants.' Sawyer and Wood (eds) 1977, 139–58

Sawyer, P 1978: *From Roman Britain to Norman England*. London

Sawyer, P 1983: 'The royal *tun* in pre-conquest England.' Wormald *et al* (eds) 1983, 273–99

Sawyer, P and Wood, I N (eds) 1977: *Early Medieval Kingship*. Leeds

Scharer, A 1982: *Die angelsächsische Königsurkunde im 7. und 8. Jahrhundert*. Vienna

Schütt, M 1957: 'The literary form of Asser's *Vita Alfredi*.' *English Historical Review* 72, 209–20

Shephard, J F 1979: 'The social identity of the individual in isolated barrows and barrow-cemeteries in Anglo-Saxon England.' *Space, Hierarchy and Society* ed B Burnham and J Kingsbury, BAR International series 59, 47–79

Shippey, T A 1979: 'Wealth and Wisdom in King Alfred's *Preface* to the Old English *Pastoral Care*.' *English Historical Review* 94, 346–55

Shoesmith, R 1982: *Hereford City Excavations vol. 2. Excavations on and close to the Defences* CBA no 46

Sims-Williams, P 1983a: 'Gildas and the Anglo-Saxons.' *Cambridge Medieval Celtic Studies* 6, 1–30

Sims-Williams, P 1983b: 'The settlement of England in Bede and the *Chronicle*.' *Anglo-Saxon England* 12, 1–41

Sisam, K 1953a: 'Anglo-Saxon royal genealogies.' *Proceedings of the British Academy* 39, 287–346

Sisam, K 1953b: *Studies in the History of Old English Literature*. Oxford

Smith, R 1903: 'Anglo-Saxon remains.' *Victoria County History: Essex*, I, London, 315–31

Smyth, A 1977: *Scandinavian Kings in the British Isles 850–880*. Oxford

Smyth, A 1984: *Warlords and Holy Men: Scotland AD 80–1000*. London

Stafford, P 1981a: 'The king's wife in Wessex 800–1066.' *Past and Present* 91, 3–27

Stafford, P 1981b: 'Charles the Bald, Judith and England.' *Charles the Bald: Court and Kingdom*. ed M Gibson and J Nelson, BAR International series 101, 137–51

Stafford, P 1985: *The East Midlands in the Early Middle Ages*. Leicester

Stancliffe, C 1983: 'Kings who opted out.' Wormald *et al* (eds) 1983, 154–76

Stenton, F M 1913: *The Early History of the Abbey of Abingdon*. Reading

Stenton, F M 1918: 'The supremacy of the Mercian kings.' Stenton 1970, 48–66

Stenton, F M 1925: 'The south-western element in the Old English Chronicle.' Stenton 1970, 106–15

Stenton, F M 1926: 'The foundations of English history.' Stenton 1970, 116–26

Stenton, F M 1927: 'Lindsey and its Kings.' Stenton 1970, 127–37

Stenton, F M 1933: 'Medeshamstede and its Colonies.' Stenton 1970, 179–92

Stenton, F M 1934: 'Pre-Conquest Herefordshire.' Stenton 1970, 193–202

Stenton, F M 1955: *The Latin Charters of the Anglo-Saxon Period*. Oxford

Stenton, F M 1958: 'The Anglo-Saxon coinage and the historian.' Stenton 1970, 371–82

Stenton, F M 1959: 'The East Anglian Kings.' Stenton 1970, 394–402

Stenton, F M 1970: *Preparatory to Anglo-Saxon England: being the Collected papers of Frank Merry Stenton* ed D M Stenton, Oxford

Stenton, F M 1971: *Anglo-Saxon England*. 3rd ed, Oxford

Stephens, J 1884: 'On remains found in an Anglo-Saxon tumulus at Taplow, Buckinghamshire.' *Journal of the British Archaeological Association* 40, 61–71

Stevenson, W H 1904: *Asser's Life of King Alfred.* Oxford

Stewart, I 1978: 'Anglo-Saxon gold coins.' *Scripta Nummaria Romana. Essays presented to Humphrey Sutherland.* ed R A G Carson and C M Kraay, London, 143–72

Stewart, I 1984: 'The early English denarial coinage, c. 680–c. 750.' Hill and Metcalf (eds) 1984, 5–26

Stewart, I 1986: 'The London mint and the coinage of Offa.' Blackburn (ed) 1986, 27–44

Stubbs, W 1862: 'The cathedral, diocese and monasteries of Worcester in the eighth century.' *Archaeological Journal* 19, 236–52

Szarmach, P E (ed) 1986: *Studies in Earlier Old English Prose.* Albany, New York

Tacitus: *Germania.* ed J G C Anderson, Oxford, 1938

Talbot, C H 1954: *The Anglo-Saxon Missionaries in Germany.* London

Tangl, M (ed) 1916: *Die Briefe des heiligen Bonifatius und Lullus. Monumenta Germaniae Historica* Epistolae Selectae I, Berlin

Tatton-Brown, T 1984: 'The towns of Kent.' *Anglo-Saxon Towns in Southern England.* ed J Haslam, Chichester, 1–36

Tatton-Brown, T 1986: 'The topography of Anglo-Saxon London.' *Antiquity* 60, 21–9

Taylor, C S 1957: 'The origin of the Mercian shires.' *Gloucestershire Studies.* ed H P R Finberg, Leicester, 17–51

Taylor, H M 1987: 'St Wystan's church, Repton, Derbyshire. A reconstruction essay.' *The Archaeological Journal* 144, 205–45

Thacker, A 1981: 'Some terms for noblemen in Anglo-Saxon England, c 650–900.' *Anglo-Saxon Studies in Archaeology and History* 2, 201–36

Thacker, A 1983: 'Bede's ideal of reform.' Wormald *et al* (eds), 1983, 130–53

Thacker, A 1985: 'Kings, saints and monasteries in pre-Viking Mercia.' *Midland History* 10, 1–25

Thomas of Elmham: *Historia Monasterii S. Augustini Cantuariensis.* ed C Hardwick, London, 1858

Thompson, A Hamilton (ed) 1935: *Bede: His Life, Times and Writings.* Oxford

Thompson, E A 1979: 'Gildas and the history of Britain.' *Britannia* 10, 203–26

Todd, M 1987: *The South-West to AD 1000.* Harlow

Turville-Petre, J E 1957: 'Hengist and Horsa.' *Saga Book of the Viking Society.* 14, 273–90

Ullmann, W 1969: *The Carolingian Renaissance and the Idea of Kingship.* London

V Cuthberti (Anon): Colgrave (ed) 1940, 60–139

V Cuthberti (Bede): Colgrave (ed) 1940, 142–307

V Guthlaci: Colgrave (ed) 1956

Vierck, H 1980: 'The cremation in the ship at Sutton Hoo: a postscript.' Rahtz, Dickinson and Watts (eds), 343–56

Vince, A 1984: 'The Aldwych: mid-Saxon London discovered.' *Current Archaeology* 93, 310–12

Vollrath-Reichelt, H 1971: *Königsgedanke und Königtum bei den Angelsachsen.* Cologne

V Wilfredi: Colgrave (ed) 1927

Wainwright, F T 1959: 'Æthelflaed, Lady of the Mercians.' Clemoes (ed) 1959, 53–70

Waitz, G 1887 (ed): 'Rudolf of Fulda, *Vita S. Leobae.*' *Monumenta Germaniae Historica* Scriptores XV (i), Hanover

Walker, H E 1956: 'Bede and the Gewissae: the political evolution of the heptarchy and its nomenclature.' *Cambridge Historical Journal* 12, 174–86

Wallace-Hadrill, J M 1965: 'Charlemagne and England.' Wallace-Hadrill 1975, 155–80

Wallace-Hadrill, J M 1971: *Early Germanic Kingship in England and on the Continent.* Oxford

Wallace-Hadrill, J M 1975: *Early Medieval History* (collected essays). Oxford

Wallace-Hadrill, J M 1983: *The Frankish Church.* Oxford
Wallace-Hadrill, J M 1988: *Bede's Ecclesiastical History of the English People. A Historical Commentary.* Oxford
Ward, G 1938: 'King Oswin – a forgotten ruler of Kent.' *Archaeologia Cantiana* 50, 60–5
Warner, P 1988: 'Pre-Conquest territorial and administrative organization in East Suffolk.' Hooke (ed) 1988, 9–34
Waterhouse, R 1986: 'Tone in Alfred's version of Augustine's *Soliloquies.*' Szarmach (ed) 1986, 47–85
Welch, M 1971: 'Late Romans and Saxons in Sussex.' *Britannia* 2, 232–7
Welch, M 1983: *Anglo-Saxon Sussex.* BAR 112
Welch, M 1989: 'The kingdom of the South Saxons: the origins.' Bassett (ed) 1989b, 75–83
Werner, K 1985: 'Les rouages de l'administration.' *La Neustrie: Les pays au nord de la Loire de Dagobert à Charles le Chauve (vii–ix siècles).* ed P Périn and L C Feffer, Créteil
West, S E and Scarfe, N 1984: 'Iken, St Botolph and the coming of East Anglian Christianity.' *Proceedings of the Suffolk Institute of Archaeology and History* 35, 279–301
Whitelock, D 1951: *The Audience of Beowulf.* Oxford
Whitelock, D 1969: 'Fact and fiction in the legend of King Edmund.' *Proceedings of the Suffolk Institute of Archaeology* 31, 217–33
Whitelock, D 1972: 'The pre-Viking age church in East Anglia.' *Anglo-Saxon England* 1, 1–22
Whitelock, D 1975: *Some Anglo-Saxon Bishops of London.* London
Whitelock, D 1978: *The Importance of the Battle of Edington, A.D. 878.* Edington
Williams, A 1978: 'Some notes and considerations on problems connected with the English royal succession.' *Proceedings of the Battle Conference of Anglo-Norman Studies* 1, 144–67
Williams, A 1982: '*Princeps Merciorum gentis*: the family, career and connections of Ælfhere, ealdorman of Mercia 956–83.' *Anglo-Saxon England* 10, 143–72
Williams, J, Shaw, M and Denham, V 1985: *Middle Saxon Palaces at Northampton.* Northampton
Winterbottom, M (ed) 1972: *Three Lives of English Saints.* Toronto
Winterbottom, M (ed and trans) 1978: *Gildas: the Ruin of Britain and other documents.* Chichester
Witney, K P 1982: *The Kingdom of Kent.* Chichester
Witney, K P 1984: 'The Kentish royal saints: an enquiry into the facts behind the legends.' *Archaeologia Cantiana* 101, 1–22
Wood, I N 1983: *The Merovingian North Sea.* Alingsæs
Wood, S 1983: 'Bede's Northumbrian dates again.' *English Historical Review* 98, 280–96
Wormald, P 1976: 'Bede and Benedict Biscop.' Bonner (ed) 1976, 141–69
Wormald, P 1977a: '*Lex Scripta* and *Verbum Regis*: legislation and Germanic kingship from Euric to Cnut.' Sawyer and Wood (eds) 1977, 105–38
Wormald, P 1977b: 'The uses of literacy in Anglo-Saxon England and its neighbours.' *Transactions of the Royal Historical Society* 5th series, 27, 95–114
Wormald, P 1978: 'Bede, Beowulf and the conversion of the Anglo-Saxon aristocracy.' *Bede and Anglo-Saxon England.* ed R T Farrell, BAR 46, 32–95
Wormald, P 1982: 'The age of Bede and Æthelbald. The age of Offa and Alcuin. The ninth century.' Campbell (ed) 1982, 70–157
Wormald, P 1983: 'Bede, the *Bretwaldas* and the origins of the *Gens Anglorum.*' Wormald *et al* 1983 (eds), 99–129
Wormald, P (ed) (with Bullough, D and Collins, R) 1983: *Ideal and Reality in Frankish and Anglo-Saxon Society: Studies presented to J.M.Wallace-Hadrill.* Oxford

Wormald, P 1984: *Bede and the Conversion of England: the Charter Evidence*. Jarrow Lecture

Wrenn, C L 1941: 'A saga of the Anglo-Saxons.' *History* 25, 208–15

Yorke, B A E 1981: 'The vocabulary of Anglo-Saxon overlordship.' *Anglo-Saxon Studies in History and Archaeology* **2**, 171–200

Yorke, B A E 1982: 'The foundation of the Old Minster and the status of Winchester in the seventh and eighth centuries.' *Proceedings of the Hampshire Field Club and Archaeological Society* 38, 75–84

Yorke, B A E 1983: 'Joint kingship in Kent c. 560 to 785.' *Archaeologia Cantiana* **99**, 1–19

Yorke, B A E 1984: 'The bishops of Winchester, the kings of Wessex and the development of Winchester in the ninth and early tenth centuries.' *Proceedings of the Hampshire Field Club and Archaeological Society* **40**, 61–70

Yorke, B A E 1985: 'The kingdom of the East Saxons.' *Anglo-Saxon England* **14**, 1–36

Yorke, B A E 1989: 'The Jutes of Hampshire and Wight and the origins of Wessex.' Bassett (ed) 1989b, 84–96

INDEX

(The following abbreviations have been used: archb. = archbishop; b. = bishop; bro. = brother; d. = daughter; f. = father; k. = king; s. = son; St = Saint; subk. = subking; w. = wife.)